# Faillandia

*for M.*
*once more*

# ONE

The telegram telling Gideon of his wife's death was pushed under the door of the room in West London where he and Kathy had been living for eight months or so by their landlady. His first thought was that now he could marry Kathy, and perhaps return to Failland which was his homeland. His second, to be fair, was an agonising pang, recalling those times, few as they were, when all had been well between him and Lydia. Failland was also Kathy's homeland, where before coming to London she had worked in her father's hotel in the capital city. Indeed, Gideon may have seen her there when he was still living with Lydia in the country and had occasionally dined at the hotel restaurant.

Neither he nor Kathy mentioned the question of marriage, Gideon, out of a conventional deference, did not wish to appear to himself or Kathy as if he responded to Lydia's death primarily as a solution to a problem. As for Kathy, he knew it was what she wanted, but that she would wait for him to mention it.

First, though, he had to go to the funeral, which his daughter had announced in the telegram was the day after tomorrow.

Setting out through the early morning London streets, deserted in that strange lull between Christmas and New Year, for the journey by train and boat his heart sank at the thought of taking part in the ceremony that under different circumstances would have been solemn and even religious, marking the end of a unique relationship whose beginning had been consecrated. When he recalled their marriage, into which he and Lydia had been pressurised by their respective families

7

after their return from a trip abroad that in those days was considered scandalous, he recalled the lack of response with which he, and he thought Lydia, had gone through it.

His daughter, Laura, met him at the station and drove him through the city and suburbs to the old house in the hills where he'd lived for nearly fifteen years and where Laura and her sister had been born.

They were all gathered when Gideon arrived (conspiring against him, was his absurd impression), members of his disapproving family-in-law, Laura's genial husband, with whom at least he could pretend to talk, old friends of Lydia's who now regarded him warily, or not at all.

The coffin already rested there on trestles when, hanging back a little, he entered the small church on the side of the hill.

What had been the very heart and intensity of his life lay inside, cold and still, beyond his reach, and now he found that he could recapture none of the joy and pain of those years. It wasn't, he surmised, that time and later intensities of emotions had annulled those memories, but rather that thick clouds had descended, a layer of insulation that cut him off from his earlier life. He had a foreboding that at a future date a memory of how it had been with her at its best would return to him in all vividness, but for the moment he didn't dwell on the thought.

On the return to the house from the graveyard the solicitor from the city had been followed into the dining-room by the close relatives to hear the reading of the will, while Gideon had remained in the big living-room with a glass of sherry in his hand listening to Laura's husband, who hadn't accompanied his wife next door, talking about, Gideon thought, St. Jerome. He lectured somewhere it seemed on the earlier Church Fathers.

Gideon had to stay the night of the funeral, sleeping in his old room at the back of the house that looked out on the yard with the horse-boxes where, with a couple of stable-lads, he had carried on the never more than precarious business of a small stud farm.

That night was the worst part of the whole visit. Unexpectedly, he was beset with unreasonable fears in regard to Kathy. He should not have left her to come to what, as he saw, he had no real part in, and where his presence caused awkwardness and even hostility. Whatever had impelled him to leave the small haven of their furnished room and adjoining kitchenette with their bed in an alcove to come here where it struck him such a fragile world as theirs was threatened?

Gideon shivered and couldn't sleep, the room was cold, which he never remembered noticing before, or else the bed-covers were insufficient. Laura had promised to drive him to the city after breakfast, where he might have time for a quick visit to Kathy's father at the Hotel Aphra. But the land and sea journey to London was a comparatively long and tedious one, and he'd only arrive early the following morning. He now wished he'd gone to Heathrow on the chance of getting a return seat on a plane as the girl at the travel agency had suggested, even though the air fare was more than he could afford or wanted to ask Kathy for.

If only she were still in bed in the alcove when he arrived. If she was up and fully dressed, ready to set out to work, it would be like their first encounter all over again, the memory of which sometimes returned to haunt him. He had failed on that freezing evening to illuminate the drab, lonely world that had been closing around him, and, only his luck (though wasn't it more than that?) in that he went to the hotel to get the articles of clothing back, which he didn't need, had provided a second chance.

And now if he arrived back and she was having breakfast in the little kitchenette, her mood orientated towards her job, he would have failed to slip into the new London day by way of her and the secret dimension which put the outward scene and busy hubbub into perspective.

Gideon was driven back to Aphrin by his daughter, Laura, and her husband who were returning to her home in another part of the country.

After some hesitation he resolved to go to the hotel and

ask for Leo Gadbally, Kathy's well-known (at least in certain social and gastronomical circles) father. What he would say, he left to the inspiration of the moment. Perhaps he wouldn't mention Kathy at all (then how explain the call?) or he might mention having met her and wait for her father's reaction.

Mr. Gadbally asked about Kathy before Gideon had more than started to introduce himself. Having given an at first sketchy account of how she was getting on (such as a casual acquaintance might have ascertained from mutual friends) he paused.

"She writes regularly to her sister and tells her everything," Leo Gadbally said. "She got a note today about you coming here to attend your wife's funeral."

Now, relieved, Gideon told Leo of the cool reception he had had from most of the gathered mourners.

"Gideon, if I may familiarise our relationship, haven't you heard of the amendment to our Constitution?"

"Well, yes."

"And haven't you been committing what may soon be the crime of adultery with our little Kathy?"

Leo, who seemed to take a personal interest in the matter, told him there was a pressure group of, as he put it, frustrated spinsters and indeed men and women of all ages whose sexual urges had become demonic by inhibition and whose sense of order (in some cases their sanity) depended on having branded as criminal the acts that their subconscious so longed to perform, who had suggested to the leader of the party previously in power that adultery should be made a criminal offence punishable in certain cases with a prison sentence.

"And this leader of ours, fearful of being seen as leaning towards liberalism, an attitude condemned as gravely sinful, as you know, by our local Catholic Hierarchy, gave his solemn promise to introduce an anti-adultery amendment if returned to power, which he and his party were last month. If your wife hadn't died and you'd come here say in a couple of months, and they could prove that you were cohabiting with Kathy as no doubt they could through their surveillance, bugging and several intelligence agencies, you could have been arrested and made a test case of with an unwelcome publicity for your father-in-law whom I believe is a very respectable politician."

Gideon warmed to this character as he gave his half-exaggerated account of what things were coming to in his beloved and hated land.

Later in a corner of the empty hotel restaurant Leo entertained Gideon to an early meal. He was quite different to what Gideon had expected. If he was passionately interested in politics he didn't show it. In fact he was meditative, but he also had the same zestful nature as Kathy, though the word Kathy had used for the family characteristic was temperamental.

He asked about his daughter, looking Gideon straight in the eyes without a sign of pretence that he mightn't know all that was to be known about them.

"I've another little girl. You wouldn't have got off with her like you did with Kathy. Always keeps her lights at 'Stop', never at 'Go' and, as far as I can make out, hardly ever even at 'Wait'! Of course she takes things seriously, doesn't go in for clowning like Kathy."

"Kathy?"

"You must have noticed by now. Why, when she told us about your first meeting, how you picked her up and took her back to your flat and how she kept asking for more things to put on, she thought it hilarious."

"The heating had failed and it was a bitterly cold evening."

"She said that, but she was making the most of it just to see how you'd take it. I'm not embarrassing you, am I?"

"No, you're not. Only I didn't know Kathy confided so frankly in you."

"Not me. But I happened to read a couple of letters she wrote to Pieta."

Good Lord, the old sneak-thief, Gideon reflected.

"Neither of you have very brilliant jobs," Leo remarked.

"No, though Kathy's at the hotel, which she got, I think,

11

because of being your daughter, is a bit better than mine, which anyhow helps provide a living."

"There might be something here, now that you're free to return, more in both your lines."

What did he suppose Gideon's 'line' was? How, for that matter, did Gideon see himself? While married to Lydia he'd had a small thoroughbred stud, and in the latter years had, with the help of a few friends, brought out a weekly paper, intermittently serious, comic or satirical, called *The Tablet of Stone*. Then, when after a year or so, that failed, partly for want of readers, and, after selling the stud farm at the time of his separation from Lydia, he'd become a car sales representative and, not too successful at that, manager and general go-between at a fairly large city garage. When he'd gone to London with Kathy he'd at first worked as a filing clerk in a hire-purchase firm and then as warder (he'd have preferred to be called 'warden') in the Geological Museum, South Kensington. Which, if any of these jobs, had he been suited to? None, really. The nearest he had come to a sense that he was fulfilling whatever in the way of a true gift he might have been endowed with, had been during the time he edited the small weekly.

"Yes."

This was hardly an adequate response to Leo's suggestion, but Gideon had been momentarily preoccupied in getting 'to grips with the question of his own qualifications, if any, before considering it seriously.

"Perhaps you're quite happy in your present job. Perhaps wages aren't everything to you."

"You mean as a museum attendant?"

So he'd read a letter from Kathy reporting that too.

"Why not? It sounds a tranquil kind of occupation with time for meditation."

Gideon was surprised at the other's insight. He felt like that about it too. He suspected he needed a lot of time for introspection, or perhaps fantasising, a less respected tendency, and one hard always to distinguish from idleness.

12

"It doesn't involve all my energies."

Better put in a word rather than sit there like a zombie.

"I never missed a copy of your . . . "

*"Tablet of Stone."*

"Yes, indeed, your lampoon sheet." Leo finished his sentence.

"Lampoon sheet?" Had it been no more than that? No, Gideon's own estimate of its worth, looking back, wasn't high. There had been in all, perhaps half-a-dozen good numbers, vibrant (he thought the word was right) with a new beam of light, however narrow, shed on some aspects of the local scene.

"If you'd like to stay the night (you could phone Kathy), I'll arrange a meeting in the morning with a couple of interested and influential parties."

Add an extra twelve hours to the period which kept him apart from the dove whom it was essential to hold between his cupped hands if the sense of dereliction, that the atmosphere at his old home had left him with, was to be filled. That, of course, was a manner of speaking, a symbolic or metaphoric utterance, as in the Song of Solomon, for a more directly sexual experience. Where was the ache? In his mind and in his flesh. It was hard to say which was the more tormenting.

If she was in bed when he opened the door of their room, and all he had to do was to strip and get into it, she would grasp everything because of his violent shivering. He wouldn't have to say a word. Not about his in-laws, the funeral, the journey, or his longing.

Gideon shivered slightly as he sat at the table at the thought of it going like that. And here was this character suggesting a postponement. Certainly, with the best will in the world, and his welfare at heart.

"No, I suppose not. I see you want to get back to London as soon as possible."

He had hesitated a moment before saying 'London' instead of perhaps 'Kathy'.

# TWO

For the whole of the all-night journey the time of his arrival became an increasingly desperate preoccupation.

His whole future had shrunk to the size of a tiny object which could turn either to a brilliant diamond or a splinter of carbon. He saw in the dim alcove Kathy's contour beaneath the bedclothes, he imagined the feeling of quickly undressing and going to bed, while she was still warm with sleep. To be inside her; was that an impossibility, some totally imaginary beatitude he was tormenting himself with? The ostracism and tacit condemnation he'd met with the day before made his need the greater.

When he found Kathy still in bed he made love as if his life and hers depended on it, until the whole hostile world was having its foundation washed away in the tidal wave of the orgasm.

Even if Kathy hadn't had to go to work, they probably wouldn't have stayed in bed. So complete and final until next time had been their love-making, so all-absorbing and all-else obliterating, that they came to themselves fully renewed for the daily routine in to which would be carried part of the tidal wave that was still washing against their nerves.

"What a hunted creature you were, burrowing and burrowing in such a panic into me!"

"Not exactly a panic, more a high-tuned pitch."

"How was it?"

"You know very well, utterly reassuring!"

"Not that, silly. The funeral and your old home."

"Oh, those. Sad and desolate."

"Did you recall some of the happy times with Lydia?"

"Did I? I don't think so, I was too miserable."

"You can tell me this evening."

He want back to bed as he was on night shift and had only to be at the museum at half past six.

Later, he went out to buy provisions for their evening meal and a bottle of wine, glad to be back in these familiar London streets where there was, as it struck him, less tension and edginess than at home.

In the light of Leo Gadbally's suggestion, Gideon asked himself what qualifications he had for a more gainful job than his present one. Had he any original gifts or unusual qualifications that might recommend him in preference to many others? If so, it wasn't much in the way of positive skills but this constant sense of dissatisfaction both with himself and, perhaps even more, with the community in which he lived, with what he saw as the prevailing mediocrity, hypocrisy, greed and hardness of heart, all of which became the more marked the higher the social, economic and political standing.

As for his judgement of himself, he might have a certain savage indignation at the corruption he saw in his own society, but how would he fare by ordinary standards of humanity and compassion?

He made himself recall a scene that self-evasion had caused to slip from his memory. He was visiting with his wife their dying baby daughter in hospital. Had she recognised Lydia? Had she not for a moment looked up at him with an animal-like appeal between her moans? Had she sensed a presence that might have protected her (how?) had there been more love in his heart?

These were thoughts he had never mentioned to Lydia. He had meant to but as time passed they seemed less important and, besides, there developed a gap between them across which it was harder and harder to communicate.

Finally, the death of Sabina hadn't been something they shared but that isolated them further.

He had an irrational feeling that it still wasn't too late. For what, though? The baby was dead, as was his wife, and he was in the midst of life and the living. He had Kathy, however tentatively, but at the end Lydia seemed to have had nobody and nothing. At least when he was there, at the back of the tension there had been, hidden and hardly discernible, an intermittent hope. He thought, looking far back, that after the baby's death, Lydia had never been fully involved in the world of the living again.

They had never talked of these things, or if they'd approached them hesitantly, they had soon appeared to take different sides (as if there were arguments even here) and instead of their sharing the grievous thoughts and apprehensions that such a death as Sabina's fills all but the most fickle and trivial minds with, they fell even further apart. And that meant Gideon indulging his current preoccupations with a defiant zest and Lydia retreating into a kind of defensive apathy.

That evening when Kathy returned he had put the small table against the wall of the tiny kitchen and left out the provisions he'd bought for her to cook. At the meal he didn't speak of the funeral but told about his meeting her father and what he had suggested about their returning to Failland.

"Would you like that?" she asked him.

"He seemed to have better jobs for both of us than we have here."

"For you, too?"

"As editor of an opposition magazine, of all things."

"Opposition to what?"

"I suppose to the whole set-up there."

"He has always been involved in politics, or not politics exactly, but in liberation, or is it, liberalising, movements?"

"How should I know, Kathy?"

"He was friendly with some deputies who used to dine at the hotel and hold discussions long into the night."

"What do you think, dove? Should we go back?"

16

"To that awful country? The hypocrisy and the prurience! The place overrun by a tribe of witch-doctors in black exerting what they call their God-given authority, encouraging superstition and observances instead of true religion which if it happened to catch on might make them redundant."

Gideon was surprised at the vehemence of her outburst. They had never discussed these things and Gideon didn't know much about Kathy's life before he'd met her. And that itself had been an event he'd not yet talked much about.

It was only a few months after his leaving his home and family and he was living in a room in the city and working — one of his several jobs — in a garage. He was at a low ebb, drinking, reading, often thinking of picking up a girl one evening, but getting drunk instead.

Then in desperation he drove his not unimpressive car, that, with some pieces of cheap furniture was the only property he had taken with him, slowly past the long bus queues at the evening rush hour. It was a bitterly cold evening with a bleak spring lingering late as sometimes happened in Failland despite its normally mild climate. As he drove slowly with the wipers sweeping the sleet from the windscreen in whispering arcs, he was overcome by desire. Desire for what, he wasn't sure. To commit the sin of adultery that had been looming up in his thoughts since the publicity it was getting in the papers? In his present state it seemed to him that it must be some sort of enormity since the state was considering having a clause making it a crime written into the Constitution. Had the local Catholic Church — always allotting to sexuality a greater mystery and importance than it had come to have in popular practice — advised the Government that to forbid it would help to establish a more law-abiding, conforming, tranquillised society?

He envisaged a time, perhaps not far off, when adultery would be committed (even the verb was full of dark possibilities) behind locked or guarded doors, a kind of black rite performed in utter privacy — in distinction to the approved and licensed conjugal act — and which, at each commission, weakened the power of the state.

17

But, however awesome and sensational his fantasies could make adultery seem on a night like this, there was more in what Gideon was seeking in the freezing evening streets.

At one moment his desires seemed so vast that only some unearthly revelation could satisfy them, such as the turned-low music on the car radio being interrupted, not for a commercial, but for a voice addressing him personally. Saying what?

"Come, Gideon, arise from idle slumber, you have been chosen to inspire the downtrodden and with words of truth expose the corruption of those in high places." No, that didn't sound convincing even in his present vacillation between euphoria and nervous anxiety.

There were queues under umbrellas at the tram-stops. Supposing he pavement-crawled past one, might not somebody, a woman, not elderly, but not immature or giggly either, step out and get into the car when he opened the door?

The idea was certainly daring, and would take resolution. But that he had when pushed to extremes, as he felt that he was now.

Without starting a detailed consideration of the pros and cons of such a manoeuvre which would have ended in doubt and weakened his power to act, he slowed down at the next queue and, shivering violently, sailed close to the waiting commuters.

A woman sidled out into the sleet and when Gideon stopped with the passenger window opened — he'd not risked opening the door — had asked for a lift.

She was sitting beside him and he'd driven off without another word having been spoken, or if it had he was too tense to have registered it, though he'd an idea that he'd made some comment intended to be casual and reassuring such as: "What an evening!"

His next impulse was to ask:

"Going far?"

In a sudden backlash to his previous fantasies he wanted to get rid of her. She might be a street girl who had infiltrated herself among the homing office workers for just such an opportunity. Better look at her, just a side glance. What he saw was fair enough, at least she wasn't a hard-faced grinning harridan. Nor one of those mixtures of gentility and avarice that he imagined round every corner or, rather, as being stranded with at parties, if, that is, it wasn't the other kind who seemed to frequent them, the haggard with a twitch at a corner of the mouth who kept asking him to have her glass refilled. No. In fact all was well, the cat was safely in the bag and the bag was . . . But to indulge in such suppositions was equally unbalanced. Calm down, become reasonable, practical, be honest. What did he really want from her?

Instant sex, up against the wall of the sitting room of his flat the moment after he'd ushered her safely into it?

Well, no, though the idea was by no means distasteful. So little so in fact that it gave him courage to ask her if she'd care to come to his apartment which was only a couple of streets away for a hot drink before driving her home.

"I wouldn't mind a coffee, without cream or sugar which I've given up for Lent."

God almighty, had he got involved with some kind of a crank, with a handbag full of religious tracts, perhaps a proponent of the Constitutional Amendment! What an irony, and just the sort of situation with a nasty twist to it that could happen to him on such an evening!

But she was looking at him and laughing.

"I was joking."

A rather feeble joke, but let it go, as long as it hadn't included the first part of the sentence. Better not enquire if it did or not, just drive on and see what eventuated.

Nothing. He parked at the side of the apartment block and all was well until the concierge met them in the hall. Gideon thought that the elderly woman was going to tell him that it was against some regulation for him to take a woman, other than his wife, up to his flat at this hour (or, for all he knew, any hour). At the same time he knew that this was another of his fantasies, a morbid one, caused by his nervous tension.

19

What the concierge was telling him and apologising for on behalf of the management was that there had been a breakdown of the heating system.

Gideon hardly took in what she was saying. It was only when he opened the door of the apartment and followed the woman, who had told him her name was Kathy, into the small hallway that, hit by what seemed an icy blast, after the warmth of the car, he realised that all wasn't going smoothly.

Gideon felt the radiators. Not only were they cold but, as if whatever liquid they contained had frozen, they struck him as even more icy than the air in the rooms.

No question of relaxing beside her on the couch, with the coffee, or other more potent drinks, on the glass-topped table, while he unbuttoned her blouse. Though, hot, warm or cold, the chance of his relaxing was anyhow remote. What he did was, in order to take stock, to leave her in the sitting-room to sink or swim, as he put it to himself, while he escaped to the kitchen, and somewhat half-heartedly started making the beverage.

"You haven't got anything warm I could put on?" she asked as soon as he returned.

"Yes, of course."

He went to his bedroom. What on earth in the way of woollies did she expect? A thick pullover that he had bought on a trip to the islands and never worn, was one item. He hurried back with it, looking in to the kitchen on the way to see how the filter was going. He'd a fear that with the central heating breaking down, none of the gadgets might be functioning.

"Wonderful. Would you have anything I could pull on under my skirt?"

She was wearing flimsy-looking tights and no doubt the lower part was also vulnerable to the arctic conditions. Nothing for it, but a pair of pure wool (he hoped) slacks he'd bought to wear with the dark, whipcord blazer that Lydia's father, whom it didn't fit, had once given him. Gideon brought them and showed her where she could put them on.

20

What a travesty! There she was in the bathroom, not taking off her clothes, or some of them, but putting more on, covering herself up, top and bottom, and so making even the more modest of his fantasies unrealisable.

Such a farce, he supposed, could only happen to him. And yet, the situation − if that's what it was − took another twist. He was hardly aware of it at the time, but thinking and re-thinking the evening over, it was clear to him that, despite the apparent disaster, something had happened to him that was important, perhaps vital and evidently, by comparision to all recent events, unique.

He couldn't, though, say at first what it was. They had talked in a desultory way, not, it seemed, managing to find a topic that gripped them both.

Literature? No, she wasn't all that mad about it. The motor car and its extraordinary influence on the lifestyle of industrial-ised nations? Which would bring them circuitously back to the part this greatest of modern inventions had played in their meeting this evening. Make comparisons with the medieval knight on his caparisoned steed who rides past as the maiden signals her distress. Then ask her the question to which an honest answer would give him a clearer picture of her.

"Aren't you afraid of getting into strange men's cars on cold nights?"

## THREE

When Gideon had called at the hotel ostensibly to retrieve the apparel he'd lent her, it wasn't at all easy between them. She was engaged at the reception desk and could only join him for a very few minutes at a time at the bar across the hotel foyer.

He did mention the evening they had met, but she didn't seem interested in the subject and as for Gideon, he foresaw that they weren't likely to come to a satisfactory conclusion about it.

Satisfactory? What, in any case, did he mean by that? Did he want to assure her that he wasn't in the habit of curb-crawling to pick up stray women and driving them home with him? Or was he even more anxious to hear from her that it had been a joke from the start and that, had all gone as envisaged, she wouldn't have let him make casual love to her? Which, after all, was unlikely, seeing that her father managed one of the top hotels in the city and that she obviously had a congenial job in it, meeting all sorts of people.

She sipped her drink, sitting on a stool beside him, clutching a sheaf of papers, keeping an eye over her shoulder on the comings and goings in the hall.

One morning after a disturbing — to say the least — evening spent in this on-and-off way with Kathy, his daughter Laura rang him up. Gideon had taken home no more definite an impression from the previous night than the suspicion that Kathy was, consciously or unconsciously, keeping a kind of no-man's land between them. Laura had been on a visit to her mother and was now back at home in another part of the

22

country where she lived with her husband. She seemed to find it hard to express herself, and this Gideon understood because he too disliked conversing on the phone. But she kept talking and he thought he grasped the reason for ringing him. Lydia was depressed and, though Laura did not put it so directly, it might be a good thing for both of them if he went home, at first on a visit, and then, though he might be taking the suggestion further than Laura was actually doing, achieve some working reconcilliation or arrangement, and live there again.

The idea brought back the frightening failures in communication that he and Lydia had gone through. Some of the darkest times in his life re-appeared in a threatening flash as he held the dreaded instrument to his ear.

How explain to Laura the true situation? The circumstances could hardly have been less propitious. Why had he left it so late? Couldn't he have tried to make the girl, who after all had always seemed to feel sympathetic to him in her own scattered thoughts, see, not 'his side' of it, but the impossibility of retrieving anything from the ruins of his and Lydia's marriage?

He would try now, by long-distance call, at this hour of a morning when the thought of Kathy was weighing on him and what gifts he had of communication were at a low ebb.

"Listen, Laura: It was hopelessly wrong from the start. The gulf was too great, though neither of us knew anything about it for a time. Two different kinds of being, that's what we were. Your mother with much of the child in her, a not-at-all complicated nature, but unsocial and full of reserve, who loved and looked up to her father with that single-heartedness of hers. Then, I came along, somebody utterly different from both of them, complex, outgoing and at times excessive, sceptical of much of what your mother treasured, including her father, a not-very-intelligent politician with a one-track mind.

"Yet we were attracted to each other. It's irrelevant now, Laura, to tell you about my side of it, but she, who till then had thought the sun rose and set on her father, and cared for perhaps no one else, except her cats, was suddenly in love with

23

me, who, as it soon began to appear, contradicted and even threatened her father's simplistic world. Her father she saw as courageous (which he was), as a knight who braved the mean assaults of rogues and vicious men, whereas he was a rogue among rogues, who, with luck on his side (which meant becoming the mouthpiece for a rather unenlightened section of the populace) was, as you know, Laura, for a time very much in the public eye. Not that Lydia was somebody impressed by success. But she harboured her secret ideal, which she felt was being dismissed as impractical in this materialist age and which, indeed, was outmoded. Although that made her deeply conservative nature cling to it all the more, and with it, to that old renegade, her father, as well."

Gideon paused. Was he getting anywhere? He didn't know. Was Laura still there? He plunged on.

"Then, there I was, quite unsuccessful (none the worse for that in Lydia's eyes had it not been for her father for whom it made me a good deal the worse, and who told her so).

"I knew about race-horses and bred them, and this interested her too in a way. But she distrusted my judgement even about them, when it looked as if I was making a mess of the business. Which, in turn, made me even more sceptical of her father and his apparent success.

"Listen, Laura, I'm not really making it clear. I know that. But the fatal thing for us both was that she loved these two people, her father and me, and we dragged her apart, she couldn't, of course, make it out, she was trying to accompany him in one direction and me in another, and it was too much for a basically simple nature.

"Naturally she parted company with me, to use the conventional phrase. But it was a prolonged and agonising process, emotional surgery would be a better way of putting it. The worst of it was that she, at least, never believed it was inevitable, supposing quite sincerely that it came from my perversity, my lack of seriousness (an accusation she sometimes made), and an excessive sexuality which she didn't share. These were,

24

as almost everything else between us, misunderstandings. I was aware of the pain, hers and mine, and was therefore more guilty than her father who was aware of nothing but the ups and downs of his own career. I may have been as corrupt, though in a quite different and far more complex way."

Gideon paused and drew breath. Was there any use in telling Laura all this? Hadn't she inherited more of Lydia's simplicity, innocence· even, than his own multi-layered consciousness with its facility for grasping quite alien ones? But now he had to go on to the bitter end.

"I'll tell you, Laura, that the final and deepest hurt I inflicted on her was when I started bringing out the weekly sheet that on her black-and-white, one-dimensional screen registered as an attack on everything she loved and believed in."

"Can you really justify that, Daddy?"

"I'm not really trying to justify anything, Laura. The self-justification act is not in my repertoire, and the lack was something that your mother resented, and called my 'revelling in dirt', or sometimes my *'Gout de la boue'!* Lydia just couldn't imagine anyone with any conscience not being greatly concerned to defend themselves against charges of moral, or any other turpitude. Her father was endlessly doing so in the popular press, which in his case consisted in posing as an idealist."

"She's alone and miserable."

Whatever she had hoped for from her phone-call, and whatever he had intended by his long exposition, Gideon saw that neither had achieved.

A few minutes after they had hung up, he dialled the reception desk at the Hotel Aphra.

Kathy answered, which for him was a sign and a wonder, though where else would she have been at this time of morning?

"Will you come for a drive with me into the country on your next day off?"

"What for?"

What response would have been more discouraging, he wondered, apart from an unambiguous 'No'?

He hesitated. Not that several replies didn't come quickly to his mind: 'For the outing', 'For us to clear the air', 'For a sea breeze', or, but here he was fantasising, 'for a bit of fun, my sexy dove.'

"So that I can talk to you without constant interruption."

"What about, Gideon?"

"Do I have to submit a synopsis?"

"You didn't tell me you're married with children."

"With one child, a girl. But it wasn't difficult to find out."

"Yes."

"Yes, what?"

"If you park the car round the corner at ten the day after tomorrow I'll join you as soon after as I can."

Why the secrecy? Because she didn't want him to meet her father? Another father, equally successful in his way! But that was all irrelevant. Gideon was transported, the word was the only one he could think of as at all expressive of his sudden transference from gloom and acute anxiety into a comparative respite, if not quite assurance.

# FOUR

The idea of the outing preoccupied Gideon for the next couple of days, casting a secret glow over the routine tasks and forming the centre of meditation when he was disengaged from them.

He'd read of such states in the lives of saints who even at the most menial tasks were conscious of being enveloped by a supreme benediction. He was adopting some of the remembered phrases.

Such a prospect had never been promised him before. With Lydia it had all happened in confusion and semi-trance.

The blessed Henry Suso (was it?) had been transported as he stood before the tub, a lay brother washing the dishes in his monastery, and Gideon, explaining to a customer the faults the mechanic had found in his car, was likewise in the grip of an interior transport of some kind.

The morning dawned and it was one of the first warm days of spring. When she appeared he saw she was wearing a summer dress.

Keep calmly casual. Don't contrast her getting into the car with that first time. Nor, as much as rest a hand momentarily on her printed cotton-covered thigh just above the knee, and, above all, don't get a fit of the shivers.

At last, and at least, Kathy was sitting beside him and he was driving out of town through uncongested morning streets.

"I didn't want you to meet Father."

"No." (Though he wondered why not.)

"He knows all about you."

"Ah!"

"He's met your father-in-law, who is in the other political camp. When I asked him about you, without saying I knew you, he told me you were married with a family."

"I wasn't hiding it from you, Kathy. It hadn't come up."

"There's something in your favour as far as he's concerned."

"Oh?"

"The weekly you used to bring out. I don't know what it was he liked so much about it, but he did. He was surprised, considering what he called your background, at the outlook expressed in it. Didn't your father-in-law vote in the assembly for this referendum to make promiscuous sex a criminal offence?"

"Adultery, actually."

This was not the sort of turn to the conversation that Gideon had hoped for.

"Well, whatever it is, it seems crazy. He thought you and your wife had separated over the business of the weekly."

"I'd have told you about it myself if you'd asked, Kathy, which would have been better than a second-hand account."

"Why should I have had to ask?"

Why, indeed? This was getting beyond him.

"You never stayed long enough on your stool at the bar for me to make more than a couple of consecutive remarks."

She laughed and looked out of the window for the first time.

"Where are we going?"

"What about the mountains?"

"There aren't any for a hundred miles."

"That's no more than an hour or two."

"Too far. Besides we don't want to be dashing down the motorway."

What did they want? What did he want? He wanted to say to her: 'Kathy, my dove, I'm not hoping to commit adultery with you — the fatal word having been brought up — even if I once was; all that is far from me now. I'm humble and modest in my needs, because of all the pain. What pain? The call from Laura had revived the old one. All I want and I don't really expect it, is the promise of your company from time to time!'

28

He didn't come out with it, though. Not through lack of resolution. Perhaps because he wasn't yet sure how close they were, how much in that kind of accord which he dreamed of having with a woman but had never had.

Once on the motorway, he headed north for the mountains, gradually increasing speed so that perhaps she wouldn't notice or might even be transported into a state where her nerve-rhythm adapted to the smooth power of the car in full flight. Would something like that happen if he made love to her? That was a secret, though, that couldn't be elucidated by facile comparisons, and moreover one that he didn't want to introduce into his thoughts — or more accurately — blood-stream.

The faster he drove and the further they sped from the city, the more alone the two of them seemed to him to be. Everything he saw and felt was reflected through her. The forest through which in this part of the country the road ran was dark and silent with her hidden reserves, and the instruments on the dash-board flickered as though registering her subtle nervous balances and reactions.

The blue wall of mountains began to build itself higher ahead, and though Kathy had earlier demurred about driving so far, she was now as eager as he to reach them. She told Gideon of a trip there with her sister, Pieta, to visit a valley where long ago a battle was fought in the struggle for national independence.

"She knows the history of Failland and all about our national saints and heroes."

"I could find it on the map and take you back there."

"Oh no. I'm not that taken with all that. Let's take a side-track when we get there into the foothills and enjoy the peace and seclusion."

Alone with her in seclusion! The prospect, as she suggested it, would normally be enough to open the way for whatever it was that entered into him, demon, fallen angel, or uprisen beast, taking over nerves and senses. But because of Kathy's evident innocence about words having any other interpretation than her

29

simple one, and also perhaps because of his having been con-
strained from as much as laying a hand on her by an instinct not
to take the initiative, he shut his mind to the beast's first
beguilings. After a short, brief inner struggle, it was unexpectedly
easy. He seemed to forget, or was able to ignore, the other side
of her, to be ready and glad to neglect the wonderful oppor-
tunities of the outing.

He drove, as she'd suggested, along a narrow road that led
uphill across one of the first ridges, through a woodland of
smallish oaks with pale new leaves and, at ground level, the
opening yellowish fronds of giant ferns.

When the road started to level out and even to descend
slightly, Gideon was about to park the car on the mossy verge,
but Kathy told him to drive on down the slope that got steeper,
into a valley that turned out to have a stream flowing through
it, with the beginning of the mountains looking both feathery
and rocky in the soft bluish air.

Nowhere would do her but the most inaccessible, isolated
spot. She must, he reflected, have some idea of the provo-
cation she was inflicting, especially in the light of their first
encounter. Was it in part to try to annul that memory that she
was encouraging him to take her ever deeper into this wilder-
ness?

Finally he stopped the car where the road appeared to end,
although when they got out and began to walk on round a
bend, it did indeed stretch beyond them and, after crossing a
bridge over a stream, rise steeply towards what looked like a
high pass. But it wasn't the distant view that Kathy was
admiring. She had stopped and was studying a bank over-
hanging the track at the opposite side of the stream covered in
a coarse-looking growth of grass and weeds.

She stooped and picked a small spray of leaves, the colour
of deep mourning, lyre-shaped with a sharp spike at the ends,
minute drops of darkness in the bluish-grey silence of the
mountains.

She held the sprigs towards him as if she had discovered a

treasure, or, rather, he imagined, as if she had known of its existence and come all the way here for it. Her face looked rapt, and he waited.

"It's called Fael," and she spelt it out: f - a - e - l. "There's a legend that relates how it came to give its name to our land." Now that she had opened his eyes to it, Gideon could make out clusters of the plant among the dense growth all along the bank. He thought he could just about share the fringe of her thoughts which he interpreted as a mixture of wonder, sadness and delight at the very existence of the weed in its secret habitat. Beyond that he couldn't follow her, couldn't quite account for the look he'd seen on her face.

For those minutes Gideon wasn't concerned with his own part in this. He was free from the burden of self that often weighed so heavily on him. He experienced a clarification of his usually confused and opaque emotions. And in the sudden un-self-regarding clarity he supposed what he felt for her might, without the false and self-serving connotations that clung to the word, be called love.

"How lovely and modest!" he exclaimed at last, whether of the plant or of her, he didn't wait to consider. "It puts things in a new light," he added. Was he thinking again of their first meeting that had weighed on him?

"You're really quite wise after all," she told him, looking up.

God almighty, what a thing to say! Something that in all the years Lydia had never said, nor had he expected her to. Not only because he never saw himself like that, but because to have done so would have implied that her father and the very different world he represented was not wisdom's realm after all, as she was convinced it was.

Gideon drove more slowly back to the city, extending the hours alone with her. They didn't speak much, and as he left her at the hotel she gave him one of the sprigs of Fael, as what he took to be not a promise but a souvenir.

31

# FIVE

Promise or not, from then on, it never entered Gideon's head that he and Kathy were anything else than lovers. However, the technical and recognised achievement of this state was far from smooth, let alone automatic.

There were practical obstacles. She was very busy at the hotel that Spring, besides which it was inadvisable that her father should be faced with a situation in which somebody at one of the meetings of opposition politicians held at the hotel might have heard that his daughter was allowing a married man, the son-in-law of a respected public figure, to commit the very act with her that the Government, with the help of the Hierarchy, was about to persuade the electorate to decide was a punishable crime.

It was beyond Gideon to grasp the political or social logic behind all this, but he left the reasoning to Kathy because he was convinced it wasn't an excuse on her part but a genuine desire not to embarrass her father in what were evidently delicate and confidential negotiations.

There were also difficulties, strange as it may seem, to her visiting him at his so-called flat, which in fact was little more than a bed-sitter with kitchenette, though he did have a bathroom of his own. One of the other occupants of the house who claimed to know Lydia — though Gideon hadn't heard of her — knocked at his door one day, no doubt out of curiosity. Rather misguidedly, as it happened, he'd pretended that his wife, though out at the moment, was with him, that they had moved to the city where, owing to the recession in the thoroughbred

32

industry, he had had to find an executive appointment in an engineering firm, and they had taken this accommodation while looking for a more commodious one. Why he'd gone in for this little fantasy, unless just to disappoint the lady, he didn't know. But the result was she was probably keeping an eye out for Lydia and might well spot somebody who bore her no resemblance.

Gideon's demon was still being kept aloof, which was made easier because the opportunities for more intimacy between them and the conditions conducive to intense sexual impulses were absent since the outing. But the problem was there in another guise. Gideon was wondering about the full validity — as he put it — of a relationship devoid of the physical. As long as it was only wondering and speculating there was no real crisis. It was only when sex shifted from an idea to be considered in all its diverse aspects and entered the blood stream and the nerve system, reversing the order of priorities, overturning the normalities and restructuring the world around a different centre, that the situation would become out-of-hand. So far Gideon was keeping the ravaging demon, or fiery angel, depending on in what mood he imagined his desire, at bay. In a way, this wasn't difficult, though it meant a certain discipline, such as not going with Kathy to sex films — they didn't go to the cinema at all — not getting drunk, though it was a morning hangover that was the critical time, when the mental processes were sluggish and more easily taken over by fantasies.

It was a comfort to think that in many of the great love stories the couple had never consummated their passion, as the saying goes. Hamlet and Ophelia hadn't slept together , as far as Shakespeare recorded, nor did Raskolnikov and Sonia in Dostoyevsky's novel. A less comforting consideration was how to feel a full and close relationship with a woman he hadn't slept with, lacking the intimate memories of her that any of the couples along the bar counter possessed of each other?

Both Kathy and he were aware that the expedients he made

33

use of were only temporary. They discussed the situation when they met in cafés or occasionally in restaurants for a meal. Every solution, and there weren't that many, was looked into and weighed one against the other, being finally summarised thus:

Gideon could take an apartment and Kathy come to live with him while still working in the hotel. This required her father's approval which she didn't suppose would be forthcoming. To continue as they were but spending the weekends together in the country. The weekends were when she was busiest at her job and Gideon couldn't take a regular mid-week break from his, even if Kathy could have worked out such an arrangement. To go abroad. This seemed the simplest, and was also the classic expedient, not that that would have weighed with the more practical Kathy had he mentioned it. But it was the most exciting, which weighed with them both, although their hearts sank quite unexpectedly, at least in Gideon's case, at the thought of leaving Failland for what might be a long time.

Where should they go? Sweden and Switzerland were out, however attractive either of them had found one or other during a holiday. So was Finland for the same reason that neither of them was likely to find a job there, and certainly not both.

"My old fellow could fix me up at any of several pleasant spots along the Côte d'Azure."

"What old fellow?" put in Gideon, with a pang as he imagined some rich elderly Frenchman whose mistress she had once been.

"Daddy, who else? Say at the Carlton in Cannes or the Negresco at Nice."

She was showing off to him, as she sometimes took it into her head to do when he was watching her from the bar at her job and seeing how the Aphra revolved around her.

"Yes, but what about me?"

In the end it was London they decided on, and she told him that she thought she could persuade her father to use his in-

34

fluence there too, although there was sure to be all sorts of pleas and arguments against it.

"Pieta will support me, he always listens to her. Although it will be my sister who'll really miss me."

Gideon hadn't met Pieta either; he wasn't sure whether or not on Kathy's negative initiative. She took shifts on the elevator, Kathy told him, but the few times he'd been there, the girl he'd glimpsed once or twice as the door closed and the lift rose looked too unlike Kathy for a sister. In the end, it was suddenly settled and accomplished, before Gideon in his slow pondering had really taken all the vital implications and the lesser effects in.

Kathy, on her father's recommendation, besides that of an influential client of the Aphra called Kemp who also stayed at the London place, was engaged by a small but exclusive hotel in the Notting Hill neighbourhood, where she'd be manageress, but could live out if she wished. Technically it was a promotion, as she pointed out to her father, besides giving her more experience in the many-sided business, thus persuading him of the advantages of the move, if not its necessity.

She travelled to London before him, and Gideon followed a week later by which time she had rented a small flat and was settled in her new job.

Unlike the later journey back from his wife's funeral to Kathy in London, Gideon was hardly conscious of the sexual implications of arrival (certainly not wildly impatient on that score), which this time, as because with all the attendant expenses, there seemed no point in skimping on the travelling, was at Heathrow.

They met during her lunch hour, at an Italian restaurant in Holland Park avenue where she was waiting, as his flight had been delayed.

For almost, but not quite, the first time, he kissed her on the mouth. He hadn't meant to, but as he was about to touch her cheek as usual with his lips, she must have turned her face quickly so that their mouths met.

35

This set Gideon thinking, or if that is making him out too simple or naive, it indicated that the great upheaval in their relationship was not just a place of their own in a foreign city, but, to put it biblically, there was this new wine in the new bottle.

New wine, yes, but also new and unexpected doubts. Oh, not emotionally, he was overwhelmed by delight when reminding himself that when she left to return to her job only a few hours would elapse before they were locked into the flat, that he hadn't yet seen, together.

Everything was looking propitious. Or if not everything, what mattered most at the moment. The boldness of her kiss he'd taken as a promise that this, their first night, was going to live up to his expectations which she fully shared.

How wonderful to be sitting there, the dinner ordered, awaiting the carafe of wine, with such an evening and night before them and, just below the table top, the seal of reality added by his muscular response.

Not the time nor place? Time enough, but that had never in the old days precluded the phenomenon taking place. There were miles to go metaphorically before it became 'for real'. No need of a private rehearsal without the scenery. There were the more disturbing objects to be revealed, her breasts for a start.

After the meal, Kathy gave him the keys and he walked through the early summer sunlight to the abode she had found for them that wasn't far distant. It was a modest double bed-sitter with a kitchenette and use of the bath. The furniture was on the drab side, or so it struck him when compared to where he'd been living in his native city. Not that it affected him. He'd have perceived the difference between an elegant West End mews or a single basement around King's Cross, not being indifferent to such matters as living standards and social scales, but what penetrated to where he was vulnerable were atmospheres, something quite different.

Seeing some of Kathy's personal belongings, the summer dress she's worn on the outing over a chair, and a satiny nightgown on the double bed in the alcove (left there to catch his eye, and perhaps reassure him?) he felt at home. So much and yet so fragile seemed the craft on which she was setting out with him, that when he sat down in the one other chair, a reclining one, and stared at the wall-paper, his eyes filled with tears.

There is no need for a reconstruction in words of their first love-making, which would be no more than a sketch for what has already been recorded of Gideon's second arrival at their room with the alcove bed.

Sexual scenes tend to be repetitive, in reality as well as recollection, one can serve for another, unless on the rare occasions when place or circumstance makes it seem unique.

In the first weeks of their working honeymoon, Gideon spent the mornings in an exhausted sex trance in a couple of jobs, neither of which was tenable. Finally he was engaged through the local labour exchange as warder at the Geological Museum in South Kensington. It was shift work, three eight-hour ones which alternated weekly, and this he thought suited him, as did the actual job of patrolling the floor and two galleries among the exhibits displayed in cases.

On his first days there he met a fellow Faillander in the basement warder's room where he went for one of the two-hourly breaks. A tall youngish man, with long hair under the hard topped, peaked cap which was the only article of uniform they had to wear, introduced himself as Frank Everett, though some days later when they'd had longer talks, he told Gideon that when he'd taken his first job here in London he'd changed his good old Faillandian name (that's how Gideon thought of it) of Karel Paulhen for the present one.

"Why?" Gideon asked.

"You, of all people, must know how it is with that country of ours making itself ridiculous in the eyes of the world."

Why 'of all people' Gideon wondered. Frank explained that while still in Failland he'd been, as had some of his work-mates in the civil service department, a devoted reader of *The Tablet of Stone* and had been delighted, if astonished, to see the name Gideon Spokane among the new-warder roster pinned on the notice board.

The conversation which took place when they were both on night shift wasn't the sort that Gideon felt like expanding. So he stopped and addressed a few words to the old, black museum cat called Winnie that had followed him up from the basement to the main exhibition floor. There was a legend about its mother, or perhaps grandam, having been officially adopted and put on the expense account as rat-catcher in the far-off days when Churchill was said to have had his wartime bunker under what were now the Museum staff tennis courts. The atmosphere was one of tradition and legend, which, in addition to most of the warders being retired officials of some sort, with a proportion of naval petty officers, made the place more tolerable for Gideon. It was reassuring to know that when he made his coffee, the heavy kettle from which he poured the water into his mug was reputed never to have been off the simmer, day or night, since the Second World War.

He spent most of the night shift on a bench near the cases that contained the precious stones and pieces of jewellery, one of which was a gold cigarette case encrusted with diamonds around a painted minature of Czar Nicholas. Invisiable X-rays criss-crossed between the cases which, if interrupted, set off alarm signals. His duties took him through the basement storerooms and once each hour to the offices and chemical laboratories on the upper floors.

On the night after his return from his wife's funeral, although in a state of extreme nervous exhaustion, Gideon had not fallen asleep even for a few mintues as sometimes happened on nights when he was only tired. When Frank approached him as he lay on the bench with his hands under his head, and remarked: "Aren't you wasting yourself here?", it was as if, coming softly in his old tennis shoes across the polished floor unseen by Gideon until he loomed up in the circle of light that shone on the display cases, Frank had divined the direction of Gideon's thoughts.

"It's all experience, as it is for you."

Yet as he said it, Gideon knew that this wasn't quite an honest reply. So did Frank, for between them there was an instinctive, if limited, understanding.

"You could say I'm finding my feet again."

Gideon took him to be referring to his recently having served a prison sentence, for subversive activities back at home, after which he was making another start. At the same time Gideon, or at least his unruly imagination on its own, projected fleeting pictures of Frank in which the most defined object seemed to be a key that might have been of the door of a prison cell, which made the little scenario into a fantasy in which Frank was a member of the guerrilla group sworn to free Failland from the politicans — among them Gideon's father-in-law.

It might, however, open the steel cover of the alarm system in the basement that operated the rays that criss-crossed between the show-cases of jewels.

"These tangible commodities, is that what you're after?" asked Gideon with a nod at the cases.

"Commodities? Tangible?" Frank laughed, and went on. "I've a ticket in the lottery, if that's what you mean. But to draw a winning number like that you need a bit of luck."

"And resolution," Gideon suggested.

But his companion pulled his peak cap over his eyes and lapsed into silence. Gideon saw that his remark had been too direct to elicit any elaboration of what Frank had been saying. There it was again, it was he himself who usually proved the less alert and sensitive in these intimate, late-night discussions.

Down in the warders' room Gideon made himself the main meal of the night and while he was eating he read the paper from Failland that he'd brought back with him. One page was devoted to letters to the editor, many of them in support of the proposed Constitutional Amendment making adultery a criminal offence. These exuded a secretion of acidity and bile, independent of the actual words and arguments, as if some secret gland was overactive, and he assimilated an almost physical sourness from the page.

He began to think of the more recent history of his land, of what he had learnt of the bright promise that had appeared as a star above the community at the time that the country had finally liberated itself.

What had happened then?

The capital had changed its name from Aphraburg to Aphrin, some street names too had been altered, the pillar boxes turned yellow and black, and the local Catholic Church greatly increased its hold on the hearts, if not the minds, of the rural population. And the press with one voice exhorted the people to live together in peace and share a glorious future in the Comity of Nations.

Instead, his country had soon become a province or dependency of European reaction, a mixture of political corruption and spiritual puritanism. Neither a Kingdom of God on earth nor a socialist community appeared, as had been prophesied by differing visionaries. A strict censorship was imposed and the few good writers were banned. A general standard of mediocrity was adopted by the new government and was warmly greeted as though that was just what most people had been waiting for. But there was also here and there pockets of resistance. A few courageous spirits, like Frank, still hankered for a promised land.

The two political parties, after years of alternating in the possession of an authority used for their own agrandizement, were only preoccupied in how to keep it or to wrest it from the other, although by now discredited in the eyes of a bemused and sceptical electorate. And now, at what Gideon saw as his country's lowest ebb, both parties were backing this new bill, in the hope of winning the approval of the rural and middle-class-middle-age-middle-mix sections.

A couple of years earlier there had been rumours of division among army and air-force officers, but all news of it was censored, though it was acknowledged that two or three potential leaders had left and taken up posts in more progressive countries, one of them a Colonel Klotz. Gideon had liked reading of him in the foreign press where he was compared to certain older revolutionaries and he had thought of writing to him in Israel where he was said to be training the air-force.

Timidity, hypocrisy, a high nationalistic tone, these had flourished everywhere in the state. The new generation of writers, after the virtual silencing of the dissidents, had nothing to say of all that Gideon knew was waiting to be said.

Ah, how shameful and sickening to him, was the tone of the papers he read! And the leading articles were the worst, full of caution and common sense, an eye fixed on circulation, indifferent to the real movements of the heart, that are inhibited by such inertia, avoiding the depths around which the writer was stepping, complacent in his assumed role as moral and social guide.

A movement of the heart, yes, it was something like that that Gideon was aware of, painful and without an outlet. While he knew intuitively that lies were taking over, how could a word be put in for the truth? Was there still somebody who might arise out of the blue?

Had not Lenin been called back to Russia at the moment of national crisis and, arrived at the Finland Station to address the welcoming committee in a speech that both disturbed and shocked them, but which gave a direction and vision to the revolution. Then there had been Castro and Guevara landing on their beloved island and establishing, by the unbiased historical account, a just and exciting new way of life in Cuba.

He was not comrade Illyich or Fidel, he was indeed nobody, with no special gift of any kind, with only this passionate contempt for the condition to which Failland had been brought, a negative and perhaps evil one.

One day the following week when Gideon had the ten to six shift on the top gallery, Kathy came round in her lunch time.

Seeing her there unexpectedly, first as a moving reflection in

41

the glass cases of carboniferous rock and quartz which stood at that end of the gallery, and then before him, he was momentarily apprehensive. The few times she had come to the museum before had been either, once, to make up a bad quarrel (ah, that had been a marvellous reconciliation!) or with unpleasant or threatening news. On one of the latter occasions she had brought the envelope of a letter from her father that had evidently been opened and re-sealed. It had been addressed to her at the hotel where she worked and where he supposed she lived, as she had only given their actual address to Pieta. This was in case on one of his business visits to London he should call unexpectedly and discover she shared a room with Gideon.

One of her duties was to sort the mail when it arrived so that there was no question of her letter having been tampered with after delivery. At first Gideon had thought she was making a to-do about very little. Her father might himself have reopened it to add an afterthought. But she told him that a year ago they'd discovered several of the rooms at the Hotel Aphra were bugged on order from the Department of Internal Security because members of the opposition party, including a shadow minister, Lucius Canavan, a friend of her father's, used to meet there. And when she worked at the switchboard she'd found that lines were being tapped.

This time she had with her a letter from her sister, which, whether opened by an intelligence agent or not, contained exciting news. Pieta had been to the Dominican Monastery on an island a half-hour's boat trip from Aphrin, where, at the neighbouring convent, she'd gone to school. She'd talked to an old monk who'd been her father confessor, as well as the Prior himself, and he had agreed to have the marriage celebrated there — apparently a rare privilege — if the couple wished it.

"What couple?" Gideon asked stupidly. It had come suddenly, not just the suggestion of the religious ceremony but mention of marriage at all.

Kathy read out the rest of her sister's letter which actually

42

contained the main news that their father would be glad to have Kathy back to take over some of the responsibility of running the hotel from him. There was even a reference to Gideon and the possibility of a position in his old line of work being available for him.

It was almost too much, the quite unexpected prospect of a return home, and, on top of that, getting married.

Yet however exciting, it seemed to him a forsaking of their familiar routine, the upside-down timetable that, when on night shift, turned their one meal together into his breakfast and her supper. The rather spartan days had become a precious ritual with its accompanying totems such as the kettle that had never been off the boil or simmer, the cat, Winnie, with her historic connections and even certain of the exhibits in the museum.

Gideon was trembling. Or rather it was part tremble and part shiver. He was vulnerable to this kind of shock which might to most people have caused no more than a pleasant ripple in their thoughts. Once adjusted to a certain way of life, he had a fear of it coming to an end, as though all change was fraught with unknown dangers. And, perhaps, looking back, this had been so in his experience.

He pulled Kathy behind a tall glass case in which a reflection would warn them of anyone's approach, and clung to her. Because of the ambiguity of their first meeting he never quite knew what would be her sexual response. While they were still in Aphrin she had shown little interest in arranging meetings where they'd be alone, and had introduced another kind of mood or tone into their one outing so that he had thought she might have been as indifferent in these ways as Lydia. But the first time he had slept with her had been a different story, with no hanging back on her part, but rather showing the way.

Now Gideon was shivering and clinging to her, and when she took an arm from around him he thought it was to gently disengage herself, until he felt her pull up her skirt. This shocked him, and the shock of the news, added to the possibility of discovery, combined to overwhelm him — and, he thought, Kathy — with an almost immediate orgasm that was still reverberating around his body as he withdrew from her at the sound of approaching children.

# SIX

To return to Aphrin in the first and tender days of Spring was, Gideon supposed, a great step forward, but the more immediate effect was deprivation and a nostalgia for their old way of life in London.

Above all, he and Kathy were no longer living together. With much increased responsibility at the Aphra that sometimes kept her up late into the night, she had to share a room there with her sister. What, it turned out, Leo Galbaddy had tentatively arranged for Gideon was a job as stud manager at one of several farms owned by the elderly, wealthy couple called Kemp who spent part of each year at the hotel. This would have meant him living in a comparatively remote part of the country and only coming up to Aphrin for a day or two each month.

"When you and Kathy are married, she won't want to go on working for me if I know anything about it," her father told him, "and you can make your own life together in the quiet of the country."

"Don't take it amiss, Mr. Galbaddy, but my heart's no longer in the thoroughbred-horse business, if it ever was."

"That's what Pieta said."

Pieta? Who was this mysterious sister of Kathy whom, to the best of his belief, he had never seen, and what on earth did she know about him? He asked Kathy.

"Oh, I told her a lot about you in my letters from London, about my life with you, of what it was like, after years of her and I sharing our small joys, sorrows and longings, to be alone day and night, or at least evenings and nights with a man.

I tried to tell her everything, as I always had, what was un-expected and what was difficult, as well as what was so thrilling, though without giving away our special secrets."

"What are they, Dove?"

Gideon thought he knew, but he wanted to hear her spell them out.

"Oh, they are things I couldn't have told her had I wanted. They can only be told to somebody who has those kind of secrets, however different in practice, of their own. What Pieta and I were so conscious and even proud of, were our physical attributes, which we used to meditate on — yes, we really did — I did most of the telling — what exciting situations and wonder-ful relationships we could get into because of them. Pieta was always a little reserved and said I was exaggerating, but she liked to listen all the same."

"*Were* you exaggerating?"

"It's hard to exaggerate in those ways. But we didn't relate sex to love. This was beyond us, although we had heard at the convent a lot about the connection between the two, we never grasped it. If you've never loved anybody but a sister it isn't at all clear what sex has to do with it. And probably that is diff-erent for each couple and can't be foreseen."

"Please, darling, come to the point."

"Oh, yes, about our secrets. One of the things I like to be for you is a haven from what threatens and harasses you. You're sometimes a shivering creature burrowing into me, deeper and deeper, an animal with its enemies on its heels to which I'm giving shelter and comfort."

Gideon couldn't have put it so clearly. She had explained it in what he thought was an apposite little parable. In making love to her he escaped into her body from what she called his enemies, but perhaps what her body shielded him from was his at time too intense consciousness.

"What an astonishing thing sex is," she went on, "When we risk making love in odd places it's because we feel it's too deep a secret for anyone to hit on it. Altogether too unlikely and

46

preposterous, if you think of it objectively. Which is why Pieta and I never got to the end of it, sometimes not by five o'clock in the morning."

Ah, he thought, lovers enter into the order of the miraculous, of parable and myth.

"It's going to be hard to manage with you living at the hotel and me in a flat the other side of the city."

"You've found a place, then?"

He was about to take an apartment in a block on a leafy avenue now that he had got his old job back in the garage.

"Whenever you need me, really desperately that is, not just for fun, give me a ring and I'll dash round on the scooter, which reminds me that Pieta damaged it while I was away and you'll have to take it to the garage one of these days."

"When are you going to let me see her?"

"This evening. We're having dinner together at the hotel, the three of us, though Daddy may join us later."

"I'm nervous of meeting her after what you've told her about us."

"Oh, there's no need. She's like nobody else you've ever met. She's not at all like me who, if the roles were reversed, would be terribly curious. She's so imaginative, if that's the word, that the picture she paints of the world is so rich and diverse that nothing she learns about it comes as a surprise."

"I'll have a look at the scooter myself. Where do you keep it?"

Gideon's thoughts were straying back to Kathy's promise.

"In the basement car-park, but if you bring it up in the service lift you could take it apart in our room."

"Take it apart? Is it something so serious?"

She laughed.

"I've no idea. It won't go. I used to fly all over the place on it long ago. I'd have used it the night you picked me up if it hadn't been snowing and freezing."

They were talking in what amounted to her office — a small sign on the door said 'Manageress' — on the other side of the

47

foyer from her father's. Now, since Lydia's death, he supposed there was no necessity for secrecy in their meetings. Even Gideon's declining the job that her father had obtained for him, Leo Galbaddy hadn't taken badly. In fact, the day after he'd had another talk with Gideon and, as far as Gideon could make out, had in mind a quite different proposition, one connected with the publication of a weekly paper.

"We'll talk it over very soon, you and I and Lucius Canavan."

"I'm not at all politically minded, you know."

There might be some misunderstanding there because of his editing *The Tablet of Stone*. But that had not been directed specifically at politicians.

The dinner was quite extraordinary, that at least was how Gideon found it. Not that he didn't admit that he partly contributed to making it so.

First, there was Pieta to take in, without, though, taking his attention off Kathy, which he wasn't tempted to do for a moment.

Her sister looked fairly ordinary, he reflected. But then, had he expected some obvious eccentric, or blue-stocking, or one of those intense young women devoted to some crusade or other, several of whom had been among Lydia's group of acquaintances?

"What do you think of it after being so long away?" she asked him.

"This place? Failland?"

"What you've been able to take in of it."

"I'll tell you: there's a breath of hypocrisy and corruption wafted along the streets that I imagine as coming from the direction of public buildings like the Government offices."

"Have you ever thought of doing anything about it?"

Strange question! Yes, he'd thought quite a bit and discussed it with Karel, alias Frank, during the long night-shifts at the Geological Museum. But this Gideon was not going to go into, partly because it would have left Kathy high and dry, and partly because he hadn't yet come to any conclusion about whether it was not better to leave society to go its own way to disintegration and decay, as it was certainly doing here, and keep a small space of decontaminated air between oneself and those close to one and the surrounding mess. But as soon as he put it like that to himself, he became doubtful about such an attitude. What if it indicated that some of the greed, albeit for something other than power, prestige and money, had got into him?

The dinner, Kathy had told him, was on the house. After the girls had ordered a fish soup, which, it appeared, was to constitute their main dish, Gideon ordered one of the most substantial choices, something called 'Porchetta Veritabile Romana', after Kathy had explained that it was a portion of roast, or baked, sucking-pig, prepared in a manner her father had learned when head chef in a famous Italian hotel, and served with a mandragora root sauce.

"Isn't that the mandrake mentioned in the Bible?"

"Is it?"

"In the story of Jacob, Leah and Rachel."

"So you read those old tales, too, Mr. Spokane?"

"For heaven's sake, call him Gideon," Kathy told her sister.

"Yes, they've a fascination about them."

"Isn't that the story where the girls' father had his elder daughter change places with her younger sister, whom the bridegroom wanted to marry, in the dark tent on the bridal night?" Kathy asked.

"Not that it mattered much. It was all in the family, and the family was everything in those old patriarchal times," Gideon told her.

Now they were all three drawn into the conversation, and, he thought, not just the conversation but into something faintly reminiscent of the ancient tribal and sibling closeness they were talking about.

"And the whole household was a part of it," Gideon went on, drawing the two girls after him, as he could tell by their air of attention.

49

"Even the flocks were involved by Laban promising Jacob the younger daughter after he'd looked after them a certain number of years."

"The hand-maidens too," Pieta put in, "When Rachel was barren, Jacob slept with her maid, and when the time came she gave birth sitting on Rachel's lap."

Gideon felt a sense new to him of being one of a little family, though whether it included Leo or not, he wasn't sure. It wasn't that his and Kathy's intimacy had become less secret but that it was extending so that Pieta was within its warm radiation.

This feeling that he sensed the three of them were conscious of wasn't dispersed by the arrival of the dish he had ordered. The lifting of the silver cover, the aroma of herbs (mandragora?), and succulent baked pork, of which the trimming had a deep golden glisten, was a ceremony that seemed to him not disruptive of their mood. When the waiter filled their glasses with the Frascati wine, they raised them, to what was not explicit. Let us each divine the toast, Gideon reflected, and drank, though Pieta took only a couple of sips.

"I'm afraid it's not a satisfactory arrangement as things are," Pieta said.

Gideon waited for Kathy to enquire what her sister was referring to, but she didn't, as if she knew, so it was up to him.

"What arrangement?"

"Kathy sharing a room with me, and you miles away, in another part of town."

"We'll have to manage."

"What I wanted to say was that you needn't have inhibitions about coming up to be with her, whether I'm there or not. Once in my cot, I sleep like a log."

"She does, that's right," Kathy added, giving her approval, and Gideon took it that the sisters had talked it over before.

"Anyhow, it won't be for long," Pieta went on — "we're going to the Island next week or the one after to arrange for your wedding at the monastery."

50

"Are we? That's wonderful."

Although it wasn't the first time that Gideon had heard of the plan, it came as a surprise, especially the mention of the monastery. While the suggestion that he was welcome to the girls' room added to his sense of being drawn into the older world, which was half-sensual and half-religious.

The girls' father and a couple, whom Kathy told him were Lucius Canavan and his wife Mamine, had come into the restaurant and were seated at a table across the room.

"We're to join them for coffee and a confidential talk," Kathy said.

"What on earth about?"

Gideon had become somewhat apprehensive at the appearance of the others. The sight of the politician, whom he knew only by repute, was disturbing to his present state of mind, warmly meditative and sensually alerted.

"Let's wait and see."

## SEVEN

When Gideon and the girls had joined the others what they talked about was, at least at first, the proposed anti-Adultery Amendment to the constitution, a referendum which the opposition party, in which Lucius Canavan was a leading light, had proposed.

Gideon was startled to hear Canavan refer to what he called 'the Christian Ethic'. In fact he was so taken out of his present preoccupation that he found it hard to follow the political nature of his talk. He was saying, as far as Gideon could make out, that what the country needed above all was to come together in a new impulse of faith and generosity which would heal the bitter division, all of which centred round the gaining of material advantage for conflicting sections. He did not seem to take the 'Christian Ethic' all that seriously in the present company at least, but believed in it as a slogan that was going to find a genuine response in the disprited and disillusioned populace.

In order not to become himself bewildered and dispirited, Gideon had to remind himself that people like Canavan lived on another level of experience and had different thought processes.

"Our first objective is to get the present administration out," Leo announced.

"As you've been living abroad, Mr. Spokane," Mamine Canavan was addressing him before he'd made up his mind about her or about the subject under discussion, "you may not realise the way the Government has been pandering to the lowest instincts of the electorate" — it crossed his mind to ask her what were those, as he would one of the girls had the subject come up in their previous conversation — "What we need is a high-class journal to re-state our traditional values."

Gideon felt dispirited. He wished he could take advantage of Pieta's offer and go upstairs with Kathy.

Lucius Canavan was now telling him how much he admired his father-in-law "for his fearless defence of public morality when faced with the introduction of measures liberalising . . ." What? Gideon hadn't caught the definitive word or words, because at that moment he caught a glance from Pieta, reflective and, perhaps, interrogatory. Was she still making up her mind about him? If so, he'd do his best to enlighten her.

"Our history has been one long misunderstanding," Gideon launched himself onto an exposition that he had little idea how to turn in his favour as far as the girls were concerned. "Our battles were never fought against any real enemy and what our revolutions achieved were the direct reverse of what those who died in them had wanted."

He was getting out of his depth, but with an effort regained what to him was solid ground: "the ideals that are valued here are those that are advantageous to the system, which doesn't change no matter what party is in power, advantageous and expedient. In art, for example, in literature in particular, the books that are praised, whether by our native writers — a poor lot, if you ask me — or by foreigners, are those that confirm popular attitudes, or those which don't confirm anything, but by their soft woolliness stifle any dissident voice trying to come through."

"Bravo!"

Who was this? Was it ironic? No, Leo was looking at him with admiration and amusement.

Encouraged, Gideon went on: "Timidity and apathy presented as high-minded conservatism, when what we need is explosive energy."

He even quoted a passage, hardly apropos, from Wilhelm Reich:

*"I have done wrong to have disclosed to mankind the Cosmic, primordial mass-free energy which fills the universe. This energy rules all living processes and the lawful behaviour of celestial functions. It determines our emotions . . . "*

He was in a state where any spark would have ignited his long-smouldering indignation, and thought it best to leave Leo and the Canavans in the bar and went to the basement where he started up the scooter. Listening to the tiny two-stroke engine, he concluded that the fault was in the exhaust system. He brought the machine up in the service lift to the girls' room and, after spreading newspapers on the carpet to catch the grime and solidified carbon, began dismantling it.

Kathy was working a late night shift but Pieta kept him company with a book that she read intermittently.

"Your friend played a trick on you," he said, and showed her the three carbon-clogged balls of kitchen scouring wire that he'd extracted from the small exhaust chamber.

"Whatever did he do that for?"

"To save the trouble and expense of buying and inserting a set of baffle plates."

"I'd have paid for them."

Gideon left it at that. He supposed she carried a diverse section of hotel patrons in her lift, some of whom would naturally try to get off with her by one means or another.

"I'll get the part and put it in tomorrow evening."

Not that there was all that hurry if he could be here with Kathy as her sister had told him.

"About the magazine," Pieta began — "It won't be much in your line by the look of things."

"You mean if Mr. Canavan has much to do with it."

"Or in mine either, which is what I want to talk to you about."

So perhaps she'd not so much been keeping him company as waiting till he was finished. But Gideon had other ideas, as they say.

"Then what about having dinner with me tomorrow night

after I've finished the job?"

"Where?"

"Wherever you like."

"What about the Havane?"

No hesitation. She was always unexpected, he evidently hadn't got the hang of it. He'd never heard of the place, but didn't say so.

Gideon found the name and address in the telephone book and, propitiously, a parking space round the corner in a narrow, one-way street called Denmark Lane, which he didn't recall ever having been down before.

The restaurant seemed a small, smart but not showy place, well-spaced tables with white linen coverings. A waiter whom Gideon recognised from the Hotel Aphra greeted him. It was, it appeared, in the same ownership.

Pieta surprised him once more by being late, which he wouldn't have guessed was a characteristic. By the time she arrived, still in the jeans she wore in the lift, Gideon had drunk a couple of gins-and-tonic and looked all through an evening paper, reading the race-course news and skimming through an article about a planned new moon expedition. When at last she appeared, looking as if she'd just stepped out of her lift, all she said was: "You must have felt like giving me up."

"Well, no. When I've a lot to think about I suppose I'm not conscious of waiting. Besides, I'm very patient by nature."

"I was thinking it might remind you of waiting in the past with the fear that the person you had the rendezvous with wasn't going to come."

Gideon laughed. Quite a convoluted imagination!

"No."

"You never waited for someone in growing desperation?"

"Oh, yes, of course."

"For your late wife, soon after you first met her?"

"I don't remember that."

What he did remember was a Russian dancer in a fur coat, and, more for something to say than anything else, he mentioned it.

"A fur coat! And here I am in jeans! Mink, was it?"

"No, I don't think so. It may have been Astrakhan."

"Still, it wasn't fur coats or fashions we came here to talk of."

"No."

He supposed not, but what exactly they were to discuss he waited for her to say.

"I want you to be editor of the magazine."

"What on earth for? I know nothing about it and you know almost nothing about me, Pieta."

"A little, perhaps enough. You can tell me something more if you like. That's up to you. The suggestion stands anyhow."

What should he say? The truth about himself? That was something he wasn't sure of. A few of the vital 'facts'. They would surely not recommend him to her, or to whoever the others were behind the venture.

"You know, I'm a nothing and a nobody."

Pieta smiled and said nothing. Then, when he didn't continue, she prompted him: "All right for a start."

"As a youth I lived with my father who carried on business as a bookmaker (you know what that is, Pieta?) in a provincial town. I was quite contented then. I liked him, indeed I must have loved him. He was known as 'Curly' Spokane. He must have been called that in derision at first, because he had lank dark hair, quite straight, that clung wetly to his forehead when he was drunk. I think he used to souse his head under the cold tap."

"There are names given in derision that become terms of affection and even admiration."

Gideon was surprised at the point in his sudden burst of reminiscense that she took up.

"I don't suppose it was that anyone ever admired my father but there were some who were fond of him. But I don't know if all this is what you want to hear."

"Of course. What else?"

56

"He died a violent death when I was fourteen or fifteen, which I won't go into. It's still painful when I think about it."

"What happened to you then?"

"My mother, whom I hadn't seen for years, appeared at the funeral. She also called on a solicitor in the town and then took me back with her here to Aphrin where she ran a shop, although I never came to know much about it or about her. I soon left the school she sent me to and was taken on as an apprentice in a garage, one belonging to the same chain where I later became foreman."

"What sort of dreams kept you going, Gideon?"

Yes, she guessed where the crux of the matter, probably of many matters, lay. And here, if he was honest, was where, Gideon thought, he'd spoil his chance of being given the job. That didn't worry him, because he thought he knew, if she didn't, that he was quite unfitted for it. He went ahead.

"Since my father's death I'd become — though I didn't know it, nor the word to describe the condition — some sort of subversive. Not the usual or what a little later became the fashionable kind. I'd no social or political leanings, or even knowledge. I was very much alone and kept my thoughts to myself."

"Girl-friends?"

"Not to speak of. You know, looking back, I wonder if I ever had what's called a girl-friend in my life. When I'd earned some money, and had a room of my own, I spent my holidays in a foreign city, staying the nights at a cheap hotel and spending the days walking the streets. Sometimes I had a map but more often I just walked down the streets and avenues, the back streets and alleyways that looked promising."

"Promising what?"

"Hard to say, Pieta. That they led to places where a life different to the one I knew was being lived."

"They didn't."

"Perhaps not. But is there such a life anywhere?"

"That's something our magazine must discover and reveal."

57

This needed thinking over, but there wasn't time now.

"I'd better tell you in case of a serious misunderstanding, Pieta, that I'm not of what's called a religious disposition."

"There's no misunderstanding, Gideon."

She said this with great confidence.

"Each year I explored other cities in this way. When I realised I wouldn't discover what I'd started out looking for, I began fantasising about being the leader of a group of barbaric invaders, of forcing my way into expensive apartments on some of the fashionable boulevards, of raping and stealing. If we're speaking of dreams, not very elevating ones."

"There are dreams and there are fantasies."

Better, he thought, let that pass.

"In one of these cities at midday I was in a café to have a rest and a snack. At a nearby table there was a woman with an older man, the first girl whose face I'd really looked into on my travels. Very pure and pale it looked, and aloof. Not for me, evidently. The man got up and left and I regarded her boldly. I was near enough to look into her eyes which I couldn't have if she hadn't held my gaze in return. That was a long moment of shock and realisation such as happens very rarely in a lifetime."

"This is what you'd been after?"

"It was, as you've probably guessed, Lydia, whom I married a year or two afterwards and who was with her father. After my marriage I gave up the garage job — though I returned to it later — and dabbled in horse-breeding when we lived in the country."

"What about *The Tablet of Stone*? That's how father first heard of you."

"The scurrilous little rag, as it was called. It increased the gap between Lydia and me. Not, I've an idea, that she'd have objected to it if it hadn't been for his Excellency."

"Who was that?"

"The Right Honourable Deputy, or whatever her father was called."

"I never saw a copy."

"Oh, it was soon banned. Then I brought it out again with a slight change of title to *Tablets of Stone*. It's tone was meant to be satirical, but not embittered. In accord with its name, it printed a couple of the Ten Commandments in each issue alongside with what seemed to me less phoney ones."

"Like what?"

" 'Thou shalt not commit adultery', a precept very relevant at the time, became: 'Thou shalt not presume to sanctify thy lusts under sanction of Church and State.' "

"For 'Thou shalt not covet thy neighbour's wife, nor his ox . . . ' and all the rest, we had: 'Covet whatever you lack with your whole heart in all honesty but without scheming or malice, and be ready to give your neighbour whatever in a similar spirit he covets of yours.' "

"You let lapse the biblical phraseology."

"Did we?" Gideon hadn't noticed, he went on: " 'Thou shalt not kill.' 'Thou shalt not put on any garment the wearing of which permits you to kill on the order of authority.'

" 'Thou shalt not bear false witness.' 'Thou shalt not bear any witness nor take any part in the deliberations of those appointed to uphold unjust laws by corrupt rulers.'

" 'Thou shalt love the Lord thy God with thy whole heart and thy whole mind.' 'Thou shalt listen in silence and alone until thou hearest a whisper from thine own God. Thou shalt not worship the officially approved and publicised one.' "

"Amen."

Was she gently mocking him? Had he shown himself up as quite unsuitable?

Gideon had some of the fillet left, but no croutons to go with it. Pieta passed him her plate, which, he saw, she'd scarcely touched.

"You're eating nothing."

Her head was bowed. What was she pondering, Gideon wondered? About what he'd been telling her?

"When can you come and meet a monk who's a friend of mine?"

59

"Oh, I don't think . . . I wouldn't have much to say to him."

"It's not the Prior of the monastery where you and Kathy are going to be married."

"No? Another holy man? I still don't think we'd have much in common."

"He thinks you might. I told him something about you."

So it wasn't only Kathy who thought him of sufficient interest to write or talk about.

"I can't imagine what you had to tell him."

"Partly what Kathy told me, and a little on my own. For one thing, about your contempt for the whole set-up here."

"I'm not very unique in that attitude."

"Your reaction isn't political or even social, it's personal and psychic."

Was it, Gideon wondered? He knew it was more passionate and seemed at times to involve his whole manner of thinking, than the sceptical talk to be heard all over town. But he didn't know how such a passion could have any positive release. He'd certainly no desire to join one of the guerilla groups who operated by occasionally bombing an isolated barracks or shooting the odd intelligence officer. All that amounted to was pinpricks in the thick hide of officialdom.

"Well, so what?"

He still didn't see where he fitted in. Surely Pieta wasn't interested in the sort of weekly her father and Canavan seemed determined to launch.

"It's going to be published."

"By whom?"

"By you and me, and Frère Emanuel, with the help of those like the Prior and my father, at least at first, who don't share our longing for the start of a new era, but who will help by their standing and also, of course, by attracting certain sponsors."

She had gone into it seriously, it seemed. How had she guessed that he had a longing for the start of what she called 'a new era' so solemnly that it made him smile and forged a bond between them?

## EIGHT

The following night Gideon fitted the exhaust system to the scooter in the girls' bathroom and then waited till he thought Pieta would be asleep.

He settled down first on the stool and then, when he found that too hard, astride the scooter, and read several of the poems from the book he'd brought with him without taking them in. It was only when he came on the following lines about women that the counter-spell began to work:

'Their calling: to accompany the dead,
To be first to meet the risen,
And we should trespass to command caresses of them,
And to part from them is beyond our strength!'

'Amen', he murmured, seemingly ignoring the fact that he was about to 'command' caresses from one of them. But it was of Pieta the lines reminded him, and indeed when it came to saying good-night to her just now, if it had not exactly been beyond his strength, it had required resolution.

He became calmer, almost serene, though that might be to confuse the mood of the poem he was meditating on with his own. Strange, how the senses could be subdued, at least temporarily, by certain books!

Perhaps the analogy wasn't felicious, but he recalled how occasionally when making love to Kathy and, for one reason or another, she didn't seem to be keeping up with his tempo towards the orgasm, he slowed himself down by concentrating on one of the psalms.

Soon after midnight, having partly undressed, and taking his discarded jacket and trousers with him, he opened the door into the bedroom.

A momentary shock or setback. In which of the small cots or guilded cages were the respective birds? He should have checked on this earlier, even the other day when he'd brought up the scooter, though, come to think of it, what indication was there then?

Both girls had red hair, though Kathy's tended more to auburn, at least in certain lights, and Pieta's to bronze, but how could he detect the difference spread against the pillows in semi-darkness?

He tiptoed to the bed on the left and pulled back the covers.

"Holy spirits protect us!"

Kathy's exclamation terrified him in the state of mind he was in. He'd been trembling for the last half hour or so in the bathroom and the Mandlestam poems had only seemed to add to his anxiety.

"Come on," she whispered, "what's wrong with you?"

Had she sensed something wrong? Had she detected something in him, or in the air, that he, haunted by desire for her, had missed. Haunted was the word, fearing up to the very last minute that there would be a hitch that would prevent him entering her. In the past these fears had driven him half crazy. There had been an afternoon on the museum gallery when he'd been in the grip of desire for her and, though not expecting her, had seen her. But he was convinced she had come to look at some of the exhibits and might merely greet him in passing with a smile. By the time Kathy had reached him Gideon was shivering so violently that he could hardly greet her. By now she knew the symptoms which, although she only told him this later, were accompanied by a special damp pallor of his face, 'like that first time', she had added. Gideon had noticed her hesitation and has associated it with his dread that hadn't completely cleared from his thoughts. But then she'd led him by the hand between a tall glass case containing a diarama, as it was called, of an Arabian oilfield, and the gallery wall where they were out of sight, unless a visitor actually came to look at the rather neglected exhibits in the corner.

This was the second time they'd made love in the exhibition hall of the Geological Museum and he knew these were events he would remember when much had faded in years to come.

After she'd made herself decent and he was in his right mind, as she put it, they had stood talking happily, about the model of the oil-field of all things, which he explained to her in some detail, in order to complete the sobering-up process.

Now, tonight, after their rather violent love-making, which Kathy had to tell him to moderate for fear of waking Pieta, they were conversing contentedly. She told him about a picnic that her father was arranging for them on the island of Dominicus.

"It's to be quite a lavish little party."

"Who's going?"

Not that he cared all that much. It was part of the attraction of their pillow-talk that nothing factual was gone into. The world looked different to him in the relaxed aftermath of sex, lying with Kathy in his arms, touching her here and there as they whispered, without urgency or the thrill of desire. Now patient to the point of saintliness, he felt free of the fever and fret, the whole business of sexuality had a different feel. It was simple, natural to the point of being semi-conscious, with no sharply defined frontiers. All they had to do when the fancy took them was a lazy, co-ordinated shift, quite slight, and they were once more performing the eternal miracle, without fuss or forethought, almost accidentally.

She was recounting some of the dishes her father had told the chef to prepare for a picnic, as Gideon lay there listening, and imagined more than the words conveyed. He made his own pictures of a fictional picnic at which he and Kathy reclined beside each other on the grass, peeling plovers' eggs on a napkin spread over their knees, which distraction allowed him with hardly any re-adjustment of their relative positions to enter her without the rest of the company having an inkling.

This fantasy was no sooner evoked than he had an urge to enact it, carefully as if, in fact, the others were present, though without the plovers' eggs, and with the cover of the napkin now becoming the more commodious sheet. But he delayed the slight move and thrust for a moment to ask her whether this excursion was the one to the island that Pieta had proposed, but without mention of others accompanying them, let alone a lavish lunch party.

"The very same, my love, but each guest with his or her axe to grind."

As far as Gideon could make out, in his state of growing impatience to reach the vital point in his own fantasy, the launching of the magazine was one of the matters to be discussed, by her father and Canavan with the Prior, by Pieta with her former father-confessor, now a semi-hermit, and there was also the arrangement for their wedding to be confirmed.

Suddenly the lamp beside Pieta's bed was switched on and for a moment Gideon supposed she had overheard some of the conversation, and wanted to give her own account of what she saw as the purpose of the expedition. But she was slipping out of bed in her nightdress and padding over to a box on a table in the far corner of the room.

Kathy put her mouth close to Gideon's ear: "It's O.K. She's only feeding the bloody bird."

"What bird, for God's sake?"

If Kathy explained, he didn't really take it in, but perhaps she'd not bothered to make it clear, and had in fact dismissed his question by starting some insidious, or at least muted, caressing on her own.

Soon after Pieta had returned to her bed and switched off the light, Gideon rose, got into the things he had discarded in the dark, and crept out of the room.

On his way through the foyer where a few night-hawks and their companions were still sitting around at glass and ash-tray-littered tables, Gideon ran into Leo coming out of his office.

He was somewhat embarrassed, but the girls' father greeted him as if it had been mid-morning and drew back with him into the small room.

"I wanted to tell you about what's been arranged for the excursion, though I daresay the girls have let you in on 'the secret'."

"The secret?"

"I'm only joking. They wanted to keep it as a surprise, but the fact is I need your advice, not just about what to take in the way of food and drink, I can take care of that, though of course if you've any special fancies, just let me know in good time. It's not just a matter of Caspian caviar and snails from Perigord as in the old days, we've got to manage with what's available."

"The old days," Gideon repeated, rather besmusedly.

"Yes, indeed. As manager of one of the three great hotels on the French Riviera, the Negresco at Nice and the Carlton in Cannes were the others, and with two lovely young daughters by a Russian mother, I brushed shoulders — and more than shoulders where the titled women were concerned — with high society. Kathy, even then, was a great help and consolation to me, my little nectarino, but Pieta has always been bad news for would-be admirers."

As Leo was talking there came through the half open window the distant sound of firing. Slightly bewildered, partly exhausted, and yet elated, as he was, Gideon was startled, though Leo seemed to take it as an unwelcome interruption in the till-now one-sided conversation.

"That's somewhere up north, they've been occupying the station there."

Gideon knew that there had been a number of street demonstrations and even some rioting, though they were not reported in the newspapers. These were presumed to be mindless acts of violence stemming from the growing level of unemployment in some working-class areas of Aphrin. But it seemed, and was indeed a source of hope, to Gideon that this might be a logical supposition and one that allayed the fears of law-abiding citizens, but that it didn't take into account the underground revolutionary movement, and the rumours of the imminent return of Colonel Klotz.

This was the first time he'd heard shots fired, possibly because he slept in a district further removed from the dissident areas than the Hotel Aphra.

Leo poured them each a glass of Armagnac which he said was a spirit he preferred "to any of your famous cognacs, a taste you must also appreciate, old son, with your refusal to be impressed by the pressure of informed opinions, so-called."

Although Gideon didn't think his faculties were functioning anything like at their peak, he thought that when Leo was in this expansive mood was a good time to try to clear up one or two matters of concern to him.

"This monk that's such a friend of yours . . . "

"Father Celestine, one of the finest minds . . . "

"Yes . . . "

It wasn't his intelligence that Gideon was questioning but the reason for his close association with Leo, not ostensibly a religiously inclined person, which extended to allowing the apparently rare privilege of having his daughter married in the Priory Chapel, and, equally surprising to Gideon, his evident interest in the launching of a weekly paper.

"If it comes to the worst and the crowd of malicious nonentities that call themselves a government should declare a state of emergency and vote themselves extra powers, then there'd be nothing for it but emigration for people like us, you and Kathy back to London, myself and Pieta to Dominicus which, by ancient charter, has its own constitution."

"With an authoritarian government here in Failland?"

Gideon used a phrase he'd often heard and wasn't quite sure about.

"Autocracy, Democracy, Mediocracy, call it what you like."

"I see."

He was hardly holding his own in the conversation. How far

better he'd be doing if he and his dove were still pillow-talking! It wasn't, he reflected, that he was unintelligent, or a dunce as his father-in-law had considered him, but that his mind was sluggish where politics were concerned. He had this conviction that they involved a fairly superficial and very active part of the cerebrum so that many people preferred the ideas that could be tossed about there in a stimulating, and not too demanding, game to the thoughts that move more slowly at a deeper level.

"The Prior and the mainland bishops don't see eye to eye, and he'd welcome a magazine in which there'd appear occasional informed support for a Gospel-based Christianity."

Which, Gideon supposed with relief, at having at least grasped something, was where Pieta came in. But, as usual, he was over-simplifying.

Pieta hadn't mentioned the Prior but another monk whose name Gideon had forgotten and he couldn't be sure that these weren't also rivals. What *was* sure, as Kathy had said, was that there were several factions among those invited to the picnic, and he wasn't even certain whether arrangements for his and Kathy's wedding or for the publication of a magazine was the principle object of the outing, or whether indeed it had as its principle aim to give Leo a chance to indulge his culinary skills and celebrate what he nostalgically called 'the old days'.

## NINE

On the short voyage to the island there was no sign of concern among the tourists, either foreign or Faillese, who crowded the boat, despite the morning papers for the first time carrying news of disturbances in the city.

Gideon sat between Kathy and Pieta on a slatted wooden bench in the bow with a strong wind and the sun burning their faces that from time to time were cooled by salty splashes as the boat, lifted on a wave, crashed down on the following one.

Kathy who had brought a newspaper with her had folded it small and, holding it on her knees against the wind, was glancing down at it between gazing around at one of the passing yachts or ahead at the low profile of the island of Dominicus in front of them.

"It says here that a large crowd of demonstrators gathered in front of the North Station calling for a Colonel Klotz to come out and address them."

"Why should he be hiding at a station?"

The name raised a recollective response in Gideon, but whether the Colonel was returning as a government 'strong man', or as leader of one of the factions of revolutionary guerillas, he still wasn't sure.

"He sometimes used to dine at the hotel restaurant."

"A friend of your father's?"

"That's three or four years ago."

"Let's have a look."

Why he wanted to read the report of the incident for himself, Gideon didn't know. Not having as keen eyesight as Kathy, he held the folded sheet up closer and it was spattered by a shower of spray at the moment he came to the words 'Colonel Klotz' that were in heavier type than the rest of the paragraph. No, he was none the wiser. Why then, did his glance linger on them as though expectantly? Because the darker letters eased his eyes? He turned the sheet to see if this giving of proper names and titles in heavier print was a habit of this newspaper.

In a similarly short report he read of a robbery at the Geological Museum, South Kensington, London, in which valuable jewellery of a historic nature had been stolen the previous night and not discovered by the night watchman owing to the thieves having managed to disconnect the alarm system.

He showed the paragraph to Kathy as he handed back the news sheet. She smiled at him and Gideon knew that her chief response to the report was to recall their love-making up on the second gallery. She had never met, or indeed heard of Frank Everett, let alone Karel Paulhen.

Leo Galbaddy and the Canavans had crossed to the island in the Prior's small boat, with the provisions.

Gideon and the two girls disembarked with the throng of excursionists who dispersed in various directions, while Pieta led the way to the Priory.

Gideon asked her to show him the whereabouts of the Dominican Convent where she had spent two or three years finishing her education and where, as he'd heard, she'd come under the influence of the monks, one of them in particular, this friar who used to say Mass at the convent and hear the girls' confessions. Kathy herself had also been there, but for a short time only and had left under a cloud, 'though a quite small one', as she put it.

Gideon had naturally wanted to hear the details and had pressed her.

"Some of the pupils resented the questions put to us in confession, not by Frère Emanuel, Pieta's spiritual father, but by one of those little nobodies in monks' disguise with nothing but prurient curiosity behind their pious air and expression.

69

"We teased our poor friar to distraction. When we confessed to petting parties in the holidays and he asked how far it went, we always said, each putting it differently so that he wouldn't suspect collusion: 'Oh, Father, never beyond the mini-orgasm'. 'What do you mean by that, child?' 'Just a tiny *frisson,* the nuns who give sex-education say it's only a venial sin.' "

When they reached the Priory wall they rang the bell at the door and it was opened by Leo in a white linen suit he'd put on for the occasion. A gravelled path led between tall palms that gave Gideon the impression of an exotic rather than other-worldly atmosphere. But the monastery was still some way off and it was to an out-building that Leo led them.

He brought them into a long, narrow room where there was just space for a table and wooden chairs down the centre. On this the contents of the hampers were laid out, rather disappointingly for Gideon who had supposed the constant reference to a picnic had meant a cloth spread on a sandy beach at the water's edge, with glasses firmly wedged into the velvet sand at their elbows.

The Canavans were seated at the table, looking (especially Mrs. Canavan) somewhat disconsolate. Leo said they would have to wait for Prior Celestine to join them. Until then, nothing must be touched, not a bottle opened nor a crumb dropped on the polished oak surface.

Gideon's recollections (and they are what this whole report is based on) of events that day on the island were selective, not a little ambiguous, and perhaps biased.

Prior Celestine was an old man, with a lined, ascetic (the word came to Gideon's mind automatically and was not perhaps the most discerning one) face framed in a white woollen hood or cowl. He drank a glass of wine but ate nothing, although encouraging the others to take part in the feast, as he put it.

Almost at once they were discussing the political situation, the clashes between the military and guerilla groups the night before, on which Lucius Canavan was listened to as the one

70

with the most accurate information.

"The Government won't admit the strength of the support for the revolutionaries," he told them.

Gideon's heart jumped with a small secret thrill, but he kept a grave face.

"They've got some popular backing in the city" — mine too, reflected Gideon, anything rather than the present lot, including the Canavans — "and evidently don't lack arms. Luckily for us all," Canavan continued "they're without a recognised leader to give them a clear objective, nobody with a sense of history."

"What about this Klotz whom they say is a neo-Trotskyite?" the Prior asked.

"For one thing, he isn't here, Reverend Father. And you must remember that even Trotsky himself wasn't, like Marx, a great original thinker. He had administrative capability but lacked imagination and could only operate inside the ideology established by Marx and Lenin. He could not have created or developed one of his own."

"Do you really think, Mr. Canavan, that Communists are behind what is happening?"

"There isn't, as far as we know, any other powerful enough group here or abroad to openly challenge, as it looks now as if they're ready to do, what is after all a very well-trained and equipped army totally loyal to the ideal of law and order." (Gideon: 'to preserving the deal made between your lot and the Government by which you all in turn get a share of the loot.')

The Prior took a sip from his glass of wine with a grimace of distaste that struck Gideon if nobody else. He seemed the only one of the company unimpressed by Lucius Canavan's summing up of the situation.

"I've an idea, Mr. Canavan, that our politicians aren't quite sure in what direction these new winds, not just here but in other unexpected places, are blowing."

"That may go for the Government, but we of the opposing

71

parties are very conscious of the moral nature of the struggle. That's why we suggested the Referendum."

"There's no hope of stemming the disruptive tide by imposing moral sanctions." The Prior then launched himself on what, it seemed, he had come to say.

"There's a quite different conflict going on than the one that has been agitating us here between so-called pagans and those for moral rectitude. It centres around conflicting dreams, Mr. Canavan, such as the dream of social justice and security, the technologists' dream of a world liberation through applied science, the artists have their dream too, though it hardly counts down in your arena; and there's the dream of the Kingdom of God. And they all, and others too, have determined, and some even ruthless, adherents. But as for the old ideas like the Dictatorship of the Proletariat, that, or the other old ideologies have lost most of their power. They never really penetrated and became rooted in the deepest areas of the human psyche because they can't be transferred into a dream."

"Your insights, Reverend Father, are of great interest, but are they not based on the ideas of modern theologians and how, may I ask, can the ordinary people, the electorate, be persuaded to accept them?"

(Gideon: 'The electorate. Yes, the counting of votes is never far from their minds.')

"As I said, there are indications that even the ordinary people — as you like to call them, though I'm not sure if that isn't an out-dated fiction too — are feeling breezes flowing from unaccustomed quarters. And one of the things we're here to discuss, the weekly magazine, will help in the process."

Gideon took a couple of long draughts of the specially selected red wine from the Aphran cellars, then folded a thinly-carved slice of underdone, cold beef onto a slice of wheaten bread from the Priory, and hesitated a moment — the Prior's talk about dreams and their power had reassured him and he wanted to reflect on it — before putting it into his mouth.

"I'm old-fashioned enough to believe that a political party

72

closely united with the Church can still ensure the necessary ethical basis of peace and justice."

Gideon began to see why Canavan was interested in the weekly.

"At times of upheaval the Church is only as strong as the spirit of its secular clergy." A remark by Mamine Canavan of which no notice was taken.

"The magazine," said Gideon, unexpectantly emboldened, "what tone should it take, what kind of sermons should it print?"

"Nobody listens to sermons anymore or reads leading articles, except those who need sustaining in their half-hearted attitudes. And they won't be our readers. These are the ninety-nine we shall leave in the fold," the Prior continued, "to go after the one who has absented him or herself from it. Multiply the parable figures by several thousand and you have some idea of our potential readership."

"Yet you must admit, Reverend Father, that here in Failland we are still a religious people in the midst of societies given over to materialism," Canavan put in.

"Oh, the sheepfolds are full. But full sheepfolds aren't a guarantee of docile flocks anymore. The voice of the shepherd is no longer the only one to reach them. Sermons and leading articles haven't the same reassuring, sedative effect they used to. Now there are ways of relaying all sorts of other voices to them, some of quite unheard-of disruptiveness. One of the weaknesses of most systems of control, secular and religious, is that the administrations are cocooned in their well-insulated capsules and have little idea of any changes in the weather outside.

"Now, you might say the same thing about me, the head of a house of enclosed contemplatives, on an island, what's more, where there are neither newspapers nor television. But partly just because we lack these instruments for the propagation of complacency, it is easier to catch some of the other signals. And because each of us is here, I think, to give a true report from our own area of observation, I want to say that, though I cannot prophecy how long it will take, the upheaval that is coming in ways of thinking and apprehending, of judging and comparing, of feeling and responding, will be more extreme and radical than anyone can foresee."

Because of something very serious without a trace of assumed authority in the tone of the Prior's words, they came as a shock, though to Gideon at least one of subdued delight – subdued because even he felt a slight shiver of apprehension. Canavan was the first to fill the pause with phrases like: "We, in our party . . . the Christian ethic . . . "

Gideon didn't bother to listen, and anyhow Kathy was telling him in a whisper that it was rumoured — the Hotel Aphra was an exchange centre in this respect — that Lucius Canavan had paid for two abortions for a girl called Nella, Nonna or Masha — Gideon didn't quite catch every word — who worked at the Ministry for Security and with whom he had sometimes dined in the restaurant.

"When back in power and exercising responsible leadership . . . "

Gideon again heard a sentence here and there of what Canavan was saying, but there were also blanks into which he substituted phrases of his own that came to him from the utterances of politicians he'd read in the papers. It struck him that they were interchangeable, not just as members of the same party, but between those in Government and Opposition. The policies advocated might appear in conflict but that was an illusion, the scale of the matters being, in respect of overall reality, so minute that to the non-washed brain, or averagely independent intelligence, one was roughly the shape, had the feel and, if touched by an organ of sense, say the tongue, would have much the same old, tepid and somewhat stale taste as another.

Canavan had stopped talking and was saying something to his wife in a low voice, while she raised her hand to her tightly-waved hair, every coil of which, Gideon noticed, returned to its place after her beringed fingers had passed through it.

Gideon concluded that he hadn't eavesdropped on a tender interchange, perhaps in the nature of a reconciliation after an earlier disagreement, but that Mamine Canavan, at the instigation of Leo, was already slightly intoxicated and had been told by her husband to go easy.

" . . . Klotz . . . "

Had it really been Kathy who had opened her mouth — after which he hankered but not yet desperately — and again set off the sound of this name like a small explosion two feet, say, above the well-spread surface of the table?

"A minor demagogue, Miss Galbaddy."

Lucius Canavan's tone was contemptuous but mitigated by a patient and patronising tone which, Gideon supposed, it wouldn't have had in the Chamber of Elected Representatives, to give the assembly building its official designation.

"A loud-mouthed nobody," Canavan added, supposing that Kathy had accepted his first judgement unquestioninly.

"He'd very little to say when I met him."

"You met him?"

Canavan looked at Kathy reproachfully as though a favoured pupil had let him down in front of the class.

"When he was dining at the hotel with Daddy."

'Daddy' glanced at his 'little nectarino', but said nothing. There was a bond between them as Gideon knew; she was his favourite, in contrast to Pieta, he shared many of her instincts and attitudes. Rather surprisingly the subject was dropped, and a little later Pieta suggested he go with her to see Frère Emanuel, leaving her father and Kathy to talk to the Prior about the other matter to be discussed, the marriage celebration.

Frère Emanuel, it turned out, though Gideon may have been informed of it without it registering, had his cell, not in the Friary itself but in what was known as the Fortress, an ancient square block with immensely thick walls built on an outcrop of rock a short distance from the shore.

He was awaiting them, which accounted for Pieta's hurry, with a small boat in which he rowed them the fifty yards or so to a cove below the fort which, he told Gideon, had housed the community for a hundred years or so during the era of raiders and pillagers though, with so much to take in, Gideon failed to register which century he was talking of.

He hadn't expected the monk to be so old, though Pieta had probably never mentioned his age. He had certainly lived eight or ten years longer than the Prior, whom Gideon took to be over seventy.

He led the way up the stairs carved in rock without fuss or difficulty, pausing at the open door at the top to welcome them over again, not with an open-arms gesture, or the sign of the Cross, but with a benediction from the Sermon on the Mount: "Blessed are those who hunger and thirst after righteousness."

They entered a large, stone-flagged room that had once, Frère Emanuel said, been the refectory.

There was a raised dais at one wall below a narrow window (from where the *lecteur* had read out to the monks at table?), a long wooden table, grey-white with age and a tank containing what, at a glance, looked like several large crustaceans, presumably lobsters.

In such a place Salomé danced while Herod lounged on his throne and the drunken company applauded.

"Is there a dungeon below?" Gideon enquired.

An inconsequential question, an impulse perhaps to relieve a sense of claustrophobia.

"Like the one where John the Baptist had to listen to the revelry above?"

How had Pieta entered into his rather bizarre fantasy, sharing with him the very fragile assocation? He was shocked and glad at the same time, as when Kathy entered into his very different fantasy.

"John the Baptist, the last of the ancient prophets and the first of the Christian martyrs," the old man exclaimed. He then paused as though to let his visitors take this in. Or perhaps in order to meditate for a moment on what evidently to him was a historical fact of deep significance:— "A link between the old and the new, the people of Israel and the people of Jesus, to whom you, *Kinder*, belong."

Was he German? Pieta hadn't said so, nor was his accent non-native. He studied, no doubt, the contemporary theologians who nearly all were German, and wrote, or had their works translated into that language. As for 'the people of Jesus', Gideon didn't think of himself as one of them no more, though perhaps no less, than as a member of any of the sects, factions or groupings that he was sometimes taken as belonging to.

"Don't let his words distract you," Pieta said as the monk led them up more stone stairs, "from the silver radiance that shimmers on these stones. Invisible to the naked eye."

The moment she mentioned it, Gideon was aware of what he took to be the slant of sea-reflected light through a window higher up.

The stone stairway led into the library above, against three of whose walls from floor to ceiling were shelves of books, and along the fourth cupboards containing — the old man told Gideon — ancient manuscripts and scrolls in Greek, Hebrew and Aramaic to some of which the Vatican had laid an unsuccessful claim in the last century.

Gideon would have liked to know whether Frère Emanuel read these languages, but abstained from asking him. There was about the Friar an air of seclusion and self-containment, although, unlike the Prior, his shaved grey head was uncovered, that any such personal question seemed inappropriate. Pieta would tell him later.

Gideon had gone over to read some of the titles of the volumes visible from that level — there was a mobile ladder for reaching the higher shelves. Sections were numbered by Roman numerals to which he didn't have the key. Gideon had arrived at a shelf of volumes whose category was hard to determine from the names of the authors and the titles were mostly, as he had foreseen, but not all, German. So the sections were not arranged by language.

"*P. Hoffman, Studien zur Theologie der Logienquelle; D. Lührmann, Die Redaktion der Logienquelle; E. Auerbach, Mimeses, Dargestellte Wirklichkeit in der Abendländischen Literatur; R. Formesyn, Le semeion johannique et la semeion hellenistique.*"

Having failed to establish the common subject to which these books were devoted, Gideon continued to stare at them, anxious to gain some inkling of their contents, but ending by wondering why, in the last title he'd read, the word 'semeion' whose meaning he didn't know, had a 'le' before it at its first appearance and a 'la' the second time.

"May I leave you here a few minutes, Mr. Spokane, while I hear Miss Galbaddy's confession?"

The Friar had come up behind without Gideon hearing him and was speaking over his shoulder.

Gideon, surprised in his grappling with half-forgotten tongues was about to reply: '*bien sûr* or *natürlich*', but only nodded.

What could she have to tell in the way of sins?

"It's the pre-nuptial confession as is customary."

It was only after the Friar had left the library and gone into a small oratory, which Gideon was shown later, that the expression 'pre-nuptial' seemed to him strange in relation to Pieta.

Was there a confusion on the old man's part? Did he think that it was Pieta who was getting married, as perhaps their leaving the others and visiting him together might suggest?

The mistake could, of course, be easily corrected, but that the idea had arisen disturbed Gideon. He paused in his examination of the outside of the books to try to discover why. He recalled, quite irrelevantly and absurdly, Leo's comments about what he called 'her signals'. Turning to the shelves again, the first title he saw in his own language was 'The Mystical Marriage'. He didn't pause at the volume but raising his glance a couple of tiers, he noticed a thick volume titled *Jesus, het verhaal van een levende* by Edward Schillebeeckx, and beside it *Jesus,* evidently the English translation of the same book. He took it down, opened it and saw it had been published in 1979. Encouraged by its comparatively recent appearance, he looked through it at random and came on this sentence: 'What will they have to say after they have first of all listened to what the non-church people have to tell them of Jesus of Nazareth?'

Who were 'they'? Gideon realised he was out of his depth. Despite which he was impelled to push on, as years ago he had taken those long and fruitless walks through foreign cities.

As far as he made out, there was the Church with all its bureaucrats, highly disciplined in the exercise of powerful influence on the minds and psyches of those belonging to it, and on the other the historical Christ, powerless vis-a-vis the institutions of his time, very vulnerable and making little impact in his short lifetime. The Dutch theologian with the curious name appeared to be saying that the Church and Jesus of Nazareth were not necessarily the same, a proposition that seemed to Gideon (who admitted he was hardly an expert in these matters) self-evident.

The conclusion that followed he tried to summarise: This Church, or perhaps the Pope, was not, as it claimed, the final arbiter in this game (as Gideon thought of it) of deciding who was who in the heavenly hierarchy. For those who agreed with the Dutch theologian, the Church was exceeding its original charter (Gideon knew he was using the wrong words) in some of its latter claims. One of the more restrictive and unacceptable of these was that made by the Vatican that all intimations and spiritual revelations concerning reality granted to believers (such as the theologian or the friar) otherwise than via the institutional channels were mistaken, mischievous and probably heretical.

He was interrupted in these unaccustomed reflections by the return of Pieta and Frère Emanuel. Gideon, with the thick, theological volume in his hand, put the question that puzzled him, and that he had an instinct might concern him, to the

79

monk.

"This writer refers to 'The Galilee Fiasco'? Could you tell me what is meant by that, Reverend Father?"

He used the form by which he had heard Lucius Canavan address the Prior, though he realised it might not be correct in the case of a simple monk.

"Read the account as related by the evangelists and you'll see that failure dogged Jesus in his journeys through Palestine, ending in the fiasco of the final period when his disciples came back from the mission he had sent them on to report nothing but rejection or indifference.

"So it had to be. He had failed to persuade any but a hand-ful — and even most of these recanted — of the coming of the Kingdom of God; and then there was failure staring Him in the face as he was executed with a couple of common criminals while He Himself doubted whether He hadn't made a mess of the whole enterprise and been abandoned by His God."

"That's the first I've heard of this side of the story," Gideon said.

It didn't seem to make sense, yet he responded to it in a way that he never had to what he'd heard, or occasionally read, of the New Testament.

"Failure, fiasco, deteriorations of the brightest hopes, erosion of the deepest faith: these are the signs that we are truly within the shadow of the Kingdom of God."

These words came as balm to Gideon though he knew he might be misapplying them to his own private concerns. He resolved never to forget them.

When Pieta reappeared, Frère Emanuel returned to the oratory, perhaps, Gideon thought, to leave them alone for a few minutes. Not that at first he could think of anything to say to her. The few passages he had read from the Dutch theologian, followed by what the friar had been saying, left him confused but exhilarated as did anything he came across that contra-dicted the more widely-held assumptions of the time and place.

It was Pieta who spoke: "He believes you are the person to

be in charge of our magazine."

Is that what they'd been talking about?

"Which magazine, Pieta, for God's sake? Surely not the same one that the others have in mind?"

She laughed.

"There won't be two, that's certain. The backing will come from them, but not the words of life."

" 'The words of life', isn't that rather vague and pretentious?"

"Oh, yes, as I put it. It's for you to see that what actually gets into print has nothing like that about it. You see, Gideon, one of your principle assets as editor is that you've a very critical and negative side, but, unlike most sceptics, you're not without passion."

"Is this what you told the old monk?"

"I didn't have to make out a case for you, just a short recommendation, and he saw how it was for himself."

# TEN

Kathy was waiting for Gideon outside the gate into the Priory enclosure by the time he arrived, having parted from Pieta on her way to visit the convent where she'd been educated, at an intersection of paths between cedars.

How relieved he was to find her! He'd been afraid that she might have gone off with the others, perhaps catching a boat back to the mainland. But, no, there she was in her beige blouse, low and loose at her breast — she'd draped a scarf over it at the meal — a white skirt and rust-coloured tights of the same shade that she'd been wearing when she'd stepped out of the tram queue.

Ah, what a leap! Talk about the gulf, as Frère Emanuel had, between heaven and earth! From the fortress-hermitage with the old friar, his books and Pieta, to being alone with Kathy in a secluded part of the island, was like going from one pole to the other, one extreme of sensation to the other. He was still in the spell of the earlier one.

"Do you believe what it says in the Gospels, Kathy?"

"Why ask me? Ask your undefiled one."

Yes, it was a foolish question. He wasn't quite himself, not that that was a valid excuse.

Kathy put a hand to the back of his head and drew it down so that his nose and mouth came in contact with her bosom just above her blouse, which, with the scarf removed, seemed to have opened, or slipped lower, so that he breathed in the warm aroma that wherever he sniffed it, in whatever unlikely place, in dream or reality even, were that possible, on his death

82

bed, he'd recognise as being wafted from between a woman's breasts. Warmish and lately washed, or at least with a faint hint of soap, which might well be the trace of some talc.

It did the trick, as he put it rather crudely to himself. He was fully back into his relationship with her, or, anyhow, into the sexual side of it.

"Where are the others?"

"Gone with the last boat. I was coming to fetch you, you were so long."

"What did you arrange?"

"The wedding will be on the twenty-fourth at eleven in the morning. Where's Pieta?"

"Visiting her old convent school where I think she'll stay the night. What about us?"

"The Prior said we could go back in his private boat which will be leaving quite soon."

When they arrived at the small wharf, it was already there, a small boat painted blue and black, with a wheelhouse like a telephone booth amidship. They were helped on board by the skipper, a lay brother in a boiler suit, and shown into the little cabin aft where there were already a couple of Dominican nuns sitting on the forward-facing benches.

Once out of the sheltered, wooded bay, the vessel was swept on the long, low waves coming in from the open sea, raised and tilted, left a moment in the air as a wave slid from underneath, and falling back with a soft crash into the water.

They were settled on the rear bench facing the brown-robed backs of the nuns a couple of rows in front. Through the forward window of the little saloon the helmsman was visible in his booth.

"It's O.K.," Kathy assured him.

To what was she referring? To the slight dizziness that had overcome him, something far short of sea-sickness that caused him to feel that the seat was collapsing under him? To her brief expression of irritation at his delaying so long with Pieta and her spiritual guide? To the settling of the date for their wedding? Was it to do with the magazine? None of these mattered to Gideon greatly just then.

"They can't look round," she added.

"Why not?"

Nothing was very clear to him.

"Look how frozen to the bench they are! If they raised their heads, let alone turned them, they'd throw up."

Yes, that was what Kathy had in mind. She was raising her skirt, suggesting they do what he had thought was far too risky. But how on earth was he to make the necessary movement in the narrow space when he was still intent on keeping a grip on the bench?

"Go with the waves, not against them," Kathy told him.

She was swaying backward and forward, her legs drawn onto the bench. He got to his feet but could only stand with difficulty by holding on to the back of the seat in front.

"Not like that! Relax and be ready to slide with the next tilt of the boat."

Gideon couldn't work it out, but to his guidance came precepts he didn't know from where — let everything slide! Cast yourself on the waters, or waves, and give no thought for anything but ending up inside her!

One moment Gideon was kneeling facing her on the bench, the next he was slipping down it, as it see-sawed towards him. It was a far gentler and more rhythmic movement now that he was part of it, than when he'd been trying to keep his upright seat.

Sea and wind were in accord with them. She hooked one of her legs over the back of the bench and helped brace herself with the other foot on the floor, thus containing his slide with a firm resilience. The shudder of the next wave hitting the boat caused a slight adjustment, as if by chance and they were fully conjoined.

By the time the boat sailed into the bay of Aphrin, where the sea was calm, the couple of religious day excursionists were sitting side by side on the bench and peering out at a white cruise-liner anchored there.

On disembarking they passed a queue lined up on the quay and were told by the attendant at the car-park that these were tourists from the liner come to dine on shore who were being screened because the authorities believed that armed subversives from abroad were among them.

They passed two armoured cars on the drive from the harbour to the hotel.

"There's something in the air," Gideon remarked, not very subtly, as Kathy more factually suggested by pointing to two grey helicopters that were circling the seaward part of the city.

On the way she had Gideon stop outside a building a couple of blocks from the Hotel Aphra, which the island conference had decided on renting as the office of *Faillandia* as — also decided at the conference — the weekly was to be called.

It turned out that two small trade magazines that had been published from this address were going out of business, or moving out of town, and the premises together with a printing press on the floor above were ideal.

The next days were mostly taken up with arrangements for the launching of *Faillandia*. Gideon was working out his month's notice at the garage, but the evenings were spent with printers, representatives of newsprint suppliers, business dealings with which in a smaller way he wasn't unfamiliar, the acquisition of extra office equipment, and finally, a secretary. Staff was to be minimal to begin with, though there were to be literary, sporting and political correspondents, the first two to be selected by Gideon.

When he asked Kathy where all the money would come from, she said that her father and Canavan had both wealthy acquaintances in the business world, ready to back any project likely to prove an effective opposition.

For the moment he left it at that, not even asking: 'opposition to what?' What he noted, in one of his private meditations far removed from this outer activity, was how quickly the impact of the sensual incident on the boat was fading.

It seemed that sexual experiences, no matter how intense, needed continual renewing if they were to influence the prevailing mood. All-important at the time, they were in retrospect unmemorable. When he thought of the years he'd lived with Lydia, though admittedly their marriage had been less than averagely full of love-making, he could only recall three or four of the actual occasions.

Sex can't be that important, he reflected banally. Yet if deprived of it, it haunted him to desperation. But, another point to note (when he came to compile his treatise *Sex and the Human Psyche,* ha! ha!) was that the attention, his at least, was easily attracted away from the sensual. For example, this was just what was happening now while he was busy with the magazine, in particular considering how to ensure a first-class horse-racing column, a feature that, Leo agreed, was essential, especially as the elderly Kemp couple, who were among the magazine's sponsors, were deeply involved in the thoroughbred business.

He got in touch with a French woman journalist, Marthe Delaunay, who wrote for *Paris Turf,* and whom he'd first met in the press box at Chantilly and on a few occasions in Paris, in his days of dabbling in race-horse breeding. By telephone he arranged for her to come over for next week's important race meeting at the course just outside the city, expenses paid by *Faillandia,* where he'd meet her to discuss the matter.

Then he advertised for a literary editor, setting out briefly the qualifications, and offering a salary in excess of the usual rate. Among the replies he received were several from well-known writers, some of whom reviewed for the daily papers.

The magazine was rapidly taking shape in Gideon's imagination and much that had been obscure was clarifying. Helped by his talks with Pieta and discussions with Leo who was surprising him by a shrewd business and political sense — things Gideon distrusted — and was turning out a radical rather than the more traditional liberal reformist that Gideon had taken him for.

He now understood that the magazine's purpose was to have

an effect on the thinking and feeling of a small number of its readers. He didn't suppose it would infiltrate the defences of the kind of people who were considered leaders of informed opinion in matters of politics, culture and economics.

Moreover, this uncompromising tone must pervade all its sections. People with various interests, sporting and cultural, were beginning to long for a fresh breath to be let into those closed and stale areas.

Gideon was amazed that, whether with books or horses, both reviewers and racing journalists could transform them to lifelessness with the magic touch of a sentence.

In the sports page he was going to introduce, if Marthe agreed, a new way of writing on horse-racing, not intended for those citizens who wanted a tip a day, a dream-distraction to alleviate the drabness, but for those for whom the race-course was a microcosm of the world, where they could take the smaller, though still dangerous, risks in a quest for the more insignificant, but still exciting truth.

In a similar way, he was going to have a book page that went to the root of the matter in question.

He had advertised the position of literary critic and reviewer at a salary so generous as compared to the local rate that he hoped it might attract some outstanding applicants.

And sure enough the first of these was none other than Mario Kimm who even Gideon, who had never moved in intellectual or literary circles, had heard of, though he wasn't sure in what connection. And this rather imposing figure introduced himself with the evident expectation that recognition would be accompanied by deference and, in this case, satisfaction on Gideon's part at having hooked such a big fish.

The man's appearance was a shade too Bohemian for a politician and he had (assumed or natural) too inwardly-occupied an expression for a business executive. It was, Gideon concluded, meant to dawn on those who didn't instantly recognise him that here was indeed a welcome sight: a great artist in their midst!

Full of himself, I'd say from a quick glance, Gideon decided, and what's more, one of the pretentious sort, a breed which, unfortunately for the smooth course of the coming interview, I am perhaps unfairly biased against.

Because of this he started on a negative note.

"What I don't need is somebody to mow and trim the lawns and spread fresh gravel on the paths of our literary garden. Not even, if he, or she, can attach labels to the hardy perennials and the shrubs with variegated leaves — both of which species some kind of insect pest seems to have got at — indicating the categories to which they belong."

Was this overdoing it? Trust me, Gideon reflected, to go from one extreme to the other.

"Elegance of style, plus sensitivity, plus of course, a proper concern with our national characteristics and customs, that is the kind of fiction you would like to see given place of pride, I take it."

Had they already lost touch with each other?

"Well, yes and no, Mr. Kimm. I am not at all sure . . . "

"Please give me an example of the kind of work that appeals to you and that you think should be promoted in your weekly."

"I'm not sure about being 'promoted'. And I'm not sure that I could name any contemporary novels that, had they just appeared, I would ask my literary editor to at least take special note of. You see, we're already into ambiguities and imponderables."

Gideon felt he must be sounding very negative and disorientated. With an effort of memory he recalled a passage in an old French periodical he'd read lately and that stuck at the back of his mind.

"This is what Drieu La Rochelle had to say about Anatole France when the latter was at the height of his popularity: 'Without God, without love, without insupportable despair, without magnificent anger, without definitive defeats . . . ' "

After he had finished quoting the extract, there was a pause in which Gideon waited for Kimm to make a comment, until he saw that the writer was himself waiting.

There was one of those misunderstandings, chilling to both parties, that throws a conversation, even sometimes a promising one, into confusion. Could it really be that the writer wasn't sure whether Gideon had quoted this passage as an example of a kind of sloppy, emotional writing that he wanted to exclude from the weekly — which might be, Gideon now saw belatedly, Kimm's natural reaction to it — or was it meant to indicate the critical tone that the editor wished the magazine to set?

In order to extricate them both from the predicament, Gideon broke the awkward silence.

"Disgust, as the critic George Steiner used to say, is short of breath."

"I don't quite follow."

No wonder. Gideon had said the first thing that came to mind. But he thought he could adapt it to serve as an observation bringing an interesting discussion to a not too-abrupt end.

"He meant, don't you think, that the critics who draw a wide, warm blanket of approbation over most of what comes their way weekly are those who spread themselves garrulously in the literary supplements. Whereas those for whom literature isn't stylish comments on, or about, the passing scene, or *about* anything at all, but is the thing itself, the small, pale flower that fends for itself in all weathers, have only a few words to express their outrage."

What circumlocution! He could only bring it to a conclusion by a kind of slight of hand (or mind).

In the next few days after his interview with Kimm there were some quite violent clashes between the Government forces and the guerillas in the North of the city where the rebels were reported to have occupied the North Station.

"That's where our Liberator is expected to arrived on his return," Leo told Gideon. "Like Lenin in 1917 at the Finland

Station," he added, giving a farcical twist to the preceding announcement.

Gideon's time in London had contributed to the gaps in his knowledge of political developments at home which, given his reflective rather than actively alert kind of mind, were in any case numerous.

Whether the North or any other of the city's stations were actually in rebel hands, there was no doubt about the sudden shortages in the shops of various commodities which lasted a few days, after which some other items soon became in their turn unobtainable, a sign, more than any other, that Gideon took to foretell a coming upheaval.

There were fracas and near-riots in the petrol queues at garages where armed police were on duty to see that when the attendant walked along the line of parked cars and indicated the last one which would receive a ration, that those behind were driven off in an orderely fashion. In other cases only habitual customers, identifiable by cards issued by the particular service station, were being served.

Gideon spent long hours at his place of work in his car parked in the garage forecourt, keeping check on the figures on a small computer that registered the level of petrol in the underground tanks and the rate of flow through the pumps that were being operated. By closing down some of the pumps or by bringing more into operation the rate at which the car queue passed through the station could be controlled in relation to the flow of traffic along the adjoining street.

Once he'd got the hang of it, it was not an onerous task, and he was soon spending most of the time there working out the details for the first issue of *Faillandia* due in ten days.

Sometimes when she was free, Pieta sat with him and kept an eye on the flickering hyroglyphics of the machine's small bluish screen, leaving him free to do the final priming of the other device which was to send a tremor through (he was thinking of the state of mind, already tensely expectant, ripe for a further undermining of reliance on authority) the shaken city.

It wasn't only in the streets, in the long petrol and other queues, in the brief (censored) newspaper reports, in the sound of gunfire at nights, that there was tension, anxiety and, among a section of society, a feverish search for enjoyment.

For Gideon, the two girls, their father, and the little group concerned with the new venture these were hectic days.

When the new, uncensored publication appeared on the news-stands and in the shops, given | the astute advance publicity engineered, Gideon thought, by Leo through his association with prominent people from various sections of the citizens, it was sure to sell in large numbers.

This question of not having to submit proofs for censorship, as he'd been officially informed, puzzled Gideon. Leo seemed to suggest that this had been arranged by Lucius Canavan in agreement with his opposite number in the Government. Certainly the situation might be desperate enough for Government and opposition to come together where there might be ways of restoring some semblance of law and order. But how had Leo persuaded Canavan that *Faillandia* might help in this direction? He was beginning to grasp certain extraordinary gifts in the Patron of the Hotel Aphra, of persuasion, not to say intrigue, and a network of associations to be manipulated at the vital times.

No doubt the apparent support of the Dominican Prior for the magazine had helped to influence Canavan, quite apart from whatever Leo had told him of its anti-Government orientation. And if Canavan reported to the relevant minister that *Faillandia* was being backed by influential churchmen, that too would help convince him that it was at least something a little more substantial than another straw to be grasped at.

For Gideon it was a wonderful opportunity. For the first time in his life he had a chance of putting together a symposium of his deep, instinctive and, till now, unexpressed — he had sometimes thought unexpressable — concepts on various matters, none of them directly political. He had articles, whose authors wrote with a rare mixture of scholarship and passion on such themes as the disappearance of institutional religion from its last strongholds, with a reply by a Dominican friar, though not one of those who had been at the picnic party. There was a parable, or prophecy, in which at a far future date a spacecraft cruised round the planet Earth while a lecturer related to a group of students from a distant solar system the history of the small globe from which life had long disappeared. This story as told by the professor from a far corner of the Cosmos, and the outer fringe of the future, appealed to Gideon by both its tragedy — unapparent perhaps to the group of history students — which to him, lay partly in its holding up to ridicule much of what had been fine and fragile in man's vision, and partly in the lecturer's stressing the final failure of the religion to which the inhabitants had clung at various periods. He told them the story of the Gospels — explorers from his own world had salvaged and brought back many important relics and indications of the kind of intelligence reached there before the disaster. And though keeping close to the New Testament text, as far as Gideon, not all that familiar with it could judge, presented the story to his students as proof of the superstition and credulity of this particular breed of Cosmic beings.

There was an article that argued persuasively, and whose conclusions were based on some exhaustive research, that the reading of books, especially of popular fiction, biographies and travel volumes, would quickly decline in coming years, but that the original works, from the past and, if any, from the present and future, would go on being studied by roughly the small same number of enthusiasts.

Still on the future, there was a piece demonstrating that parliamentary democracy was unlikely to last, as a system of government, the lifetime of those still young. There was also a reply, or addendum, to this in a contribution by Lucius Canavan himself, neither of which pieces really concerned Gideon.

There would be neither a racing column nor a literary page in the first number, partly because of lack of space, but even more owing to his not having found in time the sort of person he envisaged to provide either section.

He was keeping a space for a contribution that Pieta promised him would be one of the highlights in the first issue. She did not say who had written it and he didn't ask, though he had an idea it was Frère Emanuel.

Then, to add to the threat of the day of publication dawning with much still unresolved, a lady journalist who had applied from London in answer to his advertisement for a literary correspondent telephoned that she was arriving for the interview that he'd suggested, without really supposing that, as one of the more highly-regarded reviewers on a prominent London Sunday supplement, she would be interested enough to make the flight.

There were confusions from the first. He missed her in the arrival area at the airport, having made up his mind how she would look. It was only after he'd searched in the bar, been down to the ground floor and back again on the escalator and there were only a few passengers still waiting beside their hand luggage, that he went up to a small girl in a well-worn leather jacket and a mop of untidy hair and inquired more in desperation than with any confidence: "Miss Dolfish?"

Yes, it was she. Should he pretend he was late and apologise? But she'd already seen him wandering around earlier. There was a delay leaving the airport where an armed police squad were checking the cars. To increase what must be her unfavourable impression of how things were run in a country to which this was her first visit, Gideon explained that they would have to have their talk sitting in his car in a garage forecourt.

"Please understand, Miss Dolfish, that because of the rapidly deteriorating political situation we are getting out the first issue earlier than planned, which has increased the pressures on our small editorial staff."

How did that sound, Gideon wondered? Not, he feared, as he'd meant it: businesslike, relying on her understanding without being apologetic. And instead of bringing her to the well-appointed — as he thought of it — office, he edged the car through the early arrivals at the service station where Pieta was already waiting.

If it hadn't been for Leo and Lucius Canavan bringing forward the day of *Faillandia*'s appearance, and if it hadn't been for the petrol famine, he'd have fitted everything into its proper place by working shorter hours, as it had been agreed, at the garage until his notice expired in a couple of weeks.

If, after what must surely have been her astonishment at the locale for the interview, their being joined by Pieta who, with the small computer, sat at the back, was a further shock, she hid it, making a light remark about hoping there wasn't a historical parallel between the Russian Revolution being set off by the bread queues in St. Petersburg and the effect of the petrol queues here.

"Supposing," Gideon asked her, "there had appeared in St. Petersburg or Moscow between the October and February Revolutions a weekly magazine for, let's say, fifteen issues, covering all aspects of Russian life and thinking, and supposing it had caught on and that all sorts of people had read it, even Lenin and Trotsky, do you think the course of events there might have been altered, Miss Dolfish?"

The young woman turned from watching through the car window the operation at the petrol pumps and smiled at him. No, having come across too many bizarre, not to say downright crazy, ideas in some of the books from which she selected the weekly half-dozen or so she reviewed, she wasn't surprised at the suggestion, which, in any case, not being versed in twentieth century European history, she hadn't fully understood.

"Call me Hymna; Miss Dolfish sounds ridiculous, don't you think?"

Gideon didn't supply an answer. He had put the idea that had only just occurred to him in the form of a question to Pieta rather than to Hymna; had the two names a common root? Their owners, he reflected, came from different planets.

He might, of course, be quite wrong as to the Russia of nineteen-seventeen, but what he was really telling Pieta was that now was the time in the recent hisotry of their native land when a sufficiently large number of seriously-minded people from various social groupings were, mentally, emotionally and nervously, in a condition to listen, not to new solutions (because the claim to solve problems was part of the politicians' repertoire) but, to a new way of looking at the whole set-up, the perhaps unsolvable problems included.

"What we need, Hymna, is a new approach to everything, literature included. In fact, I believe literature is one of the first things of which a proper grasp and appreciation will help de-pollute our minds and spirits."

"One thing that struck me," the girl remarked — "this country of yours seems a prosperous one. I noticed some very smart-looking shops and restaurants on the way here."

"We'll have lunch in one of them."

Gideon planned to take her to the Aphra and introduce her to Leo.

"But first I'd like you to get an idea of what kind of literary editor I need and what kind I don't."

"Sounds sensible, Gideon. Start with the sort you can do without."

"Almost any of those you can probably mention, most of the big names in your national press. I'm not conversant with them and am only judging by the reviewers they evidently prefer. I don't know, Hymna, if you'll believe me, but I could write a synopsis for the kind of novel that they'd all rave about. I know the ingredients, the favoured mixture, the approved flavour. I could even, if pushed, find somebody here who could write it to my guidelines and it would be sure to be short-listed for one of your prestigious awards."

"I see."

"Do you, though, Hymna, or are you thinking to yourself that you're not going to get involved with a crank no matter how large the salary, and that his magazine is unlikely to last beyond the first few numbers?"

95

She laughed. Perhaps he really had hit on what was going through her mind. But Gideon thought there were other thoughts there too, she seemed one of that kind of 'a very intelligent girl' that he had sometimes met in London.

"Of course, if you thought I was suitable, I'd want a contract, say for a year. But please go on about how you see the way your book page should be run."

"Like the rest of the weekly, with a cutting edge to it, cutting away all the half-dead undergrowth that clutters up the scene. No precious space wasted on mediocre, meritricious, pretentious, portentous, pseudo-historical, spurious, forced-comic, vapid-profound or social-satirical."

"How to fill the page might be a problem."

"There are ways, given imagination. I don't set any great store by being up-to-the-minute. No recently published novels worth reporting on? Then a new assessment of a classic. Literature is only great if it has something new to say to successive generations. We have sensibilities now which we hadn't a hundred years ago, and the response to reading, say, *Moby Dick* today might be worth recording."

Hymna Dolfish took a small notebook from her handbag and was about to write in it.

"Oh, don't bother to note the name. There are no hard-and-fast directions in this business. Leave it all to intuition, if that's the word. What I'm saying is only to give you a hint of the kind of tone that is needed to fit into the overall spirit of the magazine."

"Perhaps I'm obtuse, but I don't think I get it."

"I don't expect you too, not right off. I myself am only beginning to, after months of thinking about it and being submitted to a number of shocks showing me how far out I'd been, most of them coming from Pieta, who, when she hasn't to concentrate on this bloody contrivance, will give you a far çlearer idea of what *Faillandia* will try to put across. Meanwhile, one more conclusion that I came to from a study of the literary criticism in your quality papers. It is evident that if an original, radical piece of fiction was to appear — not a common occurence, but also not completely unknown — either no notice at all would be taken of it, or it would be dismissed with that tepidity that many of your best-known reviewers have made an art of exuding."

# ELEVEN

Back at the hotel, Pieta took Hymna up to her and Kathy's
room to have a belated freshener-up after her flight. As she
herself was soon due on the lift and would not be joining them
at lunch, she had a snack at the bar while Gideon kept her
company.

"Promise me something, Gideon."

Not another shock, just when he hoped that the outstanding
problems were being resolved.

"All right."

"That you'll look after the fledgeling when I go to hospital?"

"To hospital! Whatever for?"

"Probably nothing much."

"Tell me!"

"You'll feed it every few hours?"

"Yes, but what's wrong?"

"Just until the tail feathers grow."

What was this? A joke, because he sometimes called her his
Dove of peace, or Dove undefiled, in distinction to Kathy who
was just plain Dove.

"With you, not the bloody bird."

"I'll tell you later, there isn't time now. It's only a matter of
dropping morsels of cat food into its beak with a sharpened
match stick; I'll leave you a supply of them, and replacing the
newspaper at the bottom of the cardboard box."

When Hymna joined them, Gideon took her to the restaur-
ant to meet Leo and the Kemps. After the introduction and the
choosing from the menu, a ceremony that Gideon would have

98

liked to have speeded up but that the Kemps, under the guidance of Leo, lingered over lovingly, the talk, instead of, as Gideon expected, focusing on the magazine, turned to horseracing. Distracted as he was by what Pieta had just told him, it was a little time before he realised the initial misunderstanding. The Kemps, and possibly Leo, thought that the young woman had flown from London to be interviewed for the post of racing correspondent, and the old man was, very tactfully, trying to find out something about her credentials.

Gideon suggested to Leo that he should intervene, but he was more concerned in explaining to the Kemp woman the recipe for the baked sardines that, rather surprisingly to Gideon, she had ordered.

"I believe you're going with Mr. Spokane for a meeting tomorrow. It's one of our most important."

When Gideon intervened to save Hymna becoming even more bewildered than he thought, one way or another, she might well be, the old fellow was somewhat disappointed.

Half listening to the talk at his other side, in the hope of an opportunity to get Leo's attention and make the conversation general, Gideon heard Helena Kemp explain that her choice of dish had something to do with today being the Feast of Tabernacles, a day of fasting for the congregation to which she belonged.

"I'd like you to tell Miss Dolfish how much space you think the magazine will give to books," he told Leo.

Anything to distract old Kemp from his evident personal interest in Hymna, as well as possibly finding out Leo's opinion of her, before he made up his mind whether to offer her a contract. At the moment, because of anxiety over Pieta, his mind seemed incapable of coming to a decision. Had Hymna taken in and responded to what he'd tried to make clear, despite the unpropitious circumstances, in the car? For instance, had he only confused her by bringing up *Moby Dick* whereas what he'd wanted to explain to her was that he believed there was a partly subconscious instinct by critics to

99

evade mention and memory of great works from the past because any reassessment of these (when there was nothing new worth comment) might explode the pretentions of the contemporary literary fashions with which they were at home.

Had he made clear that the magazine meant to try to upset some of these? That wasn't easy. Gideon himself wasn't quite sure how far or in what direction Pieta planned them to go. He was sometimes doubtful about her admiration for the old monk, influencing her to include pieces too narrowly religious for more than a handful of readers.

For his part, he saw their first task as clearing a space around them in the ugly clutter of sham ethics and pseudo-ideas, political, social or cultural, where the few precious seeds he believed were collected and stored at the back of his mind could be sown.

Gideon excused himself from the table on the pretext that he'd forgotten to make an important phone call. It had all become beyond him: Leo, Kemp, the English girl, and in the background, the friar, Marthe and the others. They seemed at cross purposes and he was now convinced that he shouldn't have become involved. Probably Pieta herself was finding it too much for her and was retiring to hospital as an escape, though this he didn't really believe. He appeared in Kathy's office in what must have been a distraught state.

"Hello, what's up?"

"Did Pieta tell you she was going to a clinic?"

"For a check-up, isn't it? If she hasn't changed her mind."

"Changed her mind? It may be something serious."

"You know how neurotic she is."

"I know nothing of the sort!"

"Sit down and I'll get you a brandy from the bar, it will help you come to yourself."

He felt somewhat drunk as it was but welcomed the chance of a short rest in Kathy's calm company.

"Yes, please do, but don't think you're going to get me to agree with you about Pieta."

Back in the restaurant Bernard Kemp was chatting up the girl beside him, telling her, it seemed, something about Failland and what he called 'her tragic story'.

"We are apt to blame our present crisis on our long history of foreign occupation, but it is as much due to what I could call the occupation of many of our minds by trivial obsessions."

Hymna, obviously not very interested, made a polite enquiry as to what these might be. Although Gideon didn't catch all the answers because Kemp had lowered his voice in an attempt to give the conversation a more intimate air, he did hear the words: 'politics, and what passes for religion'.

What it was all leading up to was a suggestion he take the English girl to a bookshop where he'd buy her an unbiased history of the country in which, among other things, a theory was presented according to which, when a pro-consul in Aphraburg, as it was then, ruled the land in the name of a foreign power, Faillese society was prosperous, tranquil and highly cultured. There were no native politicians to engender corruption, the role of the Church authorities in imposing a crude moral code and a set of tribal taboos was curtailed, and all but a handful of extreme nationalists had a lifestyle more civilised than any that a native administration would have either the will, or the means, to achieve.

Gideon was bewildered by this historic lecture — full of inaccuracies, as far as he knew — delivered by Kemp to the obviously disinterested girl. Leo whispered to him that it was a bit of improvised academic showmanship, mistaken in its assumption that Hymna was some kind of journalistic historian, put on as a reason for getting her to himself and driving her to the bookshop he had named.

"Six minutes in the car, that's all it'll take," he told her.

"Two on foot," Leo put in, the shop being only round the corner.

Hymna looked at Gideon who, despite his eccentricities, was her guide through the confusion of this strange country.

"I'm afraid I need every minute of Miss Dolfish's time before she flies home this evening."

Thinking it over later he wondered if it wasn't just the girl's company to the bookshop that Kemp had wanted? The plan had been to get her into the car parked in the underground hotel garage where the old fellow, with his wife retired to their suite of rooms to observe the rest of the day of fasting, would go as far as the little foreigner would let him or as his potency allowed, whichever was the more restrictive.

Gideon was later ashamed at how they'd laughed with a complacent superiority at the old man's plan which they'd foiled. It was all very well for him who had Kathy to share all his fantasies, but for someone like Kemp with all his faculties still functioning, as far as could be seen, wasn't the little ruse natural, if pathetic, and not something to ridicule by those who had no need of such expedients.

# TWELVE

A week or so before publication day, Gideon, whose contract as deputy-manager of the garage had now expired, was on his way to the race meeting at which he had an appointment with Marthe Delaunay who had flown over from France, partly to cover the big race for *Paris Turf* and partly to discuss her contributing a weekly column to the magazine.

Just as he was leaving the office where Pieta was putting in appearances at odd hours of the day, she handed him an envelope containing some typescript pages:

"For the magazine."

He was slightly late already, apart from which he was in a state of mind far away from the tranquil, contemplative yet critical one in which to assess contributions, especially a last-minute one:

*'If we are not already past redeeming, it will be through the imagination that the miracle will be achieved. It is our only means of escape from the small, noisy, poisoned, neon lit cell, plastered with advertisements, in which we have imprisoned ourselves. The world we have been industriously constructing by means of our undoubted technological, engineering and rationalising gifts has been constantly narrowing and hemming us into what has the feel and whiff of a coffin ingeniously wired, sanitised and fitted with our latest time-killing contraptions. This is what, in many parts of the world, passes for life. It is only by means of what imagination survives that an alternative to it can be constructed, a*

*model closer to reality.*

*The inspiration for this is once more — as always till now has happened in times of near-destruction — in certain of our art, in poetry and fiction. These writers are inevitably in confrontation with their communities. What they see and what they foretell is not at all the way society sees itself or the way it thinks it is heading. There have been these times throughout history when the redeeming vision came through prophets and artists.*

*Isaiah, Ezekiel, Jeremiah, did not only foresee the fate that would befall their people if they neglected the vision they revealed in parables. They were not mythologising about an ancient reality that now has no relevance. Read their prophetic words with an open mind and there comes to one the rare thrill of conviction and shock that accompanies a near brush with reality. They were seared with flashes so blinding because at that time there was no diluting and obscuring media, or intermedia, to intervene between them and intimations of truth.*

*What they foretold was unpalatable, against the grain of the day, against easy optimism and rational likelihood and, as always, demeaning to the powerful and vainglorious. Like all who contradict the popular beliefs and assumptions of their time, on which society constructs its fragile base, they were isolated and persecuted. And the kind of communication that at later times could be likened to theirs has always had a very minimal appeal.*

*It is an obscure process, this soothsaying, as natural and mysterious as the growing of the grass and, like that phenomenon, unremarked but for a few kindred prophets.*

*When Hans Küng spoke recently of 'the theology of literature' he seemed to recognise that these ancient prophecies are being repeated and adapted to the contemporary context.*

*Past and future are the systole and diastole of these kind of novels, their soothsayings are both interpretations of old tales and parables about what is to come. The gap between them and the writing that receives serious attention these days is wide and growing more unbridgable.*

*Our sensibilities have evolved over the years, astonishingly in the last few decades, both weaving strong threads between us and the past and thrusting explorative antennae into the open spaces whence the unexpected is coming.*

*Perhaps this inner evolution is linked to the increasing threat of exterior doom. This age has created fear and a kind of subconscious anguish formerly undreamed of. It is also seeing a literature arise whose counter-dreams and subconscious energies extend the horizon to a point where even the worst horrors can be encompassed.*

*The roots of this literature are in the past and its shoots in the future. 'I am the Vine and you are the branches.' Here is one of those sentences that reverberates inside the nerve cells, by-passing the rational and intellectual filters. It is the language that the writer giving expression to new concepts has to use. How and in what sense this 'I' is made flesh and dramatised in fiction depends on the temperament and personal experience of the writers in question.*

*If they were to be asked how they envisaged the Vine of this parable from which they draw inspiration, there would be very diverse and surprising confessions:*

*'That Person, faithful and true, supreme and ruthless Arbiter who alone distinguishes the real from the hallucinary. He may appear in different disguises, sometimes wearing a halo, at others a forage cap.' 'The Chief of a High Consistory of Dead Masters.' 'The most lonely outcast and reviled, the condemned murderer returning in the Black Maria from Court to the death cell, executed by society for a mean and miserable crime.' 'A hunted creature at its last gasp before its tormentors.'*

*The 'heroes' and 'heroines' of this new fiction will have little in common with those of the novels that still take space in the book pages of newspapers. These, though, are themselves being edged out of the review columns by what now passes for more important kinds of literature: biography, documentary, volumes of travel, anything from which imagination can be excluded.* Faillandia, *in opening its pages to the new 'prophets' is the first undoubted sign of the coming time. This was only possible in the unique revolutionary and ambiguous (politically, religiously, culturally) situation in Failland. At the moment there is a large number of people, unaffiliated to any of the former institutions propounding their various 'certainties', whose mind and hearts are catching fire from the rekindled flame.'*

He glanced through it quickly, hardly taking it all in, but registering unbelief at what appeared to him immature fantasy. Where had she got hold of this esoteric outpouring? They were bound to receive all kinds of bizarre unsolicited offerings now that the publication had been widely advertised.

"What shall I do with it?" Pieta asked.

Gideon hesitated. He had been about to tell her to drop it into the waste-paper basket, but realised from her tone of voice there was more behind it than he thought. So he said they'd discuss it when he got back.

Once through the turnstiles he saw Marthe waiting at the parade ring. Skin the shade of wet ashes, lips like dry ashes, eye whites with the sheen of peeled, boiled eggs, teeth a creamy enamel.

"Ah, Monsieur Spokane, are we going to see the truth made visiable? *La Verité!*"

God Almighty, what had taken possession of them, first Pieta and now this girl whom he'd first met in the press box at Chantilly when he'd been invited there as a foreign breeder; the French didn't know on how modest a scale.

He learnt that she had a gift for picking two-year-olds in the parade rings at Longchamp and Every that later became outstanding, and this was one of the gifts that made her valuable to *Paris Turf.*

Today she was excited at the prospect of seeing a race horse for the first time about which a lot had already been written and whose reputation had, it seemed, reached France. He was running in the big race which was the third, and it was impossible to concentrate on the earlier proceedings and indeed even to discuss with Marthe the business on which she had flown over, though he thought she might have come anyhow for a first sight of the potential champion.

At last the horses for the third race began to be led into the parade ring.

He was anxious that the truth should be revealed to him at least not later than to Marthe. She too was not relying on her race card and he saw her moistening her dry-ash lips with the tip of her pale pink tongue.

Then there he was: the king! The king? This light-framed, smallish animal that did not really fill the eye? But was filling the heart with delight.

*"Le vrai peut quelquefois n'être pas vraisemblable."*

"Eh?"

"Not what we were expecting, no? Have you too the proverb: When the truth appears it seems unlikely?"

The colt lifted his head to survey the unfamiliar scene with a lordly glance. Marthe gripped his arm.

"Voila! the eagle look of the truly great one."

Gideon suddenly knew he'd been right in thinking of her for the magazine. There must be a daring, at first disconcerting, new spirit brought to literature, sport, politics, as well as religion. And what if the piece Pieta had shown him and which he'd too hastily dismissed was an example of this too?

So far there hadn't been time to more than touch on the subject of her contributing to *Faillandia*. He asked her to do a quick piece on 'Montenotte', and her impression of him as he was led into the parade ring.

Gideon drove back to the Hotel Aphra with Marthe where he'd taken a room for the night for her. She was catching a morning flight back to Paris.

At a roundabout shortly before entering the first built-up

areas, traffic was being stopped by soldiers and it struck him that the road on which they were driving, and the railway line that ran beside it, led to the Northern Station.

There was a slow crawl to the check-point and then a young officer in airforce uniform came up to the window that Gideon had opened and asked from where they had come.

"From the races."

Like almost all the other cars, which, Gideon supposed, not only must the officer be well aware of, but that had probably been the reason for setting up the road block. If some revolutionary figure was expected to try to slip into the city via the Northern Station, where a welcome was being prepared according to rumour, what better chance than in a car travelling with the congested race traffic?

The soldier asked Marthe where she was from.

"Also from the races."

She spoke hesitantly because of her pronounced accent, as if she didn't expect to be believed.

"And before that?"

"From Paris, France."

The soldier continued to look at her as if for further information and she added:

"And before that from Martinique."

They were allowed to drive on.

"Who are they looking for?" she asked.

"A revolutionary leader."

"I thought it had something to do with this proposed law of yours I read about, that they were looking for adulterous couples."

"Do you still live at the *Hotel des Sources* opposite the station Enghien?"

She laughed.

"You've a good memory."

"Do you, Marthe?"

That was where he had thought of fleeing at those times of desperation at home with Lydia, and an imagined haven it had remained.

She had told him that it was owned by an ex-jockey, well-known in his day, who had once ridden the winner of the *Le Prix de l'Arc de Triomphe*.

After dinner at the Aphra she went up to her room to write the piece on *Montenotte* which she would give him in the morning before flying back to France.

Pieta had left a message for him with the porter, asking him to come to her room when he was free. Under the peak of his gold-braided cap the porter's face was expressionless, without being anything but deferential, and this ability to assume this attitude under all circumstances, was part of what made him, as Leo had confided, the most highly-paid member of any hotel staff in the city.

Before going to the girls' room Gideon read the typescript that he had only had time to glance through and was glad that he had, because it was about that that Pieta asked him straight off.

He told her that he would certainly print it in the inaugural issue of the magazine.

"Not just for my sake?"

"You didn't write it?"

"No, Frère Emanuel did, but I don't want you to be guided by me."

"By who else, Pieta, when it comes to matters that are still beyond me?"

"Did you guess why I asked you up here?"

She'd been lying on her bed reading by the lamp on the small table, the rest of the room was dim. Had it been anyone else, say Marthe, he'd have understood the question as one of those that can be taken as invitation to a closer intimacy but, should things go wrong, can be explained, with an accompanying teasing reserve, as having had a quite different and sober purpose. But not with Pieta, the dove without guile.

"About this, wasn't it?"

He indicated the typed sheets.

109

"Yes, but that could have waited. I wanted to show you how to feed the bird when I go to hospital."

"You don't mean . . . "

"Oh no, I'll have to wait till there's a free bed, it's not urgent and it could take weeks but I suppose I could get a call and have to go there any morning."

"Listen, Pieta, I won't feed the bloody bird unless you tell me what's wrong with you."

She regarded him out of the grey eyes that were so like Kathy's, but hers narrowed whereas Kathy's widened when she was intent on coming to a conclusion about something important he was telling her.

"O.K."

He sat on the side of the bed from which she directed away the beam of the table lamp. There was quite a long pause which he didn't want to interrupt, but finally had to.

"Not gynaecological?"

"What makes you think that?"

He hadn't; he had been impatient.

"Nothing. What did the doctor say?"

"Doctor?"

"You haven't been to one?"

"I have, but I don't believe in doctors."

"What do you believe in?"

He was trying, perhaps clumsily, to get to the centre of the mystery.

"You know well, Gideon, I trust in God."

"Which God?"

"Jesus."

"All right. What does he say to you?"

He was at sea and probably putting the wrong question, but there was now no turning back, the time for discretion and respect for what might be her right to privacy was gone, though he hadn't realised where he might be trespassing when he started questioning her.

"He says: *Come Pieta.*"

"Is that all?"

"All! It is asking almost more than I can imagine: to take a step towards Him is to step from my little ship into the sea and start to drown. But I do it."

"And then?"

"He rescues me, and for a second holds me above the waves, and I hardly survive that second."

"You mean, your heart . . . "

"No. It's a burn, an abrasion on the breast."

An abrasion! Gideon had read a little on what he thought was called the pathology of religious mania. He had come on case histories in medical encyclopedias that at one time he had studied. In medieval times such experiences had not, he thought, been uncommon, especially among nuns and women devotees in general, some of whom, like St. Catherine of Siena, had had what was called the stigmata seared into their flesh.

At first he felt depressed and anxious. Was Pieta, without whose help he would be lost in persevering with the magazine, now, at the vital moment, drifting off into a hallucinatory world of her own? Had it been too much for her and was her 'illness' a subconsciously contrived way out, so that she could escape to hospital just when it was due to appear?

Unworthy thoughts? Trust me to entertain them in an ambiguous situation, even if I come round to regaining trust a little later, Gideon reflected.

It was an incident that happened the next day that made him revaluate what Pieta had said, though the two events would have had nothing whatever in common for anyone else.

A Government minister, not, as Gideon thought, a particularly prominent one, but of course he didn't know what inner power struggles might be going on, was assassinated while driving home from a cabinet meeting. Gideon couldn't feel much one way or the other. It was the outcry in the newspapers that caused him to think again about what Pieta had related. Was her very private interpretation of what had happened to her more of a hallucination than the media's contestation that this public event had caused 'widespread grief' and 'universal indignation'? Whereas, of course, what it actually caused, Gideon reflected, was a vague satisfaction at a notoriously corrupt bully coming to a sticky end, and a momentary uneasiness among some less-hardened citizens.

Gideon made a mental note to get someone to probe into this phenomenon of so many journalists, mostly a cynical lot, conniving at these hypocritical public expressions of outrage.

The times were out of joint and, as in *Hamlet,* all kinds of remarkable events, public and private, were going to happen, the appearance of *Faillandia* not the least. And, possibly even more fraught with unforeseeable consequences, the return of Colonel Klotz.

There were varying reports of where he had been. Most newspapers agreed he had been seconded by the Failland air force to train pilots in a foreign country. There was also a report, not confirmed, that he had indeed arrived at the North Station, unknown to the authorities, and after making a brief announcement, had been driven off to an unknown destination.

The same evening the Assembly Chairman, Nording, appeared on television to broadcast to the nation, and many turned on their sets who wouldn't normally have done so in the expectation of having the mystery about Klotz and his arrival cleared up.

Instead of which, Nording spoke at length about the minister shot that morning, referring to him as if the loss to the country was of the gravest. Gideon heard the familiar sentences about somebody (never of any real importance) who had spent his life in devoted service to . . . It was only when he heard the speaker pronounce the word 'terrorists' in reference to the killers that Gideon began to take some notice.

What Nording and most politicians didn't realise was that recent history had caused most people to revise their concept of terror. With the coming of the Bomb it had lost most of its power to frighten or appal when used in condemning individual incidents. Apparently unknown to governments, the neurological climate had altered.

Once the condemnation 'witch' had brought the tremors of fear to the hearts of God-fearing citizens. At another time, it had been the word: 'heretic'.

Nording's predecessor and present leader of the Opposition, a close friend of Canavan's, also appeared on the screen to express his sense of grief and outrage. And Gideon realised that what united them, however politically hostile, was the knowledge that the only way the system that shared out power and prestige to them could be disrupted was by the increasing guerilla activity.

## THIRTEEN

All sorts of people were now turning up at the *Faillandia* offices, some by appointment, others with contributions, advice, threats and questions. There was even a journalist who enquired as to whether the magazine might not set a good example and tone by carrying the Nording address in its first number. Gideon had a secretary-receptionist, Nolla Grimmick, a former civil servant who had rather surprisingly applied for the post. When Gideon asked her why she had left her previous job, she said: "The usual reason."

He wasn't quite sure what was usual and what was not in these secretarial-executive matters. He didn't think she meant that a relationship between her and one of her superiors had gone wrong. Gideon hesitated to enquire further. There was something about her that seemed to suit from the start. Just as though he knew the kind of contributors he wanted, he had a feeling that this girl was the right person in the office.

Miss Grimmick — Gideon had't yet begun to call her by her first name — sorted out the calls with tact and intuition, dealing even with many of those with genuine business to transact herself. And surprising him by occasionally consulting him about sending into his office a visitor without either an appointment or an obvious recommendation.

When one morning in early June she announced over the intercom: "A Mr. Frank Everett to see you," Gideon's heart fell. The policy being formulated for the magazine was at a critical point — various influences exerting pressures — and he didn't want at this moment to have to listen to the views of his old colleague from the Geological Museum.

"What does he want?"

"Says he's an old friend of yours, Mr. Spokane."

"I'm very busy, you know."

"I think you should see him."

Frank appeared smarter, more self-assured. Gideon wondered how he himself struck the other after a few months. Not more self-assured, that was certain.

"Here I am, Boss."

Boss? Let it pass. Gideon was considering the other as he did most people he met these days in the light of *Faillandia*. It was absorbing him, the magazine, but that was how he was. For Gideon, there had never been a neutral space between indifference and obsession.

Had Frank come to offer the revolutionary magazine — as he would see it — a part of the proceeds of the museum robbery? And if so, would he, Gideon, accept it? More to the point, had Frank carried out the operation, using the key to the alarm system that Gideon had seen in his possession? But there had been no key. Gidoen had dreamt of, or imagined, one.

He didn't see Frank as anything but a risk as far as *Faillandia* was concerned. Wasn't the girl in the office a risk? Risks of one kind and another beset him, but what he didn't want was the support of the gangster-revolutionary he sensed in Frank. Not from any moral or civil rectitude, but because such an influence could disturb the delicate balance he meant to introduce between the various sections which he hoped to fuse into a harmony, a new way of seeing and responding, a new interior lifestyle. He decided to get rid of his visitor as soon as he could.

He recalled in a flash, while Frank was still speaking, how Lydia liked spending solitary hours tending the garden, an occupation that he'd never taken seriously. One morning, which she'd spent in a remote part of it and come in with muddy hands, passing through the room where he was working on the stud-farm book, to wash them before going to prepare their

115

lunch, he hadn't looked up or said a word although they hadn't seen each other since breakfast.

A day or two later he came on a long bed newly raked and covered with netting where she'd sown rows of vegetable seeds, and he had realised his own blindness to obsessions other than his own.

"So you see I haven't been wasting my time since I got back."

Gideon had missed the first part of the sentence.

"No, indeed, but I'm not quite clear . . . "

"How I got in with her ladyship?"

It turned out that Frank was now the boyfriend of a rich American woman who owned a yacht that was berthed with all the others down in the old harbour.

"When it gets too hot here we shall sail off in her — and this is what I came to let you know, Boss — you could join us. I've discussed it with her nibs and you'd be welcome. What I want, *she* wants, so long as it prolongs the present arrangement."

So he had been wrong again, and Frank, far from coming to ask favours, was here to offer what might after all be useful, not in the way he suggested, but in relation to the magazine, if it had to go underground.

"That's what I call very thoughtful."

That didn't sound right, just about an adequate response, but lacking the spark that should ignite between old comrades at times like this. Still, Gideon was in no condition to do any better. He couldn't tell Frank that all he wanted was his visitor's departure, so that he could go on with the musings that took up so much of his time now, but whose exact part in the production of *Faillandia* he couldn't have put into words.

"I also came to tell you something that may be more to the point. I'm behind you in this business. Not just with moral support which is something you don't need, but as an old activist who can still use a gun."

This time Gideon's heart really fell.

116

Ah, my dove-grey treasure, my fragile hope, my fledgling! You cannot be protected by guns and swords. Gideon was intent on his musing and waiting for Frank to leave.

Frank was one of a constant stream of callers. Nolla Grimmick dealt with most of them herself, receiving the messages both verbal and written and passing them on to him, towards the end of the day.

These ranged from abuse to absurd flattery, from the meaningless to what might be a piece of wisdom that he would show to Pieta.

Some examples:

*'A purely technical-cum-rational culture constitutes a serious danger, because it contains within itself a fatal impoverishment of man.'*

*'Conservative 'models' of faith will not withstand changing sensibilities.'*

*'Time is running out.'* (He'd heard that before.)

*'There stands a house*
*It's full of windows'*
*To the right of* (indecipherable),
*And that meany witch*
*Lives*
*There and doesn't write to me.'*

> — Vladimir Mayakovsky.

*'The sexiest women,*
*The fastest horses,*
*The finest writers,*
*The most corrupt politicians.*
*Viva Failland!'*

A lot of doggerel like:

*'How nice to be a mammal!*
*In a shape that's never dated,*

117

*However much it's true*
*That it may be rather banal*
*To be geared for the next screw.'*

The Day, as he was privately thinking of it, dawned like any other (Pieta reminded him that the Thursday evening, part of which Jesus spent in the Olive Garden, had been, according to Rilke, elsewhere unexceptional. Dogs barked, beggars stretched out their hands).

The weather stayed mild to muggy, traffic flowed sluggishly, breakfast was served both in the bedrooms and the hotel restaurant.

The magazine, with *Faillandia* in large red-brown letters, reminiscent of the colouring of the wild plant that Kathy had shown him, across its front, was displayed on the news stands and in the shops along with other periodicals while Gideon was getting the second issue to the printers.

Gideon's instinct told him that these were the fatal days. The time when all is in the balance, before the first bubbles float up through the wine-must, before the silent phone rings, before the beggar unfolds a crippled leg after the 'Arise' has been pronounced. And, of course, nothing might happen, and only those with a peculiar faith, or superstition, would persevere in the belief that nevertheless all had been mysteriously achieved. Nothing happened, therefore there was nothing to record, no fermenting, no whispered word, the cripple sat on beside his begging bowl and if he thought he'd caught a word addressed to him, it was a cruel jibe.

He asked Pieta what she thought.

"About what?"

"Don't pretend. About what's so much on our minds, yours as well as mine, and no doubt on the old monk's too."

"The magazine? But Gideon, I've other things on my mind and in my heart. Surely you know that?"

"You don't mean the bird?"

She didn't answer.

118

"Your going to hospital must be weighing on you, I realise that."

She shook her head.

"Undertakings far too important than ours have failed miserably, and turned out a fiasco. And it hasn't mattered, not in the long run."

"There's not been a comment, I haven't heard a word nor seen a single soul reading it."

"When there was a threat to the marriage of a couple on a popular national TV show, their picture appeared on front pages and all sorts of people were deeply involved, identifying with one or other of the human triangle. No, that's not very relevant," she added "is it? You see, I'm no good at arguing things out. Think of it like I do."

"How?"

"Oh, I didn't mean that, either. Why should you? Your own way is the true way for you, even if it is a painful one."

"We put so much into, and had such luck in getting some wonderful things for, the first number that I thought it was sure to make a splash."

"God protect us from splashes! Why did you put in that poem by Christina Rossetti with the lines: 'Safe where the seeds wait to grow'?" she asked.

"Because you told me to."

Pieta laughed. Then, after a moment, he laughed too. Without words, at least without argument, she had convinced him, for the time being, that all was well, or that if it wasn't, that was still no cause for doubt or depression.

A hundred thousand copies, on Canavan's advice, had been printed, and at the first return forty thousand copies had been sold. The second number sold thirty thousand and the third eighty.

Gideon didn't give way to any overt rejoicing when he received a note with the latest figures from the magazine's accountants. He didn't know what to make of the fluctuation. He drew a short graph and studied it, and decided that the next returns, for the fourth issue, would be an indication of the true impact.

Then came news of a raid by an armed gang on one of the main distributors who took off with an as yet undiscovered number of the fourth issue.

How was this to be interpreted? Gideon consulted Leo.

"Hard to say, before we establish who was responsible."

"You've no idea."

"I've ideas, conflicting ones at that."

"Who would you like it to turn out to have been?"

"An action group squad from the Opposition."

"From Canavan's lot?"

"He has shown signs of uneasiness at what you've been getting up to."

"But you know, Leo, we aren't engaged in party politics, our whole orientation is away from all politics as practised in this part of the world. We could be seen just as easily as hostile to the Government."

"Yes, but the Government hasn't the surreptitious means of discouragement that are available to the Opposition. And they don't want to risk an actual clampdown at this stage."

But what heartened Gideon during these days of anxiety, which they were despite his talks with Pieta, was a Pastoral Letter issued by the Archbishop of Aphrin, Cornelius Tolling. In the main it contained directions on such usual topics as family planning, indecent films and the routine condemnation of violence (of the unauthorised kind), as well as a short prayer of thanksgiving, to be recited at each Mass, for the victory of the finally passed Anti-Adultery referendum, although in the city itself the Amendment had been heavily defeated.

But towards the end came what Gideon suspected was the real reason for the Letter. Archbishop Tolling mentioned, without naming, a recent publication that he warned the faithful of the Arch-Diocese against.

*'Seemingly harmless, even spiritually-minded at a first casual reading,'* the Pastoral declared *'unlike other previous*

*anti-church propaganda, this publication is not anti-religious in tone, but, more insidious, recalling the heretical schismatics from the past, it tries to re-interpret the Holy Scripture in a manner to discredit the divinely-appointed successors to the Apostles without whom the Gospels would not have been preserved, let alone preached, throughout the earlier dark, and the present even darker, age.'*

Unexpectedly — but Gideon seemed incapable of keeping a space in his mind open to intimations of what was going on outside the obsessive concern of the moment — the date for the celebration of the marriage arrived, and the whole wedding-party sailed for the island one morning.

On the boat there were several people reading *Faillandia* and Gideon noticed one old fellow who paused from time to time to write in a pocket notebook.

This time they went not to the Priory but the convent, where Kathy changed into her wedding dress, and in the chapel of which they were married by the Prior.

Gideon, with everything still in the balance as regards what he thought of, sometimes, as the fate of the seed they had sown, only followed the ceremony intermittently. It was when, to his surprise, Frère Emanuel started to preach that he became attentive. The old friar spoke with a shocking directness and conviction. Whereas almost all that was said publicly these days by politicians, businessmen, clerics or other professionals, was in such generous terms so as to avoid offence to potential voters, consumers, clients and members of the fold, as to be largely meaningless.

At first there was nothing unexpected in the theme: the Marriage at Cana:

"Jesus performed his first miracle, as you know, at the wedding feast, one of his more simple wonders. He wasn't going to risk anything very out-of-the-way straight off. Some of you may wonder why he didn't cause the empty jars to be replenished with wine, instead of first asking the servers to fill them with water.

"I'll tell you, Fathers, Brothers, Sisters, beloved ones: to transform water into wine presupposes no great disturbance of natural laws. It is a comparatively slight re-arrangement of the molecular composition. But to create something out of nothing, to call up the molecules that are the building blocks of all matter — solid, liquid or gaseous — including wine, and arrange them in the correct pattern in the empty jars, that might well have been beyond Him at that period . In fact, when you think of it, Fathers and Children, He never took on himself the role of creator. He could re-arrange the cells or re-activate electronic charges in bodies, He was conversant with molecular physics and, no doubt, astro-physics, though that doesn't concern us here. He had also a certain pre-vision or foresight. But He never, as far as is reported, produced, if I may put it like that, a rabbit out of his hat. He wasn't here to play the magician.

"Take the incident when his little company were short of money with which to pay the tax man. He directed a couple of His disciples to catch a fish and open its jaws. And there, and what a comforting thrill we still receive when we re-read the familiar story, was a bright coin. At first one might think that it was a roundabout way to provide the sum needed. Why not just produce it out of thin air? Because, as I'm suggesting to you, Sisters and Brothers, he did not come on earth as creator. There is nothing against natural law in a fish swallowing a small shining object (fishermen use such metal lures) or that it should get stuck between its jaws. What was extraordinary was his perception of the fish near at hand. But that again implies superperceptive gifts of mind and imagination, not a subverting of nature.

"Be patient a little longer, Fathers and Brethren, I am coming to my conclusion. The great and abiding miracle at Cana was not the turning of water into wine, but the marriage of male and female. And not, perhaps, the actual marriage, but the pre-ordained miracle of man and woman.

"Meditate a moment on the physical wonder of the sexual union of a man and a woman. It is a mystery and a sensation beyond the power of the most daring imagination to have envisaged. That is to say, it is the great miracle, and, like all miracles, it is physical, material and earthy. Because in the Kingdom of God, which is metaphysical, there can be no miracles.

So, learned Fathers and Little Ones, we celebrate this wonder of marriage to be consummated by this man and woman later in the greater miracle of bodily union."

# FOURTEEN

They were given a room in the convent in which to change before the wedding breakfast at the Priory and the return to Aphrin.

"Pieta is coming with us to help me out of all this finery," Kathy told Gideon at the end of the ceremony.

"I can manage that."

"You both can."

It was one of the bedrooms that had been used by the girls but now, with a decline in the number of pupils, was unoccupied, though still sparsely furnished with a made-up narrow bed, a miniature white wardrobe in which Kathy's everyday clothes were hanging. As a former boarder in the school, it was natural that Pieta was to show them to it along corridors and up a flight of stairs.

"Behold the bridal chamber" she announced, opening the door.

Although it was half a joke, Gideon's heart beat faster. The strange sermon had already excited him with its stress on the mystery of sex and the miracle of the conjunction of two bodies.

The words of the Friar were absorbed into his veins and nerves, causing the blood to flow and the pulses to beat with, he felt, a greater urgency.

The door was shut and Pieta was still there.

"May I help Kathy undress?" she asked him.

She struck him as also affected by the sermon, though she appeared quite calm but even paler than usual, which, as he'd noted before, caused her eyes to darken.

There was a pause while Gideon hesitated as to an answer. His desire for Kathy was compelling, but so was his reluctance to disappoint and perhaps even hurt Pieta.

He sat down on the solitary chair to unlace his patent-leather shoes, the only concession to formal attire he'd made and which he wore with what he still thought of as his one good suit. He'd changed into them in the toilet and given the plim-solls he habitually wore to Kathy to stow away with her gear.

When he stood up in his socks, he saw that Pieta had un-done a couple of the hooks in Kathy's satin bodice and seemed to be waiting for him to unfasten the rest.

But there was something that came first; it seemed that this was to be as much a ceremony as the marriage; Pieta opened a thin leather-bound volume.

"Frère Emanuel gave me this for you both. I thought we should read some verses from it together, the three of us."

"What on earth . . . "

Gideon, for all his usual patience, felt aggrieved. What was all this delay when time was short with the others expecting them over at the room attached to the Priory where they had had the picnic.

"Look!"

She showed him the book, an old edition of *The Song of Solomon,* for use in a monastery choir, in large print, with the verses arranged for alternate intoning by tne monks or nuns in opposite stalls.

Gideon undid the remainder of the hooks and opened Kathy's bodice, exposing the strong stalk of her throat that rose from the flesh above her breasts, still encapsulated in a lacy brassière. Her skin was unexpectedly dark in contrast to the white material.

Gideon was trying to insert his hand towards Kathy's back, inside the still-tight bodice.

"Not like that," Kathy told him.

Without a word, Pieta with a finger inside the elastic, eased the bra down, then pulled it round till the fastener was in view. And this she left to Gideon to open.

He'd never seen anything like her breasts before, though he had contemplated them many, many times. It was as if, for all the kisses he had lavished on them, he's always missed part of their sensuality, and had never realised that all earthly rotundities that rose from a level surface were crude copies of those fragile mounds on whose darker crests the tiny buds were in bloom.

Pieta was holding the volume to Kathy, who read out from it in a rapid low tone, with short interruptions, as if, Gideon thought, gasping for breath.

*'I will sing the song of all songs to Solomon,*
*That he may smother me with kisses.'*

Gideon bent his face to her and smelt a whiff of soap and warm flesh. He took one of her nipples into his mouth and kept it there while he heard Pieta recite to her sister:

*'Let us rejoice and be glad for you,*
*let us praise your love more than wine,*
*And your caresses more than any song.'*

And it was Kathy's turn again:

*'I am an aspodel in Sharon,*
*a lily growing in the valley.*
*. . . the winter is past*
*the rains are over and gone.*
*The flowers appear in the countryside.*
*And the turtle dove is heard in the land.'*

What was happening, or could happen? But Pieta had it well in hand. She moved behind Kathy and divested her of the bodice, easing her arms out of the close-fitting sleeves.

Kathy's torso emerged from the white wedding dress, her shoulders and breasts in the full bloom of the aspodel in Sharon, the Shulamite (the very name was for Gideon an aphrodisiac) stripped by her hand-maiden and aglow in her nakedness before the bridegroom.

Pieta unpinned the veil from her sister's head and loosened

her hair, so that it fell in a dark thick halo over her shoulder
and upper arms —
   *'My dove in the cleft of the cliffs*
   *or in crannies of the high ledges.'*
The last and highest, most inaccessible cleft, that was also
the lowest and deepest cranny where moisture was gathering
in secret, was still to be revealed.
   *'Your love is more fragrant than wine,*
   *And your perfume sweeter than any spices.'*
Pieta had fastened the bridal veil on her own head, covering
her hair and part of the face. Then she stooped to loosen the
white skirt from Kathy's waist and draw it down, while her
sister stepped, in what struck Gideon as a ritual dance, raising
one leg and then the other, out of the wedding garment.

She stood naked but for white stockings that came halfway
up her thighs. Gideon wondered at her not having worn
knickers, and only then concluded that she and Pieta had pre-
arranged this consummation ceremony.

How far was it to go? What were the ancient precedents?
Would Pieta now discard what had changed from a bride's to a
nun's veil and leave them, so that he could in turn divest himself
of his inappropriate suit?

He couldn't take his eyes from Kathy's shoulders, their ridge,
the bony blades of folded wings whose feathers were suggested
by the downward fall of her autumnal-tinted hair. And then the
wide expanse of flesh that had the look, the slight flush and
surface texture, of nothing else on earth just before it divided
and rose, drawn into twin sensual artifacts, whose magical
powers were beyond him.

"How beautiful are your breasts, my sister, my bride!"

Pieta was folding away the wedding dress and putting it back
in the attaché case in which they'd brought it. Kathy walked
slowly, and with that air of calmness that is on the verge of
explosion, to the bed, pulled back the covers and lay down.

To Gideon, now alone in the centre of the room, it seemed
that they were no longer bound by the traditional social taboos.

This was the women's doing, not indeed that there was the slightest sense of perversion or voyeurism in the presence of Pieta. They had succeeded, he wasn't sure how, perhaps by transposing them in time and place, in revealing an aspect of eroticism, eternally rooted in the dreaming imagination.

He quickly undressed and lay down beside Kathy.

He was hardly inside her when he felt this was different from their other times, when, as Kathy had told him, he mostly made love to her as if pursued by demons.

Now, perhaps because of the preliminary incantations, he was composed, could take his bearings, almost meditatively, while being carried away by sensation. What did he meditate on? Well, perhaps to say 'meditation' was an exaggeration. He was this time more fully aware of her, as a dove in the cleft of the rock, but also as the cleft itself leading through the otherwise impenetrable rock — back to the beginning, where in the orgasms he was one with her, one flesh, as it was when creation was still whole, undifferentiated into man and beast, male and female.

On their return to town the ancient and ceremonious consummation of their marriage (as Gideon thought of it), and also the peak of sensuality which casual sex never had, became a memory that he treasured in the midst of the many events, both relating to *Faillandia* and the national crisis, which were happening.

Guerilla groups, foreign-trained and armed, so it was reported in the papers, moved through the northern streets of Aphrin, sometimes occupying whole, mostly working-class districts for days, and then retreating into their strongholds.

Visitors, telephone calls and messengers in a steady stream kept the receptionist busy at the office. There was a flood of contributions as well as advertisements, letters to the editor, calls from newsagents for extra copies, invitations from the more independent of the two broadcasting stations for interviews. The fifth number sold over a hundred thousand copies and the sixth a similar number.

Would sales level out and then start to fall, or would they continue to rise, though at a lesser rate? Nobody could say, not even Leo nor Pieta, and not, Gideon supposed, Frère Emanuel, who, anyhow, certainly set little store by numbers.

On the private side, life continued, both on and below the surface, in the nerves, in the senses, above all, as he supposed it should, in the imagination.

Nolla Grimmick mentioned, in the same breath as that in which she asked if he'd see the sales manager from the garage where he used to work, that old Kemp (as she called him) had offered her a really breath-taking sum of money if she'd let him, of all things, spend a weekend with her in her apartment.

"If he'd asked me to go to Paris with him, it would be more in my line."

"I don't suppose you know much about old men and their dreams."

This was one afternoon when Kathy had taken over for a couple of hours at the reception desk, while Nolla did some book-keeping and typing. They were still running the office on a shoestring, as Leo put it. Although the magazine was making a substantial profit, it was, he advised, too early to engage extra staff.

"What's he after?"

When it comes to obsessions, and that is what it looked like to him, Gideon believed his instincts were seldom wrong. But how explain it to someone so young and sexually un-complicated as Nolla seemed to be?

"To boys and very young men, women are a mystery and, as Dostoyevsky remarked, they don't dare kiss the hem of their garments."

"What's that to do with it?"

"I've started this explanation which was probably a mistake, but at least let me finish. During their years of maturity, men solve the mystery of women by sleeping with them, as it's politely called. Then there's no end to the lengths they go to get to the bottom of the conundrum."

"Of the what?"

"Oh, for heaven's sake, Nolla, don't keep interrupting!"

Her eyes widened. She was hoping, he suspected, that he'd come out with something that would give her a shock that might create the sense of intimacy between them that was lacking.

"I'm sorry, Mr. Spokane. Please go on."

"The old Russian reprobate and inspired prophet knew (none better) how quickly this youthful awe towards women changed into a longing to experience with them the filthy habits of Sodom and Gomorrha."

Gidoen thought she wouldn't take it amiss if he was more explicit and couldn't help a fleeting thrill of satisfaction which, however, quickly curdled when he reminded himself how easy and cheap — to all concerned — it was to become a hero to the secretary cooped up with him during long and, in this case, often hectic office hours.

"Finally, the third phase: that of old men whom women fascinate much in the way they do boys and youths. That is, as being beyond their reach, though now no longer beyond their shameful thoughts and fantasies.

"Old men like Kemp, no matter how full a sexual life they've lived, are still tormented by the mystery which they now have no hope of solving by direct physical probings. What the more imaginative of them might dream of is to be able to share at least a day and night in the life of a young woman. If only they could spend every moment of twenty-four hours with her! That would, they think, make them happy. They would no longer suffer from the sense of being shut-out from the secret heart of life, no longer have to pause at night in a suburban street and look up at lit bedroom windows with that peculiar pang in the heart that is inflicted on those who, through old age or chronic illness, are disenfranchised — is that the word?" Nolla actually shook her head, showing how attentively she hung on every word "from what they see as the secret order of sensuality."

Before Nolla could put any questions as to how exactly all

this explained Mr. Kemp's extravagant offer and, even perhaps how it should influence her response, his phone rang as Kathy switched through an important call.

What was this, was Leo up to one of his charades? He had a gift of mimicry and could adopt local or foreign accents, when playing some just credible role of protestor at something that had appeared in the magazine. A day or two earlier, when Gideon had been in the middle of one of the crises that were now almost routine, he'd been, for a minute or two, ready to believe that the cultural attaché at the German Embassy was ringing up to protest at a comically dismissive piece on the latest novel by the leading West German writer of the day.

"Your foreign cultural correspondent cannot have properly informed you, Dr. Spokane, that the subject of your erroneously directed jibes and jestings is an international personage and a kindred friend of several highly renowned persons in our Bundestag."

Now it was a local Monsignor asking Gideon when he could call at the Archbishop's Palace for an urgent talk.

He was about to put down the receiver and reprimand Kathy (gently, in the manner she didn't resent) for being taken in by such a poor attempt at personification by her own father with not even the right blend of clerical gentility and regional mispronounciation, when even the possibility of somebody supposing he could be summoned like that touched a sensitive spot. Gideon had never got over his disgust at the pretensions of some church and state dignitaries, and, risking Leo's familiar guffaw at the other end of the line, he said:-

"If your Archbishop wants to meet me, I can make an appointment here at the *Faillandia* offices."

# FIFTEEN

Tall, thin, with a lined, ascetic face, Cornelius Tolling had been appointed Archbishop by the Vatican on the recommendation of the Papal Nuncio against the wishes of the Government who, it was said, regarded him as too conservative and traditionalist. His initial response to the growing mood of scepticism in regard to the local Church, which however he seemed to see as part of a general sexual permissiveness, had been to help organise and direct the anti-adultery referendum campaign.

"I understand your hesitation, Mr. Spokane, to call to the Archbishoprie because of its situation close to a disaffected section of the city. If I hadn't the protection of the Papal colours on my car, I myself might sometimes be prevented from getting through."

So the monsignor had thought up an excuse for Gideon's refusal to obey the summons.

"A cup of tea, your Grace?"

Introduce a slight diversion, keep such subjects as the Papal colours and disaffection in the background until the purpose of the visit was established.

Gideon, on the way to the door to ask Nolla to prepare the beverage, glanced through the window and saw the large car, a Mercedes as far as he could make out, standing outside the entrance to the office, with a yellow and white pennant hanging limply from a tiny mast at the front of the bonnet.

Should he tell his visitor that no parking was allowed in this street? Better leave it in case the Archbishop was exempt from traffic regulations, a matter, as it happened, which might be soon decided. A squad of women police were coming down the street in their trim dark green uniforms and black berets, on their way, he thought, to take up duty as customs and excise officers at the harbour, outside of which two cruise liners had, somewhat surprisingly, anchored the previous night, and from which the visiting tourists were being carefully screened.

The officer, a slim girl whose dark curls formed a fringe round the beret worn to one side of her head, glanced at the car and then turned her pale, oval face, without breaking her stride, up to the first floor windows from one of which Gideon was looking out.

Their eyes met for a moment, but what a moment! It was one of those when what would normally require hours or days in which to mature and culminate is all at once experienced. Or so he tried to explain and perhaps de-intensify it. On a very few occasions something like this had happened to him before, but at times when he could deal with the shock and, if not explain it by reference to such authorities on the irrational as Jüng and Wilhelm Reich (his reading in this area was limited) at least consider it from various angles.

As it was, he had fallen hopelessly, in the strict sense of the word, and passionately in love with the girl police officer at the moment when he needed all his wits about him.

He knew, of course, that this violent kind of preoccupation — he would not call it an obsession — couldn't last long.

"If it wasn't that I'm convinced that, unlike other local critics of the Church, you are a believer, Mr. Spokane, I should not have come here."

*Supposing an insurgent group had come round the corner and run into the squad, apprehending, or kidnapping, accor-ding to who was making the report, the woman officer, and bringing her up to the* Faillandia *offices where, seeing Gideon in conference with the cleric, they took him into custody too, and, for want of a better place of detention, locked him and the uniformed girl into the bathroom on the second floor.*

"Not a believer in the Church which Your Grace personifies

in this city."

"In Jesus Christ, was what I meant."

*It would be cold in the upstairs bathroom that once was part of an apartment now converted into offices, though he thought there was hot water in the taps from the furnace that supplied the whole building.*

"Our main contributors see the New Testament as the Communists look on *Das Kapital* as their standby and guide in their struggle against the Capitalist system. Although I don't write any of the articles, I too believe that the only figure with the authority and stature to lead the kind of revolution we are dedicated to is the historical-mythological Christ of the Gospels."

"There we are in accord."

*Without knowing how long they were to be incarcerated in the small, tiled cell, it was difficult to plan a routine that would keep up their morale. The first thing was to keep warm, to which end they turned on the tap and filled the bath with hot water. This, he explained to the police-girl, who told him her name was Giselle, acted like a radiator because, besides the warmth from the sides of the bath tub, there was an upward movement of heat in the form of steam from the surface of the water.*

The Archbishop was regarding Gideon from under forbidding brows, against which the world has blasphemed in vain.

"You are trying to turn Jesus into your own personal property, an élitist God who gives you private insights, which you report in your magazine, of his views on our present situation that are in conflict with the dogmatic and moral theology of the Catholic Church."

It required a great effort for Gideon to free himself from his obsession and come up with the answer that he knew was there from his talks with Pieta.

"What we're suggesting is that the sayings and actions of the Jesus depicted by Matthew, Mark, Luke and John, as reported within a generation of the events, have a new relevance for

134

many of our readers, because in the present crisis all else has failed. What we see as our task is to report some of His promises and prophecies which He is repeating today to those close to Him, as He did, according to the Gospels, in those times too, that they might be recorded and preached far and wide."

"Some of your private theologians claim to be closer to the Gospel Jesus than are we, his anointed, to whom He bequeathed His kingdom on earth. Who is it, Mr. Spokane, who has kept His name known and revered for two thousand years? Without the Church the name of Jesus would have long been forgotten, and if any records of the New Testament had survived it would be as fragments of a local myth and legend which for a brief time had a small fanatical following in Asia Minor."

There was an answer to this too, completely convincing, if Gideon could only call it up from the confused and distracted back of his thoughts.

*The cold of the bathroom reminded him of the cold of his apartment on the night he'd picked up Kathy at the bus stop. But this time there were no extra garments to put on and the only way to keep warm was to fill the bath with hot water, undress and get into it.*

*Fond of classical music?*

*This was not addressed to the cleric but, in imagination, to Giselle, as Gideon having momentarily mistaken the walkie-talkie she carried, attached by a strap to her belt, for a cassette player.*

*When she explained what it was, there ensued a pause, and the silence heightened the sound of the bath water running.*

*Why hadn't she used it to get in touch with her base and ask her superior to come and rescue them?*

*Suddenly, unexpectedly, without any effort on his part, the answer came to him — not, to the immediately foregoing query, but to the Archbishop's general contention.*

"Surely it was a question of your Church's survival, not that of Jesus who told his disciples: 'Before Abraham was, I am'. Could He not have maintained His indwelling presence in those who believed in Him and His promise during the two thousand years that have elapsed? And what if that is just what He has done: Might there not have been an underground Jesus in touch with His disciples all the time? But that might have made you and yours irrelevant, Your Grace. So you proclaimed Him a founder-member of your institution and appointed the Pope as his deputy."

"This private and personal divine phantom, indwelling and hidden, isn't what abject and sinful men and women look for, those in need of healing and mercy, who come to us in their hundreds of thousands, seeking the Crucified Saviour whose image hangs in our churches and can be touched. Most of them aren't very spiritual or imaginative, as are you and your friends.

> *'Bearing the Cross, in tattered dress,*
> *Weary and worn, the Heavenly King*
> *Our mother Church he came to bless,*
> *And through our land went wandering.'*

Was this a hymn that the old man, whose eyes were closed and who himself had taken on the weary and worn aspect of 'the Crucified King', was intoning? Gideon thought he recalled it, though he didn't see how it affected the discussion, in a different context.

"Don't try to curtail His journey through our land. If there are only one or two households in this city in which, because a distraught member of it has read an article in your magazine, uncertainty and doubts are increased, because of you putting your abstractions in place of the traditional, familiar figure, yes, even that of the Sacred Heart, your magazine will have betrayed Him."

Gideon listened, and at the same time heard the hot bath water running in his imagination and, to add confusion to confusion, recalled a piece submitted, he thought, by Frère Emanuel, though Pieta didn't say so and it had no signature, that he'd printed in *Faillandia* the previous week, called 'The Legend of the Grand Inquisitor', which had been a study of

136

the famous section in Dostoyevsky's novel.

He was, of course, out of his depth, and more at ease in the imaginary bathroom scenario, which was partly why it was taking such a hold on him. If only Pieta had been present, she'd have had the right answers, chapter and verse. For her sake, if not for his own, he had to defend the magazine.

"Very many people need the security and shelter of a Church or political party. They accept the dogmas, theological or ideological, for the sake of escaping from their inner isolation into the warm welcoming arms of a powerful tribe."

"Even put in your somewhat subjective way, Mr. Spokane, is that reprehensible? Miracle, mystery and authority, that's what they're starved of in their separate lives and whoever gives them that raises them out of the drab hopelessness," the Archbishop added.

"All the same, Your Grace, it isn't what Jesus had to offer. In fact He seems to have expressly declined to use any of the three to promote what He called the Kingdom of Heaven."

"What is to be gained, what sort of guidance or hope do you give by your questionings and doubts? This spirit of negativeness goes through all your articles and essays, political, cultural, down to the realm of entertainment and sport. You belittle those of our writers generally considered to have added to our literature, you hold up the highest civil administration in the land to contempt and ridicule. In all this you are throwing fuel on the flames with which the powers bent on destruction are trying to destroy, not just the Catholic or other churches, but the fabric of the nation."

"What powers, Your Grace?"

This reference was what had caught Gideon's attention in what struck him as a rather rhetorical outburst, perhaps the style of the kind of sermons that were being preached.

"The nihilists. You know of them too in your heart. If I didn't think that, I wouldn't have come to see you. Those who seek to undermine little by little what we live by, you as well as I. They are too clever to attempt to bring everything down in

137

ruins all together by a revolution, so bit by bit they hope to diminish our spirits by denying us our hidden nourishment. Reading that piece about the Grand Inquisitor, what the writer didn't mention was how the story ended with Alyosha's impassioned refutation of his brother's cynicism. Do you remember: '*But the little sticky leaves, and the precious graves, and the blue sky, and the woman you love! How will you live, how will you love them?*' What he means is — oh, I too have studied these great writers, Mr. Spokane — without these simple natural sources of love and faith, we shall find out that there is after all such a situation as hell, and that it is on this earth."

*Just to lower himself into the warm water beside Giselle! A tight squeeze in the narrow tub, and once and for all slip out of the Grand Inquisitor's presence! While from the little device resting on top of his clothes and her uniform piled onto the toilet seat, that was a cassette player after all, came Chopin's Polonaise.*

Yet — he was back in the room with His Grace — there was an answer to this too which he must try to formulate for his own satisfaction, if not the Archbishop's.

It went like this: If, as Pieta and Frère Emanuel believed — and both seemed to have deeper than normal insights — the Gospels were historical records, then most of the important civilised assumptions and attitudes were in urgent need of revision, including — and above all — those of this cleric's.

The Archbishop had said something in a low voice (a prayer?) that Gideon hadn't caught.

"What's that, Your Grace?"

" 'Things fall apart,
The centre cannot hold.'
I'm sure you know the poem."

Gideon nodded, but what the Irish poet, Yeats, had come up with in another time and place seemed academic.

"Do you really want, Mr. Spokane, to add to the raised voices, the public shouting, that are drowning out the whispers, the rustling leaves, the sighing grasses, the cries of the children, breaking the hush that the human spirit needs in which to preserve its contacts with its traditional source of nourishment?"

"You mean with you and your fellow bishops?"

"With the peace that Christ promised His faithful through the Church."

Peace? The status quo? Complacency? A cosy mind with shutters down?

Gideon, out of the blue, recalled some lines from an English poet, Harold Monroe, that had fascinated him as a boy:

" '. . . when the lamp is lit
And the neat curtains are drawn with care,
Though the tea may be late and the milk may be sour,
The little black cat with bright green eyes
Will always be purring there!' "

From time to time Gideon had longed to live in such a household where orderliness and habits of neatness and the small reassuring punctualities ruled.

But perhaps his thoughts were still straying, though no longer to Giselle in the bath-tub. Gideon looked at his visitor, trying to take him in for the first time. His deep-set eyes were either lowered or closed, his hands clasped inside the wide sleeves of his black habit over which hung the pectoral cross. He appeared to be in deep thought, or perhaps praying, or pretending to pray? But no, there was no acting or showmanship there.

"You proclaim an 'Underground Jesus' who has not his habitation in the Church and its tabernacles, but manifests the fullness of His Gospel person in the inner lives of alienated and solitary men and women. Don't you see, Mr. Spokane, in what anguish and doubt you are leaving some of the most vulnerable and devout of your readers?"

"If things fall apart and the tranquil centre that you, and the other authorities, have imposed isn't holding, that's because it was a false one. True peace can only be snatched from

139

fear and pain."

Gideon was astonished at what he was saying. They were Pieta's words, not his, though he didn't recall having actually heard her utter them.

"Those other authorities you speak of are certainly not our allies. In fact you and I, my dear son — don't mind my addressing you thus — have the same enemies."

It was late when Gideon's visitor left. Kathy had looked in sometime earlier to tell him she was closing the office.

He sat on alone for a time, still uncertain of the reason for the visit, of how he had managed in his defence of principles that, though he instinctively and emotively shared with Pieta, he found it hard to be clear about. Much of what the Inquisitor (as he now called him) had said seemed reasonable enough. But how should it not, given the age-old indoctrination here in Failland of the doctrine from which it came?

At last he returned to the hotel and sat down in the restaurant, almost empty at this hour, where Leo, having as usual kept an eye on operations in the kitchen most of the evening, was now free.

Gideon told him, though not in detail, of the unexpected visit. He was studying the menu.

"A grilling?"

What? For a moment he thought his father-in-law — he was beginning to think of him as that — was suggesting one of the dishes.

"Oh no. On the contrary he struck me as old and tired, despondent even, and at times about to fall asleep."

"You look as if you yourself aren't long out of a coma, man!"

Gideon resented the comment. He was nervy and with a sense of the interview — if that's what it was — having gone wrong.

He ordered the *Porchetta Veritable Romana* in a spirit of defiance, ready to show Leo, and any other doubter, that he was on top of his form by filling his mouth with the crackling morsels and washing them down with long draughts of Frascati wine.

"Did he pray with you before leaving?"

"Pray?"

"He didn't suggest you repeating the *Pater Noster* together? No? Then he must have realised he had failed, for it's well known that after one of his successful missions he likes to recite this prayer with his regained lost sheep."

"It's not as simple as that."

"How's the Porchetta?"

"All right. A touch more of the oregon wouldn't have gone amiss."

He certainly wasn't in the mood to praise this speciality of the place.

## SIXTEEN

The next issue of *Faillandia* was banned by Government decree, the offices raided and the copies found there confiscated.

Gideon called a meeting of the managerial staff and backers for that evening at the apartment where he and Kathy lived. It was attended by Leo, Canavan, Kemp, Pieta, Kathy and himself, the Prior being absent because, it appeared, the ferry service to and from the island had been halted by Government decree, after one of the ships had been commandeered by the rebels in order, it was speculated, to transport heavy arms from a neighbouring land.

After reporting what he knew about the early morning raid carried out by military police, Gideon asked for proposals. What he expected was a suggestion that a delegation call on the apposite ministry (there were several, 'Justice', 'Law and Order', 'Internal Security' whose functions overlapped) to lodge a protest and, if possible, find out on what condition the ban might be lifted.

It was Leo who surprised everyone, or at least Gideon, by saying: "We shall have to go underground."

For a moment Gideon supposed he meant those present and that, through the grapevine that brought him various confidential reports from cabinet and military intelligence sources, he'd heard that some of them would be arrested.

"Even if we got out the magazine, how can we sell it without our distributive agencies?"

"We can distribute it in the city. I know of one courier firm who'd deliver it to those shops, and there are a lot of them, who'd sell it under the counter. We'd also have to distribute a proportion of each issue free. There are plenty of volunteers for that, not to mention the girls here with their scooter."

"What about our advertisers?"

Canavan, Gideon surmised, didn't like the idea, but wasn't going to say so until he saw how the others took it.

"We'll lose some, but not all. Might even attract new readers. The publicity, in spite of all the Government tries to do, will be enormous. What do you think, Leonard?"

Yes, Gideon was beginning to catch up. How lacking he'd been in that kind of acumen that takes in the signs and portents that emanate from authority in crises, and can foretell whether it is going to assert itself by force or by political means. It was evident to him that Leo and old Kemp had agreed on a contingency plan.

Canavan seemed uneasy and talked about a solution (to what?) based on constitutional political methods, phrases that for all their familiarity — or because of it — Gideon failed to transform into something palpable and with a recognisable shape that he could handle in his own tactile fashion.

But when Leonard Kemp, who it appeared had had a white Russian emigré mother, talked about the Decembrists and their attempt to depose the Tzar and, in particular, about their clandestine paper, Gideon asked himself whether, had he then been an army officer or a Russian nobleman, from whom the conspirators came, he would have joined them?

Throw away the chance to experience the life of a young officer in the Imperial Guard, or say, a count with an estate in the country, at the height of that fabulous era, and end up in a dungeon in the Peter and Paul fortress? But, of course, his imagination was, as usual, running away with him.

Supposing he had been just setting out from the capital with a teenage Masha, when word had come asking him to hurry to the cellar to give a hand in getting copies of the revolutionary manifesto from the hand press?

Life was too beautiful, too enriching and astonishing, to

143

risk losing it for the sake of getting one's own back — and that of even more unfairly-done-by people — and seeing that those so long ensconced in the seats of power as to seem invincible got what was coming to them. That, to Gideon, was more or less what all revolutionary movements aimed at. To be honest with himself, he did not feel like endangering this wonderful new phase in his life that he had experienced in recent months.

Leo was suggesting, this also had evidently been already considered, that if the magazine went underground it could be brought out from the top floor of the hotel which was, in any case, not in use, and where the authorities were unlikely to look for it.

"Do you realise the great risk you'd be taking?"

This was Canavan, though it could have been Gideon had he not decided to keep his mouth shut for the moment.

"Oh, it won't last long."

"The magazine?"

"The Government."

"But even if we come to power after an election, we'll hardly be in a position to give the magazine open support."

"Do you know, Lucius, that a big downtown bookmaker is offering short odds against any elected Government still being in power by the end of August?"

"Bravo!"

Who had raised a cheer? Kathy. Pieta was looking at him, as, Gideon now recalled with shock, she had when he'd first come to the hotel for dinner. 'That girl is taking stock of me', he thought then, 'to see if I'm a proper mate for her sister'. But he later saw that it hadn't been just that.

What was she telling, or recalling to him? Ah, he knew, though he would at the moment rather have not. It went something like this: *Faillandia* must not fall silent or the state of those few who've been listening to words of hope in the increasing gloom will be worse than when we first appeared. As for the revolutionary talk, the Decembrist nonsense and the rest, don't take it to heart, though it's well-meant.

Canavan suggested bringing out the next issue under another name and with a different layout, but this was rejected by the others as a typically political solution, losing many of the paper's present readers and unlikely to gain many new ones.

# SEVENTEEN

The next days were spent turning the top floor of the Hotel Aphra into a rather makeshift printing and publishing concern. Leo, who had contacts with the most varied types of business people in the city, had a contractor that, he said, had previously worked for the Government — on increasing security in prisons, among other jobs — and had made enemies among the revolutionaries and now, sensing the shift in the wind's direction, was glad to be involved in a subversive project that was secret, and therefore non-compromising in the event of the survival of the *status quo*.

"But which will not be forgotten when there's a takeover by those who, I've managed to convince him, are also behind the magazine," Leo explained to Gideon whom his father-in-law's gift for double-dealing surprised, though it didn't shock.

When Gideon told Pieta, to see how she would react, she remarked, "Wily as serpents, innocent as doves, that's what those who take on demons have to be."

"Do you pray that all goes well in this rather dangerous enterprise?"

"Oh, no. I don't pray for anything specific, because I'm never sure what failures and setbacks the long-term plan requires."

"How do you pray, then? What do you say?"

He needed to know, to share as far as he could, which he knew wasn't far, in her mysterious inner life.

"*Rabboni,* give me the true gifts and I'll do without the bon-bons."

A sobering request that would require some thinking over on his part.

"But there's something else."

"That you pray for?"

"Well, not pray for, just ask, and it's of you this time. I want you to take the sick bird home with you tonight and look after it for me, because I have to go early in the morning to hospital."

"What for?"

"I told you, didn't I?"

"But what are they going to do?"

"I don't know. Probably nothing, just what they call a check-up."

"You're sure it's not gynaecological?" he asked again, rather insensitively.

"You mean some kind of feminine neurosis plus religious mania?"

"If I thought that, I'd be finished."

He surprised himself at putting it like that and so vehemently.

"So you'll take the fledgling?"

Back at his flat that evening with Kathy, his meditations, such as they were, were disrupted, for the time being, by a telephone call from a Captain somebody or other; Gideon failed to register the name and indeed only just managed to take in the details of the announcement to say that Colonel Klotz would be calling to see him next morning.

That wasn't all, and Kathy remarked: "It never is," as they were awakened around midnight by a call from Leo to say that bombs had exploded in the city and that, according to his information, several newspaper offices had been blown up.

"Which ones?" Kathy, who took the call, had the presence of mind to ask.

"You don't mean that our ... "

Gideon heard a laugh at the other end of the line. After-wards, Kathy told him that her father had mentioned three leading daily papers, two of them supporters of the Government, and had speculated whether this was in retaliation for the banning of *Faillandia.*

"It couldn't be!"

Gideon was not sure whether such an indication that they had not only the moral support of those who harboured a vision of a new society, but the backing, by arms and explosives, of the guerillas, was welcome.

"Why not? You don't know some of the sort of friends father has. He'll ring again if he hears more," Kathy murmured as they settled back on the pillow.

More explosions? More about who was responsible?

Instead of asking, he put his arms round her and at once entered a state where it was all the same to him.

"You're my salvation," he told her.

"What a big word for something so simple!"

He'd been so under the stress of events from the day of the Archbishop's visit up to now that he hadn't made love to her since. He hadn't had the tranquility to recall and meditate, even briefly, in wonder at there being this hidden gap, split or slit in the solid fabric of reality. It was, even in thought, a way out of imprisoning facts and a way into sensational fantasies, as in the bathroom scenario with Giselle he'd thought up. That had been an antidote to the cleric, a very short-term salvation as now, in actuality, Kathy was an antidote to and salvation from the bombs, Klotz's visit and the other threats in connection with the magazine.

Yes, woman was salvation: Kathy, his dove, in the middle-term; Pieta, as she herself had implied, in the long-term, and imaginary ones in the shortest of all terms.

He had never got used to the youthful discovery that there was more in women than met the eye. Making love to Kathy proved it over and over, yet he'd forget this secret as soon as exterior world events took over his mind and relegated it to the slumbering senses.

If only women and the saving mystery could be put into

148

words that would never be forgotten. He recalled the Mandelstam verse he had read that evening sitting on the scooter in the girls' bathroom. But the great Russian was always on the sombre side, never a smile, let alone a laugh. Nothing much to smile at, living the sort of life that Gideon recalled reading about, branded by Stalin as an enemy of the people.

These musings were obliterated as making love to Kathy built up a sensation with which (he'd just time to form the thought) the greatest poetry couldn't compete.

Kathy rose early and went to the hotel to drive Pieta to hospital if necessary, and to find out from her father what had happened and what was likely to happen next, for the surviving newspapers wouldn't carry much news.

Having breakfast alone, as in the old days, he scanned the paper that had been delivered as usual.

'Night of Terror' (an exaggeration, of course. This was an opposition sheet). 'Bombs wreck newspaper offices'. He phoned down to the old dame to send him up in the elevator the other, pro-government newspaper, as well as a couple of her duck eggs — she kept water-fowl — not wishing the gossipy concierge to suppose that the events of the night were his only concern.

The headlines in this rival publication announced: 'City calm this morning' and in smaller print: 'after explosions and some damage to newspaper premises. Tight security control imposed, and a six p.m. curfew.'

Gideon jumped when the phone rang; this citizen didn't share the general calm. It was Kathy, not immediately with news of Pieta or the night of violence, but with a few words, sounding the more intimate on the phone, about 'the night of love and bombs'.

"Each time we made love was for me a series of explosions that rocked the room."

"Go on."

"And each time it finished I wanted you to start your revolution inside me all over again."

149

What more encouraging coded message could be received over the phone with which to start a day!

Gideon had scarcely fully recovered from it when he was roused from his trance by a noise from the street.

From the fifth floor window he saw a couple of long-grey-coated motorcyclists stopped in the roadway opposite the entrance to the apartment block, booted feet on the tarmac, engines running.

Had they come to arrest him and had the telephone call from the Colonel's aide been to ensure he was at home at the time?

There appeared from under the canopy of tenderly green, young leaves, a squat grey car, by no means impressive, with a triangular pennant with a black star on a red background which was the airforce emblem, sprouting from the bonnet!

Gideon went back to the hall and waited at the apartment door for the sound of the lift, and, of course, was there too soon, as he tended to be on most occasions, thus being exposed to unnecessary and, as now, anxious waiting.

When finally the bell rang and he opened the door, it was to a dark young man in a civilian suit who must have climbed the five flights, as there'd been no sound from the lift. In which case, Gideon reflected, he was in excellent shape, showing no sign of breathlessness.

"Mr. Spokane."

"At your service."

These were not Gideon's actual words, but there are times in this report where a strictly factual or verbatim method would not communicate the intimations below the surface.

They shook hands, and Gideon was about to ask the visitor in when he heard the lift ascending. The aide looked at Gideon and inclined his head. It was one of those nods which, though not easy to interpret, seem meant as a sign.

Recalling it later, helped by hindsight, Gideon took it as a recognition on the Captain's side of a bond between them that the imminent appearance of Klotz need not — could not? —

damage.

The Colonel was wearing an undistinguished grey uniform, without ribbons, medals or medallions. There were three faded silver pieces of braid on the shoulder straps.

"Good morning, Sir."

"Honoured."

The greeting didn't restore Gideon's composure. First the nod, and now the 'sir', what was it all leading to? So many possible interpretations and the one that came to mind was that the 'sir' was meant ironically as, when an interrogator says to the suspect: 'Now, Sir, let's have no more prevarication!'

Gideon showed Klotz, followed by the aide-de-camp, into the livingroom, and instead of choosing the comfortable chair, Klotz sat on an upright one at the table, forcing Gideon to take the one at the other side, at once making the visit a formal one. Rather mitigating this impression, the aide sat back in the arm chair and glanced at the bookshelves. Or was this appearance of being at ease a pose, and was he looking for subversive literature? God Almighty! Gideon admonished himself, I'm imagining all kinds of signs, threats and omens!

"Quite a library, you see, Paul," Klotz remarked, and then to Gideon: "I'm not a great reader, we generals, colonels and corporals seldom are, but in my case I've Captain Weissmann to advise me."

"What about de Gaulle, Colonel?"

"An excellent question, Sir, that brings us straight to the point. De Gaulle called France's writers the nation's conscience, while under Hitler the best German books were burnt and I believe Franco did away with the one or two Spaniards with any literary gift. Am I right, Paul?"

"De Gaulle was as selective as the others. He didn't consider de Montherlant or Celine as the nation's conscience, Colonel."

Ah, Captain Weissmann was not just a yes man!

"Celine, who on earth was she, Paul? But let's not get side-tracked. The point is: the writers have the last word, not the dictators. That's a fact of history."

151

"The last word, yes," Gideon remarked. "It's a pity they don't have the first word as well."

"They don't co-operate. Take the case of Stalin, he was ignorant like myself, but he hadn't a predilection for the second-rate and sentimental like Hitler. He was in awe of his Russian poets and novelists, so Paul tells me. If he'd managed to get them behind him, what a different situation we might have today."

"He didn't make much of an attempt to do so."

"Whose fault was that, Paul? You told me yourself they opposed him from the start."

Captain Weissmann, who hadn't seemed very interested in the discussion, now took what struck Gideon as an important part.

"It's not a simple matter of political or ideological opposition. It goes deeper than that, Colonel."

"Paul likes to probe into the heart of these, and other, matters that most of us take for granted," Klotz told Gideon.

"It saves a lot of misunderstanding in the long run."

Gideon wanted the young Captain to see him, if he didn't already, as an ally.

"There's an unbridgable gulf between intensely imaginative and exceptionally active, administrative minds," Captain Weissmann went on.

"Tell Mr. Spokane the story of the telephone talk between Stalin and what's-his-name."

The Captain glanced at Gideon and a look passed between them, which Gideon took to mean: Yes, I know you published an account of the famous few words in a recent number of *Faillandia* because I read it, but, all the same, I'll repeat the story which fascinates my Commander and which, as you've probably guessed, has something to do with his being here.

"Great writer or not, this character ... "

"Pasternak," the Captain put in.

"This Pasternak lost a golden opportunity through timidity and lack of resolution. The Georgian dictator wasn't one to

152

grant second chances."

Holy Christ, what was that! A faint chirping from the next room. Pieta's sick bird, emblem of *Faillandia,* her wounded Dove of Peace — in his panic Gideon was attributing exaggerated symbolic significance to it — that he was supposed to be caring for. Disorientated and distracted that morning, swallowing black coffee, studying the scary headlines, listening to Kathy on the phone, with this visit in the offing, he'd neglected to feed it.

"Excuse me a moment, Colonel."

"What's up?"

"Miss Galbaddy, a member of the staff of the magazine, before it was closed down, that is" — why this rigmarole? — "and my sister-in-law, left me this sick creature when she went to hospital, and I forgot to feed it this morning."

Was he about to lose a golden opportunity too? Nor might he be given a second chance. Gideon now knew something of the panic with which Pasternak had taken up the phone, a few minutes after Stalin had banged it down, and rung the Kremlin to no avail.

Klotz turned to what it now struck Gideon was, as well as his 'adviser', a bodyguard.

"Is this a joke?"

Gideon tried to leave the room in a leisurely fashion, half-expecting to hear a shouted 'Halt!' As he reached the hall, there was a ring at the apartment door and when he opened it there stood Frank Everett.

"Have I come at an inconvenient moment, Boss?"

He'd seen, he said, the motorcyclists waiting in the avenue and probably (though this he didn't mention) sentries posted on each floor, and still had come up. A cool cat, as Kathy had once remarked.

"No, I don't think so, come on in."

"Who have you with you, Boss? His Nibs?"

"There's something urgent I want you to do, and don't call me Boss, especially in front of Klotz."

153

"O.K. Just give me the word."

Gideon showed him the cardbox from which a shrill chirp was coming, the utensils for feeding the fledgling, and opened the lid.

The noise stopped, the bird hopped onto the edge of the container, held its head on one side, taking what seemed a long, beady look at the visitor, who, in response, held out a forefinger. The fledgling perched on it and opened its beak so wide as to appear in danger of some dislocation.

Frank, as directed, speared a morsel of cat-food from the tin on the match stick and dropped it deftly on the tiny, pale-pink tongue. And with the bird thus safely anchored, Gideon, with the cardboard box and tin, conducted the tableau into the living room.

Klotz was standing by the window looking out — about to summon some of the mobile squad? — and the Captain, it seemed to Gideon, saying something reassuring. But he jumped to his feet when he saw Frank. Perhaps his having one hand thrust out with forefinger extended momentarily suggested that he was pointing a gun.

"Mr Everett — Colonel Klotz."

To Gideon all was in the balance. He was watching Captain Weissmann rather than the Colonel.

"Didn't you have a brush with the Government a few years ago?" the Captain asked Frank.

Although Frank hadn't referred to it in London, Gideon knew that, under his real name, he'd received a prison term for armed robbery and had either escaped from jail or had the sentence reduced for some, to Gideon, unknown reason. Did the fact that the Captain knew of the incident, despite the change of identity, indicate that there had been political undertones to the case?

Frank retired without replying to a small table in the corner where he fed the bird.

"Think it over, Mr. Spokane."

"Think what over, Colonel?"

154

Gideon had, he supposed, in his panic, missed something that Klotz had said either just before he had left the room or on his return.

"The future of your magazine."

"It hasn't a future. Didn't you know, Colonel, it has been banned?"

Klotz laughed, causing Gideon to start in surprise, and suddenly the tension was out of the air.

"Of course, I knew. Why do you think I'm here? What I'm suggesting is that, in the light of your talk, it might be wise for us both to come to an agreement. If you are willing to go on publishing it under certain conditions, which you and Paul can work out, give him a ring."

What if he knew of the preparations for continuing it as an underground publication!

"Thank you, Colonel."

"Give him the number to call, Paul."

Gideon saw them out to the landing where behind the grille of the lift, which had been immobilised at that floor, two helmeted soldiers waited.

## EIGHTEEN

Gideon hurried to the hospital with the good news, although he didn't know if Pieta would see it as such. He didn't even know the conditions and hadn't dared to ask.

He entered the ward to which he was directed and at once saw her in a cot near the door. She was propped up against a bed-rest and slowly lifted her left hand, with a langour that went to his heart, a few inches from the white bedspread.

Gideon moved the tall table on rubber casters in order to slip into the space between it and the bed and noticed on it, beside a glass of liquid with a straw in it, a small, leather-framed portrait of himself. He was shocked by this. 'Ashamed' or 'guilt-ridden', might be a more accurate description. Why was it there on this narrow altar?

He sat down on a chair that was turned to the long window.

"Pieta."

A loosening of the corners of her mouth, as if it was about to open and whisper from wherever she was, but then the pale lips reformed their line of silent repose.

Nurses flitted by on the white, noiseless wings of their soft shoes, an old woman recited a mumbled litany of holy names, interspersed with complaints; another, spoon-fed against her will, gurgled and denounced the young sister.

Beyond the window a large dark tree, perhaps an olive, stood against a brass-coloured sky. Gideon's fingers rested on the back of Pieta's hand ('it's dark out there, give me your little paw') into the underside of whose wrist a plastic cannula led beneath the bandage.

A constant traffic of birds flew in and out of the great shadow of the tree in its halo of yellow light.

Against all likelihood, solace descended on the white bed, the upturned, suspended bottle of blood plasma and the table, stilling his anxiety as well as the mumbled prayers and abuse.

Where now was the 'good news'? Here, if anywhere, in spite of all appearances. The only scrap of good news he had brought with him was that the fledgling still survived. He wrote a note telling her this and left it on the table.

After a long, anxious wait in a small surgery in the basement, the doctor who had operated on Pieta appeared.

Gideon who distrusted all doctors — he may have been unlucky in his experience of them — was resolved to act the humble lay enquirer, even the grateful and admiring relative, or close friend, of the patient.

He was the beggar in the nightmare whom the lord of the castle has at last condescended to let put his enquiries or requests. And these, Gideon knew, had to be the ones that would elicit the kind of information from which he could grasp some straws of comfort. Too much anxiety or persistence in this questioning must be avoided or the surgeon would produce the kind of non-answers that he used to get rid of importunate time-wasters.

"In plain language, Mr. Spokane, I carried out an intervention which required surgery to expose the heart for manual manipulation in order to restore its functioning."

Hanging desperately on every word, as Gideon well knew, is not the best method to receive a clear understanding of a report on an obscure and unfamiliar matter. He may have misplaced or misheard some of Mr. Cadjella's (even the name had for Gideon a hint of ambiguity) words.

"There is something I must ask you," the doctor went on, reversing their roles, "has Miss Galbaddy been exposed to radiation?"

"Of course not."

But better remain the quiet, no-trouble petitioner, and

157

keep any vehemence out of it.

"That's what she said."

When? Had she been conscious when the surgeon first examined her?

"But I wanted to confirm it. She has burns on her breast consistent with having been exposed to quite severe radiation."

"But not necessarily caused by that?"

The surgeon took a look at Gideon, really seeing him perhaps for the first time, and Gideon guessed that by his question he had impinged on the other as not just one of the rather tiresome relatives of patients to whom he had to give up so much of his time.

"No. There are none of the accompanying symptoms of radiation sickness."

"Is there a connection?"

Mr. Cadjella looked up again from the open file on his desk, but now with what Gideon interpreted as impatience. He tried again.

"Between the wound and the condition of the heart."

"Yes, I see."

A pause. Was that all he was going to say? But then the surgeon went on.

"Severe shock can cause delayed heart failure, though, in my experience, such cases are rare. And then, Mr. Spokane, not knowing the circumstances under which she received the burns, we don't know where such an explanation could apply."

"But you don't rule it out?"

"I don't rule anything out . . . Has Miss Galbaddy a history of . . . I'll put it like this: has she had psychiatric treatment?"

"Oh, no."

"The remedial clinics and psychiatric institutions are fuller than ever, and they'd be fuller still if the damage to some of those under the stress and strain of our present crises didn't manifest itself in the body tissue rather than primarily in the nerve and brain cells."

A pause, while Gideon composed himself, if that's the best

way of describing it, to put the vital question that had been the principal reason for asking to see the surgeon.

"Will she recover, Mr. Cadjella?"

"There's every indication that she will. She hadn't what's called a chronic heart condition, which, I admit, I'd expected to find."

Gideon returned home depressed and confused, wishing he had never asked for a meeting with the doctor.

At the makeshift *Faillandia* offices there was further ambivalence. Returns coming in from the newsagents showed that the final issue had, after several reprints, sold what amounted to a colossal total. Gideon checked the figures with Nolla and then consulted Leo.

"What about?" Leo asked when Gideon used the word.

"First of all can you explain the sudden rush for what after all is not a magazine with popular features?"

"It hasn't been that sudden, you know. There's been a gradual increase in sales from the start that kept pace with the deteriorating political situation.

"We've reached a pre-revolutionary phase — actually rare in modern democracies — where large sections of the people who don't agree on anything else, have lost all faith in the parliamentary system and yet are hostile to somebody like Klotz and fear a dictatorship.

"A lot of the pieces in *Faillandia* are beyond them, they are transported in spite of themselves, into another way of thinking, or rather feeling, about the situation. They catch gleams of light in the darkness that they thought was impenetrable.

"They're looking for a prophet, though they don't perhaps realise it, and *Faillandia* is the nearest they've ever come to such a phenomenon. Though, of course, at the end of the day, whenever that turns out to be, they'll come to their common and bourgeois senses and adapt to whatever the *status quo* is by then, or at least most of them, and as they nearly always do, come up with some accommodation with whoever's on top,

159

and call it a victory for public opinion."

This somewhat cynical summary and forecast from Leo surprised Gideon.

"But for the moment, old son, we go underground and make hay while the sun shines."

Gideon realised that this was what he had really wanted to hear and surprisingly, that it was his father-in-law, whom till now he hadn't taken all that seriously, that he would go by for the moment until Pieta was recovered. Not Klotz or his aide-de-camp, even less any of the others.

"What shall we do?"

"Call a meeting of the whole bloody *équipe,* everyone directly concerned, including the office staff, and put it before them."

"And let them decide."

"Oh no, we've already decided, I thought you'd grasped that."

While Gideon had been sitting at Pieta's hospital bed, trying to interpret her silence, watching the traffic of the mysterious (but so much was mysterious, including her illness) birds in and out of the huge tree, vainly hoping to hear some words of reassurance from the doctor and then coming home to find that the fledgling no longer hopped onto the edge of the box when he opened the lid, a vital decision had been taken by his father-in-law.

"Klotz realised before you may have just what the magazine had become. Or rather, his chief intelligence officer, Captain Weissmann, did. Oh, yes, old son, I've my agents too and I saw some notes (by courtesy, so to speak, of the girl secretary to whom they were dictated) in which the historically-minded Captain recalled similar cases of a publication having a profound, though sometimes delayed, influence on the course of national events."

"What cases?"

Gideon was trying not to get too far behind what to him was an unexpected — unwelcome? — acceleration of the whole

160

business of Klotz, *Faillandia,* and being faced with a board meeting, while Pieta was unavailable.

"He quotes several examples, principally the propaganda sheet published by Jean Paul Marat in 1798, called *L'ami du Peuple,* which apparently helped sway the Paris populace behind the Revolution. There was also the appearance of *Pravda* in Petersburg in the year 1912 as an underground news-sheet inciting to rebellion, which continued intermittently up to the October Revolution, when it became the organ of the Party."

"You think we can outmanoeuvre Klotz?"

That was what Gideon concluded from Leo's surprising declaration of intent, surprising him as much for what it revealed about his father-in-law's grasp of the political-military situation as for the resolution to defy Klotz and his notoriously tough airforce officers.

"The printing machine is already installed on the top floor, ready to roll. I'm only awaiting your final O.K. on the assembled copy."

"Then why call this general meeting of everyone connected? Isn't that as good as ensuring that our intentions, and the whereabouts of the new offices, will be reported to the authorities?"

"What we tell them will be passed on. What I want to find out is by whom. And, of course, what we tell them at this general meeting won't be the actual facts."

"Who's running the magazine now?" Gideon asked.

He really didn't know. In fact he knew less and less about almost everything that concerned him. The one thing that remained constant was his down-to-earth — if that was the apt expression — relationship with Kathy.

"Same lot as all along: you, me, Kemp, the Abbot ... "

"What about Pieta?"

"She sets the tone, or one of them, but was never a director nor, as far as I know, aspired to be."

"And Canavan?"

"Came for the ride as long as it suited him, and us, but dropped off when he saw he was being taken past his destination."

'Taken past his destination', Gideon reflected on the phrase, one of several that came so easily to Leo, now that he was confiding in him.

The question he put to himself was: Am I too being carried past my destination? If only I knew where my destination was!

After leaving Leo to his habitual evening inspection of the kitchen — an astonishingly flexible, all-purpose mind, he reflected — Gideon sought out Kathy in her office where she was talking to a couple of members of the hotel staff, one of whom he recognised as the night porter.

She told him she would join him in what was called the snack-dock in five minutes. This was a basement room open round the clock that served various dishes at a bar counter.

To study the menu while he waited was a relaxation for Gideon, almost the first in the last few days, when most of his time had been spent passing copy for the printers without knowing whether the magazine would be published or not.

This was the task at which he shone, a fact that both Pieta and Leo were aware of, though he himself was not. He had an instinct for selecting at first glance unrelated pieces and,' by juxtapositioning, creating a unity in theme, making each issue unique in itself and yet part of an on-going serial that more and more readers awaited anxiously or excitedly each week, according to temperament.

Here the choice was blessedly simple, though wide. But why didn't the remarkable little menu card completely absorb him? Why wasn't he preoccupied in deciding between breast of duck with orange sauce and slice of roast pork with parsley and chestnut stuffing?

Because he desperately needed — a more precise description of his mood than 'wanted' — Kathy. He only hoped he wouldn't start shivering too obviously when she appeared.

162

He studied the menu all over again to stop himself turning whenever somebody entered through the glass door, and had got halfway through the third lap when there she was, lifting herself onto the stool beside him.

"I was telling Josephus to take a careful look at the background of the girls on his list. Have you chosen something to eat? There's always a wait because each order is specially prepared."

What Josephus? Gideon had hoped she'd just have a glass of wine with him and not order anything to eat. And what girls, for Christ's sake.

"No."

No to what? No to everything that was going to delay them down here.

"Well, let's choose. What about a thick slice of underdone beef with a side dish of asparagus."

"There's no asparagus on the card."

Why on earth was he letting himself get involved in selecting items, when he couldn't have eaten anything, and didn't want her to?

"Nothing for me, Kathy, I'm not hungry. Just a glass of the Frascati."

She took his hand beneath the counter, laid the palm against her thigh and, he surmised, could feel through her skirt the vibration from what he thought of as his central nerve.

"All in good time," she told him, after giving her order, which included a carafe of the Italian wine.

"Who is Josephus?"

"The night porter, known affectionately as Josh by a lot of our patrons, especially those whom he caters for."

"Caters for?"

"Supplies with a call-girl from what he calls his stable, letting them choose, I believe, from a beautifully bound photograph album."

"Haven't you seen it, then?"

"Oh no, it might embarrass him, but Daddy has, of course. It was he who asked me to impress on Josh that from now on he was to check out the girls, especially on who else they associate with."

"What for?"

"For God's sake, pay attention! I've promised we'll go home the moment I've had something to eat and shown you the machines that Daddy has installed on the top floor, which is why he wants extra precautions taken that none of Klotz's agents slip in as one of Josh's young ladies, and snoops around the place in the middle of the night. Got that, darling?"

"And who else were you interviewing just now?"

He might as well show her that he was capable of attending to what was on her mind, no matter how far it was from what was on his, and that he could even go quite calmly and rationally into details that she hadn'd mentioned.

"The head waiter, you could hardly recognise him in one of his elegant off-duty suits. He's to report anything he overhears in the restaurant that might be of interest to Daddy. Which I think he does anyhow, but I was to tell him it was all the more important just now to keep his ears open."

Kathy's slice of beef was served between two quite thin slices of non-starch bread that had absorbed the pinkish juices, with a bowl of lightly-steamed — as she had requested — purplish-yellow asparagus.

Gideon had swallowed a glass of the raw wine that left the astringent aftertaste. It was now a matter of watching her cut the sandwich in half with the sharp blade — one side with minute saw-teeth — of the silver-handled knife provided. And then bite sensuously, as he felt it, through the warm, sodden layers of bread and into the meaty heart of the *plat de Soir*, as these house specialities were called.

It fascinated and increased his tension to watch each portion entering her mouth. She seemed to prolong the enjoying of every mouthful, as if wilfully tantalising him with the message: 'Oh, I'm aware of your impatience, but you'll bloody well have to wait till I've filled myself up with this.'

Though Gideon knew with the undisturbed part of his mind that she was incapable of any such coquetry.

164

## NINETEEN

Kathy seemed to know a great deal about the surprisingly small machine which, she explained, was one of the latest, sophisticated models, capable of high speeds and printing both sides of the sheet simultaneously.

"Where did the money come from?"

"Largely from the profits on the last few issues of the magazine, though you and Pieta don't seem very interested in that side of the business, which has been quite astonishing."

"Pieta is very ill, and as for me, I've been at my wits end completing the contents for the coming issue, deciding on the layout, as well as beginning to get together the one after that."

"You know what I think about Pieta. She broods too much on herself and her afflictions, and that makes them worse."

"Have you the key to her room?"

Oh yes, Gideon knew that this was a desperate expedient, a flight from what was closing in on him into the rapturous semi-oblivion that Kathy could give him.

"No, not on me. Let's go home."

Why did he hesitate at what was normally so welcome a suggestion? What could still threaten him in the shelter of their three of four rooms? They would be scarcely home when Kathy, having undressed, would come to him like one of those angels sent on the long journey from heaven to earth to comfort an Old Testament prophet sorely beset by his enemies. Except that this angel's journey was shorter, only from the bathroom, and what she brought in the way of deliverance was a wonderfully built-in gift, not a message or communication from on high, but her own flesh and blood.

Then he remembered! The fledgling, whose box had to be opened — it was already past its feeding time — before the miracle took place. And he was afraid what he might see when he looked in, for the bird, instead of recovering, had become listless and bedraggled. So that in the end it was with that in mind that they drove home.

And when Gideon lifted the cardboard lid the bird didn't hop onto the edge of the box, but remained squatting in a corner, with the newspaper stained a bright greenish-yellow.

Gideon had hardly finished providing a fresh sheet when the phone rang, and it was the matron at the hospital telling him not to make his usual visit to Pieta in the morning on her doctor's orders.

Was she worse then? he had asked. But of course the answer was equivocal. She was simply (simply!) in need of complete rest and quiet.

"Everything's getting worse," he told Kathy, linking, as he'd done all along, Pieta's condition to the bird's, and both to *Faillandia*.

Kathy said nothing, waiting, he thought, to see what came next, whether she still had the power, not to disperse the dark clouds, but to lift him on her breast and thighs above them. And she had, indeed, more than ever. The blacker the future, the greater the loss that threatened, the more urgent and evident became his need — need? That made it sound more excusable.

He didn't want to wait till they were in bed. It made the act more incongruous and exciting, less part of the usual late-night domesticities, to have her sit where she was in a chair while he made love to her.

"That's what I wanted the night we first met."

"Yes."

"You must have known when you came home with me."

She laughed.

"If the heat had been on, it would have ended like this!"
She gripped him more tightly.

"Wouldn't it? Wouldn't it?" he persisted, instinctively provoking her on towards a climax by suggesting that *au fond,* and when it really came down to this rapture, she was no different from a street girl.

Kathy opened her mouth, not to admit in words that, yes, it was so, but to moan in the flood of sensation that obliterated all moral distinction.

All Gideon's mornings tended to be sobering. The following one more so than usual. The fledgling was still alive, but, as far as he could make out, only just. Leo telephoned to say the meeting was convened for that afternoon. And there was also a call from Frère Emanuel, of all people, asking if he could meet Gideon anywhere that was convenient to him around noon, after a visit to Pieta in hospital, whom, he explained, he was allowed to see as her confessor.

It was arranged that he came to lunch at the flat. Then, just as he was leaving for the hotel where he had still work to do on the top floor on the layout of the coming issue, there was a long-distance call from Marthe Delaunay in Paris.

She described to him the June afternoon at Longchamp — it was already well into summer and Gideon in the midst of his preoccupations had scarcely reverted to the special magic of the season — and the debut of Montenotte in France. They shared the secret about this horse that had only run in Failland, something about it had struck them and this bond would be strengthened if it ran well in this important French race.

Amost nobody else could have grasped why it meant so much to him that the colt should do well; Pieta might have, seeing she set such store by the recovery of the sick bird.

He was listening to the rapid French, all of which he didn't take in.

Montenotte, that nobody at Longchamp had ever heard of, had run green, as was to be expected, and his jockey had let him take his time towards the rear of the field for the first three or four furlongs. Only after rounding the gentle bend into the straight had he shaken up his mount with a dig of his heels and a slap down the neck.

"You should have seen the response. I'd my glasses on the colt because of how he'd excited us that afternoon last spring. He'd that look about him that we called 'the eagle look' that day at the races in Failland, do you remember Gideon, and I wanted to see if what I thought I'd seen would come true out there on the course which, as we also agreed that day, is one of the few places where truth prevails.

"You'd have been astonished and delighted as I was. The colt accelerated as if a spark inside had ignited. He overtook the others and ranged alongside L'Attaque — I'm sure you've heard of him, Gideon, he's the star of our second season colts up to now. Then, just as I thought Montenotte would take the lead, he faltered, or, no, that's not the word, I want to get it right for you, so much depends on it . . . "

"Yes, yes . . . go on . . . "

"He began looking about him, that's what I think it was. As soon as he had an uninterrupted view of the course in front, the stands, and heard the still-distant roar of the crowd, he lost his concentration. Even so, his jockey might have given him a reminder and rallied him and still have won. But I daresay he'd been told not to punish him with the whip. Anyhow, to make it brief, he ran fourth."

So it wasn't a great victory after all, though Marthe was making the most of it. To Gideon it was the sort of ambiguous news which was as good as he was likely to get during this period of desperation, with so much in the balance.

"Thanks Marthe, for a wonderful bit of news!"

He couldn't disappoint her. And it was wonderful to her who was so undemanding. Would she write a piece about Montenotte in French for Faillandia and he would translate it? Yes, that's what she'd been thinking of, because *Faillandia* was the place for it rather than *Paris Turf.* She thought the piece should first be printed in a paper not specifically concerned with racing, but where it might add its small circle of light to the more general illumination.

The piece mightn't be all that breathtaking, but at this time of deep disillusion, whatever was written with joy and faith he welcomed for the magazine. For the first clandestine issues Gideon judged the contributions on this basis, rather than that of purely literary merit.

He drove alone to the hotel, Kathy having to do some shopping and prepare the lunch to which the old friar was coming. Not that he was likely to eat much, but that gave her the more thought about what to provide.

The machines were ready to start printing as soon as Gideon passed the final sheets. When he re-read them he was appalled at what struck him as being far in advance of what most people could bear to hear. Had he lacked the patience and humility to try to understand the readers and lead them gently into new ways of thinking? Wouldn't this uncompromising 'No!' to so much that was familiar to them come as too great a shock?

When, in extreme anxiety, he confided his doubts to Leo, his father-in-law replied: "That's all right, old son. It's just this shock, the sense of outrage that at last a huge number of people are ready for. Not just ready, but longing for."

And although Gideon wasn't convinced, he let Leo have the last word.

He always came dispirited out of a discussion with his father-in-law about the magazine. Why had he become involved to begin with? Why was his heart — and it was when all was said — in *Faillandia*? Because of his nausea at the whole set-up here in Failland? No. At last he realised why it was so vital to him, although the realisation was surprising and probably impossible to make plausible to anyone else, with the possible exception of Pieta.

It was because of a small incident long ago. Because of how, when he took Sabina from her cot into his arms in the hospital she was quiet for the very last time, as the matron had told

169

Lydia afterwards. The fact that Sabina had been comforted by him for a few moments had caused Gideon to vow that he would not finally betray what he took as the dying infant's mysterious faith in him.

"Nobody else except Bernard Kemp must know where the printing is being done," Leo told Gideon.

"What about those at the meeting this afternoon?"

"There was a Judas in the divinely-appointed twelve, so what chance have we of not having an informer among us?"

Confronted with this new problem, Gideon quickly reviewed in his mind the others who were involved in the publication of the magazine and instinctively hesitated over Nolla.

"Bernard vouches for her."

Gideon concluded that she had let the old man spend a weekend with her in her flat as a kind of peeping Tom, or rather frankly observing Tom.

Gideon for a moment didn't recognise Frère Emanuel who wore an ordinary suit with a pleated white shirt and a quite incongruous bow tie, articles of clothing, it struck him, loaned from various laymen connected with the Priory.

Gideon brought him into the front room overlooking the wide avenue, and the friar at once saw the cardboard box on a table in a corner, as though that was what he was looking for.

"Pieta is anxious about her fledgling."

"She spoke to you? How is she?"

"I left her sleeping peacefully after we'd talked for an hour."

An hour! And Gideon had been told only last night that she was not to be visited! What about? But he could not ask the friar directly.

"And her wounds?"

The old man looked at Gideon with a glance that reminded him of the expression he'd only heard again that morning from Marthe Delauney: 'the eagle look'. Except that the friar's air was not proud or imperial, but meditative.

"You've seen them, *Kind?*"

"Oh no, father" (should it be 'brother', but Frère Emanuel

was a priest who said mass). "They were described to me by her doctor as consistent with her having been exposed to radiation."

"They are healed."

"I don't see . . . "

Gideon didn't finish his expression of surprise, if not quite incredulity. If he couldn't believe this old friar, then there was no one left to trust. But the only conclusion was surely that Kathy was right about her sister's ailments being self-induced, though none the less actual for that. If so, could the symptoms not disappear by an act of the imagination as powerful as that which had produced them? Yet Gideon was not completely satisfied with an explanation which, apart from seeming contrived, left him with no other way of explaining the whole thing than as hallucination.

"I was told by the hospital only last night that I couldn't visit her."

"She told me that too. She thinks it is because they know you and she would discuss *Faillandia*, a subject she takes so much to heart that the effect on her could be to retard her recovery."

The magazine, yes that was the crux. Not, Gideon thought, for the reason given, but because a communication (from the Department of Internal Security? From Captain Weissmann From Klotz?) had been delivered to Mr. Cadjella listing the names of those who at the moment were not to visit this patient, with his name first, followed by Leo's and her sister's.

From being also the first to realise the public impact that *Faillandia* was having, he might now be exaggerating the attention it was causing to the authorities.

He suddenly thought of asking Frère Emanuel's opinion which would not be influenced by political or even patriotic considerations. But first let them sit down at the table and see which of the dishes that Kathy had prepared might be to the taste, and not precluded by monastic or personal rule, of their visitor.

171

Instead, however, of taking the place offered him, the friar went to the box in the corner and opened the lid.

"It's a very sick bird," Gideon warned him.

Frère Emanuel took off the lid, reached in a hand, withdrew it with the fledgling and then held it in his two hands for a moment or two, watched by Gideon and Kathy, standing silently beside the laid table.

"Open the window," the old man asked without raising his eyes from the small feathery bundle he was clasping.

"What for?"

Was he, too, despite the deep impression he had made on Gideon at their first meeting on the island, self-deluded, (Gideon was shocked at the 'too' so easily slipping into his interior monologue) and acting the holy hermit with miraculous powers, reminding Gideon of the monk in Dostoyevsky's *Brothers Karamazov* who mystified everyone by appearing to rival Father Zosima's sanctity.

Gideon didn't move, and it was Kathy who crossed the room and opened one of the glass panels just above the top of the plane trees that lined the avenue.

The friar, who had followed her, thrust his cupped hands out of the window, opened them, and the bird fluttered awkwardly downward and alighted on a high branch.

There it perched among the palish leaves, jerking its head this way and that, for what seemed to Gideon an agonisingly long time. Then it soared up, circled once above the trees and roof tops and then flew, straight and true, away from the trio at the window.

The friar turned, seated himself at the table, though not at the place laid for him, and, without a word, tucked the napkin into the collar of his shirt as if in readiness for a good meal, reciting as he did so: "Blessed are those who hunger and thirst after righteousness!"

Nor did Gideon refer to what had happened, because at first he half-supposed that a trick had been played on them, that Frère Emanuel had brought in his pocket one of the birds

172

that congregated in some of the squares in Aphrin and are easily caught with a few scraps of food, and by sleight of hand had made them believe that what he'd let go was Pieta's sick one.

Before sitting at the table, Gideon went over to the box and peered into it. It was empty. He joined the others, hoping that the old man hadn't noticed the slight diversion.

"What do you think was really wrong with Pieta, Reverend Father?" Gideon asked once the meal was under way. What sort of man were they entertaining, he didn't know. It would require much thinking over later, but his diagnosis of Pieta's illness would weigh more with him than the doctor's.

"Don't bother with the 'Reverend'. Just Frère or Brother will do. What I think is less than I know. Thought is fleeting, whereas knowledge is gradually stored over the years. But my knowledge of Pieta is less than my love for her, and that tells me that her afflictions are blessings from God."

Not very enlightening. But this too must be reflected on and discussed with Kathy.

"She sent you a message," Frère Emanuel was telling Gideon, "about the magazine, that even if it appeared to fail, if the authorities managed to prevent its publication, seized the clandestine copies and broke the printing machines, yes, and even if they arrested you and some of the others, you shouldn't despair."

Gideon was reminded of some sentences he'd read in one of the theological volumes he'd looked through in the fortress library while waiting for the friar's return from the oratory. And Frère Emanuel's comments on what had struck him as the Dutch writer's curious summing up of Christ's ministry, or at least the latter part of it in Galilee, as a fiasco.

"I don't intend getting myself arrested, Brother Emmanuel."

Nor did he, as he planned to avail of Frank's offer of help to the extent of taking refuge with Kathy on the yacht belonging to Frank's wealthy patroness, if it came to the worst, and perhaps taking a temporary trip outside Faillese territorial waters. But not before ensuring that *Faillandia,* in some form or other, be it only a few mimeographed sheets stapled together, continued to appear.

# TWENTY

Gideon and Bernard Kemp waited in Leo's office at the hotel where the latter had asked them to meet him before the general meeting.

Rather to his surprise — but there was a tentative rapport between them — Kemp started telling Gideon about the weekend he had spent at Nolla Grimmick's flat.

"She may have given you her own version."

Did he think she'd confided in Gideon and given him an impression that the old man wanted to correct? But, no, it didn't seem to be any attempt at self-justification. In fact, Kemp seemed to look on the weekend spent with the girl as part of the research he had for years devoted himself to. Its nature wasn't at first quite clear to Gideon, not even finally, though some of what Kemp said touched a responsive nerve in him.

"I've been making a study of the relation between outward behaviour and inner experience. Nothing very original about that, I expect you'll tell me, Mr. Spokane."

Gideon had no such intention, being already out of his depth.

"While I was reading R.D. Laing I was full of new ideas, but afterwards I couldn't recall a single one of them.

"Spend a non-stop twenty-four hours with a woman in the heyday of her sexuality and throw the books out the window. But when you're young, Spokane, you'd be in bed making love to her and wasting a precious opportunity."

"Good Lord, are they really such a mystery? I know that there is more in them than meets the eye, but aren't you chasing shadows and neglecting the substance?"

"The substance? To have made love to Nolla, isn't that what you mean by substance? But it's just because I couldn't do that, I had a chance of gaining some insights into how she saw herself, not in relation to men, but in her psyche. I know she wasn't alone, but I wasn't a disturbing presence, and she assured me she went about her daily life much as she did on any weekend."

"And what happened?"

"Not a great deal, you might say. Yet by observing her behaviour — and she kept her promise that I need never let her out of my sight or reach — I tried to deduce her experience. How she saw herself, how a woman experiences her sexuality, which is obviously to her something quite different than it is to a man who is primarily preoccupied with a few parts of her body. You see, Spokane, it is total, not only genital, sexuality that I'm interested in, the mysterious radiation that pervades the places they inhabit, that percolates their clothes and makes of 'haute couture' a kind of sub-culture than can be turned to huge profit."

This was up Gideon's street, but only a short way, because he knew that Nolla had agreed to the arrangement for the sake of the handsome sum that Kemp had paid her; she had told Gideon so, and had surely put on a show so as to have convinced the old fellow that it had been a unique experience worth every penny it had cost him.

"We can never experience the experience of others, but if we can watch their behaviour closely when they are being most themselves, that is say in the privacy of their own dwellings, we can get a rough idea of it."

It's all right for me, Gideon reflected, with Kathy to share and respond to my sexual urges, to see the silliness of old Kemp's 'research', but, even with all my advantages, don't I fantasise about sharing a bathroom with a police-girl?

When Leo joined them, he explained the purpose of the

176

meeting. Briefly, it was to discover who were the infiltrators, the Establishment's agents, if any, or, more likely, those who for their own ends, wanted to sabotage the magazine and prevent it continuing underground.

"I shall inform the gathering that the new premises are above a restaurant in Denmark Lane" — which Gideon recalled as the restaurant where he'd dined with Pieta — "that is in the same ownership as this hotel, and whereof any enquirers can be headed-off from investigating and their identity noted."

Leo explained that a second false trail would be laid for a selected group comprising the Canavans and Helga Kemp (her husband nodded and Gideon saw that it was agreed between them) which led to Gideon's apartment. The real whereabouts of the new premises would only be known, besides the three of them, to Pieta, Kathy and the Prior.

"I will vouch for Nolla Grimmick," Kemp added.

"Excellent. But this isn't a matter of personal loyalties, Bernard."

There were about a dozen people at the meeting which was held in Kathy's office that was rather larger than the one her father occupied.

Gideon, who believed he was receptive to the psychological emanations of others, sensed a nervousness among them, an uneasiness in the room that he thought must be shared by all but two or three.

Rather to his surprise, Leo began addressing them, not about the imminent appearance of the first clandestine number of the magazine on the streets, but on the subject of the great impact that *Faillandia* was making on the public. And he went on to explain it by telling them that what was happening here in Aphrin was an event of great importance such as had only occurred a few times in recent history.

It could only take place when several unusual circumstances were simultaneously present, the most important of which was when lies had completely taken over, and every intelligent citizen was aware that the debates in the National Assesmbly were a struggle between power-hungry parties and factions whose outcome was determined by which could put across the most persuasive lies, without their opponents having an even more shameless untruth with which to oppose it.

"Instead of the long, slow rise of a highly educated and cultured society, as happened in Ancient Greece, and once or twice since then, which acts as a regulator on the depths of corruption to which the administration can sink, what we have here in Failland is a society deprived of their daily heavenly bread and offered instead the dregs from the manufacturers of falsities and prevarications. Suddenly, they are overtaken by nausea. They know they are sick from the prevailing scent of deception and, almost by accident, some of them get a hint of a fresh pure breath and, without perhaps recognising it, they gulp it in. That's what we are giving them after ages: the breath of simple truth. There's a rush for it. And they find it in *Faillandia* — and this saving grace takes various shapes for our various readers — some shy away from a concept as solemn as 'truth' and welcome the simple sweetness of natural things, or the innocence of the ancient myths and legends that we bring to them once more."

'Bravo!' said Gideon under his breath.

Leo was again surprising him, speaking from his heart, defying the laws of inertia according to which nothing vital changed. Everywhere there was this fixity of hearts and minds. Yet there were also lucunae in the rigidity: he hadn't got over the flight of the bird.

Gideon slipped out of the room before the meeting was over. He didn't want to be there while Leo laid traps to catch possible Judases.

Besides, it was all too much for him. He had what he supposed was a serious social weakness: having heard a case argued skillfully and convincingly, even proving what he wanted to hear, he soon became doubtful and, out of a weariness and distrust of words, his instinct was to seek out Kathy and with her reach a wordless conviction. Or with Pieta another kind of conviction that also had little to do with words.

Because of the elaborate lunch that Kathy had prepared for their guest, who had eaten his share with apparent relish, Gideon and she had a light supper, during which he told her about Kemp's weekend with Nolla Grimmick.

"That's nothing new. Old men are like that, though few of them have the money to make their fantasies come true."

"How do you know?"

"In our business you come up against all types, among them, if you're a girl member of a hotel staff, the old voyeurs who go to blue films, pore over pornographic books and, the wealthy ones, who pay large sums to see a respectable woman — they aren't as such interested in prostitution — behave as they like to imagine her in her more sexy mood when alone."

"Weren't you ever tempted to come by such easy money."

Kathy shook her red head. Gideon knew that to enquire further and risk hearing details even of propositious she had declined was itself an indulgence in a kind of titillation he believed himself above, as if the amount of offers she'd turned down increased her valuation as a woman.

Not that he didn't sometimes speculate about her past. He never supposed her to have had no former lovers, especially in the light of their first meeting, but that should remain a secret that, perhaps because of an occasional pang of irrational jealousy, intensified the spell she exerted.

So it was now as she must be well aware and even, he thought, went out of her way to add fuel to his flames, referring casually to an old Russian aristocrat at the hotel in France who, perhaps for fear of scaring her off altogether, had asked nothing more in return to an envelope bulging with hundred-franc notes, than that she should unbutton her blouse buttons.

In that magically evoked — by her? by him? — past scenario it was all the more shocking for Gideon to ask in the same tone of voice in which he'd been conversing: "What about you taking off your knickers, Dove?"

179

"O.K."

Her tone was equally matter-of-fact and dispassionate.

Afterwards, they remained on the couch in the relaxation of having temporally banished all sensuality from their systems. A state which Gideon wondered whether even an ascetic such as the friar could achieve by fasting and self-discipline.

A knock at the hall door, a shattering of the steamy, sauna swamp in which they were immersed. Snatch up the damp tissue from the carpet that Kathy had used as a substitute for a trip to the bathroom, pull on his shoes: those were some of the self-directives reluctantly issued by Gideon's sluggish mind.

He opened the outer door where the concierge was standing and indicating a biscuit tin of the large, square type.

"I thought I'd check to see if you were expecting a delivery Mr. Spokane."

"Oh, many thanks. You're quite right to be on the alert in times like these. But, yes, I was, and as it happened I was in the bath when the van-man rang the bell, and afterwards I forgot it."

"It's in order, then?"

"Absolutely, and goodnight, madame."

A wave of the hand, and the woman turned back to the waiting lift.

Don't dream of opening the lid by as much as an inch. Shout to Kathy that he'd be back in a quarter of an hour, lift the thing gingerly, it weighed a bloody ton. Had it a time-switch? Was it designed to go off when opened? Operated by remote control? Or a hoax?

Another possibility: A tin of Scotch shortbread ordered by a neighbour and left outside No. 10B by mistake?

Gideon waited until he heard the lift reach the basement, delayed another couple of minutes to allow the concierge to reach her dwelling, summoned back the escalator and carried the tin, clasped to his chest, into it. Finally, he hauled it in aching arms, not having dared put it down for a moment's respite, across the yard at the back of the block and very gently deposited it in one of the empty garbage bins.

He then took the hose-pipe used to wash out the shed after the bi-weekly rubbish collection, turned on the tap to which it was connected, and filled the bin with water.

Back in the flat, Gideon explained the situation to Kathy. Then he rang the number that Captain Weissmann had given him on Klotz' suggestion.

There was only a slight delay before the Captain answered.

"This is Gideon Spokane."

"Ah, yes. Good morning, if it is morning."

"It's just after midnight. What looks like a home-made bomb has been left outside my apartment."

"Don't touch it."

"I took it down to the basement."

A longish pause. Had he turned over in bed, deciding it could be left there till morning and forgetting to replace the receiver?

"Hello."

"Yes, Captain."

"I've alerted our bomb disposal squad."

How? On another line, presumably.

"I'll be expecting them."

"No, they'll go direct to the basement; no need for publicity until we've investigated. What does it look like?"

"A big biscuit tin, weighing six or seven kilos."

Surely an over-estimate.

"Could be bricks!"

"A hoax?"

"A warning!"

"Against what?"

"You have a better idea of that than I. Against going underground with your magazine, I imagine."

Gideon had decided to ring up Captain Weissmann on an impulse. Klotz' suggestion that he get in touch with his aide to discuss the magazine's future had remained in his mind.

He hadn't acted on it because it meant his seeming to be prepared to compromise over the contents of *Faillandia*. But he thought that there might be a bond between himself and the Intelligence officer and that if they could meet and talk without preconditions, an understanding, about what Gideon wasn't precise, might come of it.

He was also impelled by anger at the thought that somebody had tried to kill him, and Kathy too, if the weight was explosive, though he shared the Captain's view that the thing was a hoax.

"Any idea of who the joker might be, if that's how it turns out?" Captain Weissmann was asking.

Gideon hesitated. Leo had only told the Canavan couple and Helga Kemp that the magazine was being printed at his apartment.

"I'd sooner not discuss it on the phone."

"Right. Come to my office tomorrow any time."

"Eleven a.m.?"

"I look forward to seeing you. And there's no need of the 'Captain', Paul will do. I'll be able to give you details about the infernal device."

When Gideon told Kathy of the appointment, she asked if that wasn't what he'd been hoping for.

"What makes you say that?"

He didn't recall having talked about Paul Weissmann with her.

"You aren't heart and soul behind Daddy and his revolutionaries."

Revolutionaries, who were they? Gideon wasn't sure whom she referred to. Surely not Bernard Kemp? or Pieta? and of the others, he hardly knew what they really hoped for from the magazine.

"What did he talk to them about?"

"Nothing much."

The last thing he wanted was to discuss it with her. Gideon was aware that Kathy had no real interest in *Faillandia* and far

182

preferred her work at the hotel. For some reason this suited him. He wanted her apart, the dove in the cleft of the rock in the old canticle, whom he could return to from that other confusing world.

## TWENTY ONE

Paul Weissmann's office turned out to be at his private apartment and this was one of several in a large old-fashioned building in the suburbs. It might well, Gideon thought, have been built originally as a hotel with a pillared portico at the entrance where chauffeurs — even perhaps coachmen — deposited the guests.

He entered a large, bare hall, with a marble floor and a narrow strip of carpet leading across it, to which he kept to obviate what could have been the sound of loud footfalls in the rather chilling silence.

In the alcove that might once have been the reception area, a sentry in what Gideon recognised as the airforce uniform was lounging.

Having been given directions by Weissmann, Gideon walked down a long corridor that crossed the back of the hall. There were doors at considerable distances from each other off this passage, whose size and unwelcoming air made Gideon revise his guess about the original purpose of the place.

A little girl of ten or twelve let him in, not perhaps with an actual curtsey, but with a grace that was the last thing that Gideon was expecting. In a moment Weissmann, dark and elegant in a civilian suit, came to greet him.

"This is Sarah. Sarah — Mr. Gideon Spokane."

This child stretched a pale thin arm and Gideon felt the light touch of her fingers on the back of his hand like a secret sign. Intimating what? That they, with her father, were fellow conspirators?

184

Gideon pulled himself up and may even have given a slight shake of the head. It was no time to drift off on ridiculous fantasies. Weissmann showed him into a large room, a few steps lower than the hall, with tall windows looking out onto just such a park as the hotel that Gideon had at first envisaged might well have had.

There was a desk between two of the windows, bookshelves between another two, and large paintings, one evidently a portrait of the Weissmanns — Paul, his wife and Sarah.

Gideon was waiting to hear what the biscuit-tin had contained, as he sat down by a small table in a corner and his host switched on lights over the paintings. He then went to the windows and turned handles concealed behind panels which lowered what looked like steel shutters from outside.

Gideon got up again and, out of politeness more than curiosity, went over to the family portrait.

It had evidently been painted quite recently. Sarah who was standing at her mother's knee with Paul standing behind them, looked no younger than she had to Gideon a moment ago.

"That's Judith. She died last year."

Gideon was silent, finding nothing to say that wasn't either conventional or too familiar. But he was touched at what struck him as a quite unexpected gesture of — what was it, friendship? trust? and he recalled, before dismissing the impression, the touch of the child's fingers.

Weissmann did not comment on the other painting before they returned to the table at which Gideon had just sat down a few moments before.

He had decided not to be the one to bring up the biscuit-tin.

"I've been expecting you for several days. I told Sarah that somebody was going to visit us who would remind her of the special friends we had when we lived in Jerusalem, one or two of whom she can just remember."

"You thought I'd come? But I mightn't have hadn't it been for the biscuit-tin. What was in it?"

"Most of the jewels taken in the robbery at a London museum some months ago."

Gideon said nothing because further questions seemed useless.

How deeply Frank had taken their talks on night-vigil to heart! What simple and touching faith in *Faillandia*! And what would he think of his old friend and co-conspirator when he heard that the treasure had been returned to the Geological Museum?

"Why were you expecting me?"

"When I read the last two numbers of *Faillandia*, it brought back to me those earlier days in Israel. When I married Judith she was a very young volunteer in the David Division of the Israeli army, inspired, like most of her companions, by the vision of Ben Gurion who had recently left office. Each evening before being dismissed and going home, the recruits were paraded under the Star of David banner and a senior officer read one of the Psalms of Thanksgiving."

Gideon was trying to take it in, and after the first surprise, was finding it easier.

"Do you know," Paul went on, "Judith remained a virgin during the first two years of our marriage."

Gideon didn't ask why, because he thought that this was quite natural, given the great task of re-founding the Promised Land. Pieta too would have understood it perfectly.

"But can we go on publishing it? Will Klotz lift the ban?"

"He won't lift it, but I'll see that he doesn't go out of his way to invoke it."

"He seems to depend on you."

"Judith got to know him when he came to Israel to help train our young pilots, though she wasn't in the airforce. He came to our house and, in the end, it was partly because of him that we came to Failland."

"I'm surprised that you could have left after taking such a dedicated part in building the State of Israel."

Gideon could now follow quite easily and see where the parallel lay.

186

"In modern Judaism were placed all those hopes of a community whose laws and lifestyles reflected the ancient commandments of Jehovah, who after two millenia again had his temple in Jerusalem.

"For a time his words as recorded in the scriptures were holy in the minds of these newly-delivered people. Then faith waned and an interior desolation began to take over. There were still prophets, such as Martin Buber, but those voices were stifled by the babble of civil authority exhorting them to all kinds of desirable national objectives.

"For a short time the memory of the furnace of suffering out of which they were delivered remained strong, even under Golda Maier, but then a generation of shrewd, modern politicians and businessmen took over and there was a spiritual decline downwards to Menachem Begin. And the age-old victims turned into persecutors and executioners."

"But I've read of large numbers of Israelis taking to the streets of Jerusalem against the victorious invasions of their own Government. That is something unique, Paul, and shows that what you and your friends sowed never entirely withered away."

"Which, in our context, is why you're here, Gideon."

Despite his sense of ease with Weissmann, even a feeling of closeness, of what he imagined as what he might have experienced with a brother, had he had one, he wasn't sure how this would influence outer events.

"Klotz isn't a Ben Gurion."

"But nor is he the usual run of war lords. He has considerable military gifts as well as what is lacking in most of them, a readiness to learn. You saw how he relies on me. His job is to clean up the psychic scum under which Failland has sunk, and there is nobody better. Beyond that, he knows his own deficiencies. The danger is that a great access to power may turn his head, as it did with the others.

"What will he do when he hears that we've defied the banning of *Faillandia*?"

"He knows that already and if there's anything in it that he sees as a threat, he might raid it, though I think he'd consult me first."

Gideon was silent while he made some swift re-adjustments to his conclusion about yesterday's meeting and the magazine's future. Or could this be a ploy on Paul Weissmann's part to get him to give away the hideout? No. Having crossed the invisible gulf between himself and another person — and it had happened to him no more than three times before now — Gideon's natural suspicion disappeared altogether.

"Who can have informed on us to Klotz?"

Gideon had asked Leo about the credentials of the type-setter and machine operator and been told that as they were paid a full-time wage for part-time work and had little to fear in case of a raid on the premises, quite apart from their loyalty to him personally, so they had nothing to gain by turning informer.

"One of our intelligence agents, a woman, brought me the information yesterday and I had to pass it on to Klotz."

Nolla Grimmick? Gideon didn't ask. By telling him that it was a woman Paul Weissmann had gone far out of his way to consummate in a very practical way the strange affiliation between them.

If she was a doubtless highly-paid member of the rebel military intelligence agency, then it hadn't been for the money that she'd agreed to the weekend arrangement with Kemp.

Because it amused her? Because that was when she'd got him to confide in her, more likely. Gideon recalled Kemp suggesting to Leo that she should be included in the small enclave of five, not counting the printers, who knew the whereabouts of *Faillandia*'s new premises. And now it seemed likely that this was because she'd already got it out of him.

"When are we in most danger?"

It was a lot to expect an answer to that, but now Gideon saw that Paul, like his ancient namesake to the cause he had been harassing, had been converted to looking on *Faillandia*

188

as the antidote to the same malaise that had blighted his own land.

"When will you have the new issue ready and out of the hotel?"

Yes, Gideon saw that this was the decisive hour, the getting of the first clandestine issue onto the streets.

"By ten o'clock tonight."

Gideon thought that could be managed. And after that, if Pieta's faith was justified, it would take off like the bird from the old monk's hands.

"It's for you and I, Gideon, to see that the takeover doesn't become a mirror image of the regime it replaces, as history has shown is the natural process.

"Klotz is probably the only leader who can organise and carry through an armed revolt with minimal casualties. That's because he's built up a mystique around himself, and there's nobody of stature in the army who could get sufficient support from the rank-and-file to oppose him."

There is was, the dreaded and yet fascinating word had been spoken: 'revolution' — even if Paul had actually said 'revolt'. And Gideon had heard himself named by one of the instigators as a collaborator.

Here he was, being pushed to the forefront of a movement of which as far as its activist side was concerned, he knew little and certainly was less committed to its leader than Paul Weissmann.

"In the hour or so since I've been here, Paul, and I believe you're aware of this too, there's what to me was an unexpected accord between us, in our instincts and emotions perhaps particularly. Because of this, as much as in spite of it, there mustn't be a misunderstanding about my having any other part in what you call the revolt than as editor of the totally non-political *Faillandia*."

Paul Weissmann leant forward and laid his hand on Gideon's in a gesture that reminded him of the little girl's on being introduced to her. And, as if coincidentally, Sarah appeared at that

189

moment with a coffee pot and mugs on a tray.

"That's what I rely on you as, and nothing else."

"And even for that I'm dependent on my sister-in-law who's in hospital and whom I've been forbidden to visit at the moment."

"I wanted to talk to you about that too."

Again Gideon found himself surprised and wondered what he was to make of this? That all that had gone before was of less concern than something that Paul Weissmann hadn't yet spoken of? And, it seemed, wasn't in a hurry so to do, because he was pouring coffee into the mugs that his daughter held out, and when they were filled, asking Gideon if he'd like some brandy in his.

"I was waiting for you to mention her, Gideon. I thought it might seem impertinent of me to be the one to do so. But, of course, I remember the incident when the Colonel and I called on you, and your obvious concern for the sick creature — a bird was it not? — that your sister-in-law, Pieta, had entrusted to you before going to hospital. And I guessed — yes, we had the beginnings of an understanding even then — that it was she whose purity of spirit — something long absent from all our deliberations, both political and intellectual — shines out from the pages of *Faillandia*.

"A surprisingly correct intuition."

"Since then I've had it confirmed."

"You mean, by the same agent as told you of the whereabouts of our printing press?"

"And, as I'm bound to with such information, in distinction to what I may sometimes surmise, I passed it on to the chief."

This, Gideon supposed, explained the ban on his visits. Paul hadn't answered the question directly, but Gideon saw that this wasn't necessary.

"Judith spent several months there before her death last year."

Where? Once more Gideon had to collect himself.

"Where Pieta is?"

"Yes. The master, Dr. Karl Roggan, is her brother."

190

Gideon had seen the name on the mahogany notice-board under the entrance arch of the hospital. The names of doctors were slotted into place beside the hours when they were on duty.

"What did she suffer from?"

"From injuries received in a car accident."

Gideon's heart, which he sometimes feared was stony because it seemed so seldom moved, went out to Paul, as his imagination quickly encompassed the whole long alternation between hope and near-despair, the waiting for the slightest indication, the almost abject dependence on the doctor's words — in this case a friend — the visits, both humbling and inspiring; Gideon naturally thought of his own to Pieta.

"My suggestion, Gideon, is that you move your printing press and the rest of the equipment there early tomorrow. I've spoken to Karl and he has an unused ward waiting where he will admit you as one of his patients. The other members of your entourage can come and go with the hospital visitors quite unremarked upon."

## TWENTY TWO

The Olive Tree Clinic was part of the larger hospital where Pieta was a patient, run, as Gideon had been told, by Paul Weissmann's brother-in-law.

As he waited in the room he'd been given for a promised visit from Dr. Karl Roggan, Gideon reflected on the unanswered questions, as well as on what were not so much questions as unresolved problems. One that might seem the least important occupied him first because it contained a secret source of reassurance. Had the clinic got its name from the tree that he'd been so aware of while watching from Pieta's bedside. If so, it was remarkably large for an olive tree. If the doctor turned out to be a person of perception, in Gideon's sense of the word, he would ask him.

Next was the news of the extraordinary demand for the clandestine issue of *Faillandia* as soon as it had appeared on the streets of the city the night before.

The young men and women who distributed it for a percentage of the money collected — Frank and some associates had volunteered to take batches into Government-held districts — had at times been mobbed. When Gideon had last seen Leo in the early hours of the morning, he'd estimated that ninety or a hundred thousand copies had been bought, apart from those sent to provincial towns by road.

Reports had come in of clashes between groups delivering batches to apartment blocks that the residents didn't dare leave, and troops trying to enforce a curfew that was mostly being ignored.

192

Making some final personal arrangement with Paul on the phone before leaving the Hotel Aphra Paul had said: "It's got to a point where any sentence printed across one of your pages would be taken as a clarion-call."

That, Gideon thought, was an exaggeration, but what Paul meant to imply was that the sensibilities of a lot of people had been tuned to a peak. There was hope and expectation in the air, as well as revulsion and contempt for what, after decades of disguise and dissimulation, was at last exposed as the Black Plague institutionalised by political liars of almost all parties, and given a façade of rectitute by Church officials.

A question which Gideon was only one of many in asking: who were loyal to Klotz, the troops or the guerilla militia? He concluded that in fact both were now co-ordinated under the Colonel's command.

Another, to Gideon even more vital one: Was Klotz going to take action — belatedly as it had turned out — against *Faillandia*?

Against these imponderables was the fact that he had been down in the basement and confirmed that the press, which would be idle for the next few days, and a few bundles of the magazine, were safely there. The remaining copies would be dispatched later to private distribution agents.

Should he get in touch with Pieta's doctor, Mr. Cadjella, and ask when he could go across to the main building to visit her? Better first consult Dr. Roggan. It seemed he was suddenly surrounded by medicos, an exaggeration, of course, but Gideon knew he was not at the top of his sober self.

And then there was Kathy, whom he had to arrange to meet here to tell her to move from their apartment to the hotel, at least until the situation had stabilised.

Why was he using jargon like this to himself? Because, no doubt, he had not the necessary tranquillity to construct a lucid and flexible prose style for his present interior monologues.

Memo One: The bomb outside their flat. The tin had had a picture of an old world garden on the sides and the name of a

193

brand of biscuits he had seen advertised on television on the lid. It now struck him as an example — if an extreme one — of the deception being everywhere practised in business, in politics, in art. Nothing was what it seemed. All the promises held hidden clauses that negativised them or even turned them into threats.

It had begun long ago and gradually got to the point where everything he heard, read, breathed, eat, drank, bathed in, was in some way or other falsified. A dispririted people strapped themselves into cars and crawled through traffic-jammed streets and the women in their concrete boxes turned on their televisions and watched the commercials, which were often more subtle in their deception than the politicians and clerics.

Memo Two: Consider the suggestion that Nolla was working for Klotz.

At last — though perhaps at the appointed hour — Dr. Karl Roggan turned up.

He shook hands and sat down on the bed, there being no other chair in the small room besides that occupied by Gideon.

When Gideon thanked him for all he was doing for him and the magazine, the doctor said that to help a friend of Judith's, particularly in a matter of which she would have approved, he welcomed as a way of honouring her memory. Gideon, disconcerted at the misunderstanding, may have read into 'the words a more formal tone than they contained.

"I never knew your sister, it's her husband, Paul, I'm a friend of."

"Ah . . . It was a hectic night, constantly being rung up, ambulances bringing casualties, and naturally Paul wanted to say as little as possible on the phone with the uncertainty about whose surveillance is on whom. A pity that you didn't know her: a unique creature in some ways; not at all a child of this world, or perhaps not one suited to this age. She used to make me think of those lines of the poem: 'Through the sad heart of Ruth, standing in tears amid the alien corn.' "

"Yes, indeed . . . I see." (He'd got it wrong but let it pass).

What *did* Gideon see? Nothing very clearly. Perhaps that the doctor was to be trusted. But surely that was abundantly evident already. What Gideon was thinking had nothing to do with his lending his basement to the underground magazine nor the taking-in of himself, but that he too was reassured that there were women who were sisters of those who had inspired writers like Mandelstam, Keats and Shakespeare (in his last plays).

"A lovely looking woman; I saw the family portrait. The little girl has comething of the same composed expression."

"How rare it is to meet with a composed spirit these days. You come across it sometimes in women who with their interwoven mammalian and angelic natures seem to walk through these days unscathed."

The conversation, without Gideon trying to guide it, was, he thought, of a kind into which the introduction of what was on his mind wouldn't seem abrupt.

"As you may know, Doctor, I've a sister-in-law a patient in the main hospital whom I'd like to visit."

"During afternoon visiting hours is the best time. They're not the same in all departments, so ring 'Reception' to find out the ward she's in."

The doctor evidentally knew nothing of the ban on his visits, nor had heard of Pieta.

While he waited, Gideon looked through the copy of *Faillandia* he'd brought with him, re-reading parts of a contribution that, although unsigned, he thought had come from Frère Emanuel.

The theme seemed to be the 'Underground Jesus'.

*There is no place in our Church for the outcast figure of the Gospels, often weary and dispirited, growing more aware of his failure. What he was seeking was a sign, the simplest one of all, the sign of pure, disinterested love from another being.*

*A drink of water was enough, a place where he could lay his head. The ancient religion had been travestied by a spirit*

195

*of conformism to observances. As today with us, institutional religion competed with civil institutions and organisations, promoting their spiritual commodities against the worldly ones, though both are very similar, appealing to the greed in human nature by promises of self-advantage. Heavenly rewards against, though sometimes even on top of, the glittering earthly ones.*

*Meanwhile this Person dwells among us, as He promised He would, still seeking the disinterested, spontaneous response of love without which he cannot establish the Kingdom of God He believed His Father had originally sent Him on earth to do.*

*He has now, as then, no permanent earthly habitation, and if sometimes He seems to perform miracles on behalf of those who believe in Him, He admonishes them, just as long ago, not to spread the news abroad, thus making it more difficult for Him to find men and women attracted to Him, not by His magical powers, but by words and sayings that were the very opposite of the ones that were beamed at them from every organ of authority.*

*Dostoyevsky makes it clear where the Grand Inquisitor parts company with his divine prisoner.*

*Thou didst desire man's free love, that he should follow Three freely, enticed and taken captive by Thee. Thou didst hope that man following Thee would cling to God and not ask for a miracle. Thou didst not know that when man rejects miracle he rejects God too, for man seeks not so much God as the miracles.'*

Gideon wasn't altogether convinced by this quote. He preferred the Christ that the old monk had written about in *Faillandia*, even though it was a fairytale one. Of Pieta's Christ, so far as he'd glimpsed Him, he was in awe.

In the intimations that occasionally came to him from he didn't know where he became aware of a Silent Defector, a figure emanating a miraculous balm in desperate situations mostly unrecorded except by a few poets and prophets such as

Dostoyevsky who recognised him in a drab room in St. Petersburg, Boris Pasternak in a hospital ward and Emily Brontë in a bleak nineteenth century parsonage.

The Silent Defector (as Gideon thought of him) could only manage to lead away with him those who turned to him as a last resort and didn't even ask whence they were being taken. He certainly hadn't made much headway as the Universal Saviour proclaimed by the Churches, though Gideon didn't suppose that this worried him, used as he was to what was generally considered failure.

Governmental broadcasts had ceased since the previous night, and Gideon heard a short radio bulletin announcing that a committee of airforce officers, of which Colonel Klotz was chairman, had taken over the civil administration and that the city was now quiet. What concerned him most was an additional statement that a strict censorship of all publications had been imposed with severe penalties for any evasions.

After trying to assess how this not unexpected news affected him (not, certainly, advantageously) he left the refuge of the clinic and crossed to the hospital which he entered at the back.

Pieta was sitting up in bed reading and didn't look up until Gideon was standing beside her cot. Then she dropped the book and held out her arms at whose thinness, as the loose sleeves of the nightdress fell back, he winced.

She pressed his head to her breast as if he was the one needing comfort, but he pulled it away in fear that it might be weighing on her wounds. But before he could ask about them, she enquired for the bird.

"But didn't you hear, we opened the window and it flew away."

How could she have heard? It had only happened two days ago, despite his sense that quite a time had elapsed.

"Why, Gideon, did you think it would fly straight here to show itself to me?"

Gideon saw her eyes light with happiness.

This time the tall window behind her was partially open

197

and he thought he could hear the rustling of the dark leaves of what he now imagined as a giant olive tree where the birds still seemed to be busy in and around it. But in the short silence between them that followed Pieta's exclamation, Gideon realised it was more like the sound of very distant bursts of machine-gun fire.

## TWENTY THREE

When Gideon saw in the hospital grounds that it was approaching autumn, he took it as a sign. A sign in himself, not in nature. That the change of season meant so much to him could only be that he was in touch again with one of the principal sources from which he drew strength and patience, and from which he'd been cut off recently. Another of these — or was it rather a part of the same natural power? — was his physical relationship with Kathy, from which it looked as if he might be also cut off for a time. But already he had thought of a plan in this regard.

Sheltered from what was happening in the rest of the city, and looked after by an old man who mowed the lawns and swept up the leaves, Gideon liked to stroll in this park coming back from his morning and late afternoon visits to Pieta.

One evening, two or three days after his first visit, he was returning to his own quarters by a route that took him past the furthest, overgrown corner. He was meditating on his recent talk with Pieta and how from her he drew a different nourishment than what were the more usual kinds of daily bread. With Kathy he shared the good three-meals-a-day of sweet, close companionship and had it not been for her sister couldn't have imagined more. But from Pieta and her magazine flowed to him surprising invigorating currents, metaphysical perhaps, though he was wary of using any of these vague, ready to hand, expressions.

After a visit to her he was reassured. His faith in the magazine, and especially in its effect on the struggle for the rescue of

Failland, was restored. Her faith came, he knew, from a course close to him, that she shared with Frère Emanuel. There was a whole dark area beyond his point of contact with her, the knowledge of which fascinated but also made him uneasy. And indeed, as now, his reflections were deflected from it towards another aspect of the season. He was thinking of autumn at Longchamp, with the Bois de Boulogne the other side of the course from the stands, and in particular of the gleaming colt, with the bright gloss of a chestnut just emerged from its shell, that Marthe had reminded him of.

So many different flavours in the daily bread of his imaginative nourishment, but without Pieta's contribution he'd have gone hungry!

These speculations were interrupted by his catching sight of a cluster of small dark leaves amind the undergrowth. Gideon stooped and, brushing aside the coarser tufts of weeds, revealed a spray of Fael.

He regarded it for several moments, taking in the spiral structure of the plant and the tiny, sharp-pronged, almost black leaves. He had an initial impulse to pick it to bring to Pieta in the morning, but instead he let the grasses return to their protective hiding of it.

Not that Gideon hadn't plenty to occupy him with the magazine; Leo brought him the contributions sent to *Faillandia*'s former address and re-directed to the hotel by the post office, the head of whose governing body was a friend of his. These Gideon sorted out and brought any of the unsolicited ones of which he was in doubt to show Pieta. There were also those from regular contributors, including Marthe's on the racing scene and literary reports from Hymna in London, whom he'd finally engaged as a part-time commentator.

Before the banning of the magazine, a few articles had been submitted to him, usually by hand, at his home address. Among these dropped through the letterbox at the apartment was one from an anonymous contributor with what Gideon had thought was an astonishingly inspired suggestion for the planning of a city to become the capital of a new Failland.

Ideally, it was to be built within the loop of a river, the remaining portion of the circle to be completed by a canal. This would provide one of the main public transport routes, operated by electric barges sailing around the periphery, connecting at spaced wharfs to tram lines crossing the city — there would be no private cars and no petrol engines — and running on lines set in narrow strips of lawns along the centre of the broad main streets. They would intersect at a main halt in the small central park.

The outer city, or suburbs, would consist of concentric rings of mostly single or two-story dwellings, each with its secluded garden, well-fenced and, later, bounded by hedges and trees, that ended on the next outer circular avenue. There would be pathways between every ten or twelve houses and gardens connecting the two avenues, and at greater distances apart, narrow roadways where the traffic — of bicycles and electric delivery vans — would be light.

In the inner city, or central part of the circle, around the park, the public library, concert hall, museum and two threatres for contemporary and traditional productions, would be built. Hospitals would be situated on the outer bank of the surrounding waterway, which would largely be preserved as unencumbered countryside.

Plans and specifications had accompanied the text, and Gideon had wanted to publish the entire piece, but the other members of the committee had argued that it was not the time.

So Gideon had put the long envelope in a safe place at the flat and continued on and off to think of it as the New Jerusalem, the outward and tangible symbol of what the revolution had by then achieved.

The article and plans were there at the apartment, if it hadn't already been raided. Gideon had phoned the concierge to tell her that he and Kathy had gone away for a few days — he'd considered saying 'on holiday', but hadn't — and had expected to hear if there had been any extraordinary visitors to the flat.

201

The old woman, however, had been placid and incurious.

The same evening that he'd come on the little sprig of Fael Paul Weissmann had telephoned. At first Gideon was puzzled by Paul's enquiries about how he was.

"Why, how should I be? Considering everything, I'm all right."

"Yes, quite so, considering everything. I only hope your mind, under Dr. Roggan's care, is more at rest."

It then dawned on Gideon that Paul thought there could be eavesdroppers on the line and was referring to an imaginary mental collapse. He decided not to refer to the magazine, neither the phenomenal success of the first underground number nor to the preparation of the coming one.

He did, though, mention a more purely personal concern, that about being able to see so little of Kathy and then only when she was visiting her sister.

Paul appeared not to respond and asked Gideon if he wouldn't like to have a few words with Sarah.

Gideon, somewhat taken aback, all the same managed to come out with: 'of course'.

The child herself, not surprisingly, didn't have very much to say, and, not wanting to cut the awkward conversation too short, Gideon began telling her about an event, leaving, as he knew was best with children, it uncertain whether what he was describing had actually happened or not.

Base it on fact, turn fact to fiction. Which was how good storytellers proceeded. But quickly, because the attention of children is short-lived. The Museum cat, that was it! Transformed into something larger than life and kept by an ogre called Churchhill (he'd no time to wonder where the association lay). With two such intriguing parts, the rest of the fantasy would rapidly unfold in a series, he hoped, of just about credible shocks.

The child listened at the other end, gracious, polite, and composed, as she asked him to continue, but Gideon thought that by now any agent would have tired of listening, though the whole conversation might be, he supposed, being recorded. In any case, he'd run out of exciting incidents that could be related with the persuasiveness and attention to detail necessary to hold the interest of a twelve, or thirteen-year-old. Conjuring up a sub-machine gun with a curved black magazine protruding from its underside, such as Sarah had doubtless seen cradled by members of Klotz's security guards patrolling the streets, he brought the little story to a happy enough conclusion.

Paul, at the other end again, was asking him if he had now a private night-nurse in attendance.

"I've been promised one as soon as she's available."

"I'll ask Dr. Roggan to hurry it up."

Gideon took this to mean that in no time at all Kathy, in nurse's uniform, would be spending the nights with him. It was the prospect — the pre-emptive realising of it in his imagination — and the autumnal hospital grounds that restored some of the sense of his direction that was so frequently confused by outside signals.

But, of course, he didn't know how Kathy herself would like the idea of having a couple of highly-placed officials engage in arranging facilities for their love-making.

Leo visited him to discuss some technicalities about the layout. He no longer — if he ever had — took much part in the editorial side. But he surprised Gideon by talking as if *Faillandia* was now so rooted in the hearts of the people of Aphrin that neither Klotz's militia nor any other armed group, which might emerge as the supreme authority, would dare seize it on the streets.

"You and Kathy should come to dinner at the hotel. What about tomorrow?"

Gideon hesitated. Was there really little or no danger now? Was Paul or Leo correct?

"I don't think that would be wise."

"You're not a prisoner here, are you?"

"I don't quite know, Leo. A voluntary one, perhaps."

He wondered how to make his father-in-law see that he,

203

Gideon, was the keystone in the rather frail arch that, in the form of *Faillandia* rose above the embattled city? That this had come about by accident as it struck him, in no way contradicted the fact. That he wasn't himself capable of writing a couple of the kind of sentences that were apparently burning their imagery into so many minds and hearts, had nothing to do with it.

And yet he had never been the steadfast one behind the magazine, not like Pieta, not even the convinced revolutionary, like Leo. In one sense he was a failure, he hadn't done anything but let himself go with the strong new tide whose impetus came from others, not forgetting, though here Gideon was still unsure on his part in it, Frère Emanuel.

"I'll tell you what, Leo. Either tomorrow or the day after I'll have to go home to get some documents that I left there, and, if it goes smoothly, then I'll call at the hotel on the way back and have Kathy meet me there."

If Klotz — or another — were to get hold of me, Gideon reflected, that would be the end of *Faillandia* as contender in the mental-psychic struggle for the city. He didn't take any pride in the realisation. And he didn't suppose anybody else besides Pieta, the friar, Paul Weissmann and possibly Klotz, had any inkling of this.

That evening, crossing from the hospital to the clinic, Gideon came on the park-keeper attending a mound of smouldering leaves. He stopped to watch the old fellow thrust a two-pronged fork into the pile, raising a heavy yellow-red layer, so that the breeze, which Gideon hadn't been aware of, entered the smoky cavern as if lured from afar and, igniting the leaves, turned it into a gaping, fiery mouth. He closed it by withdrawing the fork, and from the top of the pile the smoke escaped in thick, twisting skeins.

In that moment Gideon was transported back to the autumns when he lived in the country with Lydia, and one of his preoccupations had been the gathering and burning of fallen leaves.

Those twilights in the blue shadow under the back wall of the stables had been lit by the sudden flare of the flames at the heart of the damp pile, and then deepened by whorls of greyish-yellow smoke whose acrid scent stayed for hours in his nostrils.

The park-keeper, who naturally took Gideon for a patient at the clinic, seemed wary of entering a conversation with him at first. And Gideon supposed that his too obvious obsession in the proceedings, which he did not hide, added to the old man's caution.

"What about a deep prod in there?" he suggested eagerly, indicating a portion of the mound where the combustion seemed sluggish.

The park-keeper gave Gideon a furtive glance from under the hard peak of his cap, which indeed gave him an air of authority that Gideon irrationally resented. What he saw may not have reassured him, for he took a turn around the smouldering pile without reacting to the suggestion. When he'd completed a circuit, he stood still again, gripping the fork at its centre with the end of the handle on the ground and the prongs pointing upwards at a slight angle away from him.

"Did you know that this is a historic spot?" he asked.

A lovely spot, in a sense, a sacred spot, but historic?

"Well, no."

"Never heard of the second battle of Alphaburg?"

Gideon had certainly heard of it among the names of the other ancient battles fought between the foreign conquerors and the native freedom fighters. The very sound of them, now that he thought of it, had long ago depressed him, and he had never given that part of the country's history his full attention.

Now, with a sudden clarity not unlike that which he'd experienced after Leo's call, he understood why. Because, whatever the outcome, defeat or victory, it had all added up in the end to the establishment of this second-rate community, this submissive, dispirited people, by a tawdry lot of native manipulators.

"The battle raged from soon after dawn to dusk, with a pause around noon for the wounded to be carried away, and the dead buried."

This was evidently an old and well loved story handed on to the park-keeper and learnt as a recitation that was part of the precious lore of the land, even if in the circles where Gideon had moved it wasn't known.

"At the end of the day the Faillanders were in command of the ground inside these walls and of the higher ground that rises beyond as far as what is now the Observatory."

The park-keeper jabbed his fork viciously into that part of the pile that Gideon had indicated, and a puff of yellowish smoke emerged, but no flames.

"It was at this spot that the last battle that determined the outcome took place at about this time of an autumn evening with dusk gathering, as it is now." The old fellow paused and regarded the bluish smoke that he had sent billowing from the heap of leaves. He then took a deep breath as does a singer for the *grande finale* and pronounced in what struck Gideon as ringing tones: "The Faillanders drove the invaders out of the last outskirts of the town."

He added in an ordinary voice: "That was the second battle of Alphaburg, the first had been fought through the town itself a few months earlier in a sudden uprising that had taken the enemy by surprise and driven them out of almost all the occupied buildings."

He made a lunge into the heart of the smouldering leaves, and this time flames leapt high.

Gideon saw the bright tongues lick the tender blue belly of the evening and then vanish, drawn back into the smoky maw.

"This earth where you're standing was sodden with patriot blood."

The park-keeper turned and looked at Gideon for the first time. After the brightness of the brief conflagration, the shadows were deeper, and Gideon could only just see the other.

206

And with other blood. But Gideon didn't express this thought aloud.

"According to the legend, wherever this blood soaked into the land, the Fael grows."

Gideon said nothing. It was doubtful whether the keeper was even now addressing him. Besides, he was not going to tell him of the discovery he'd made in an overgrown corner of the park, where the old man was almost certainly not aware that the weed was growing.

This new role — was it new? — of keeping silent about things that he hadn't yet thought out to any conclusion, gave Gideon a sense of having gained a little wisdom since the days he was apt to blurt everything out.

## TWENTY FOUR

Gideon took a taxi to the apartment. The number of his own car, which was parked in a shed in the hospital grounds, was probably on a list of those to be stopped.

The driver at first demurred, saying he was only on the rank outside the hospital to take emergency cases. When Gideon remarked that these would surely be travelling in the in-coming direction, the young man shook his head as if this was hair-splitting. But he opened the door.

He looked to Gideon like one of the army conscripts whom he had heard had defected in large numbers from defending Government buildings and installations and, in civilian suits, were robbing and looting. If so, this one, having commandeered a taxi, had found a safer — at least temporarily — and probably more lucrative occupation.

Many, though not all, of the shops had their steel shutters lowered, there was little traffic on the streets and only a few people hurrying along the pavements. They passed through several barricades of sand bags, manned by troops, with a narrow passage left open, but were not stopped.

"Whose lot are they?" Gideon asked the driver, although he'd seen the wings of the airforce stencilled on their helmets.

"The new Government."

The young man had not pronounced the name that Gideon had expected (hoped? feared?) to hear.

On several walls and on the pseudo-imperial facades of some banks, Gideon saw the slogan: *VIVA FAILLANDIA.*

He let himself into the apartment, took a look into the rooms which were as they'd left them, and returned to the hall to pick up some letters.

There was one addressed in a hand-writing that he immediately didn't recognise but supposed was an unsolicited contribution to the magazine. Instead, it turned out to be a letter from Laura, and a quite long one at that.

Gideon took it, with the others, into the front room to read, where, on the small table in a corner, the cardboard box that had housed the fledgling still stood, and beside it a half-full tin of cat food and a couple of sharpened match sticks. He contemplated these objects for a moment and looked into the box at the stained sheet of newspaper that lined the bottom.

Gideon left the letters on the dining table and took these mementoes, as he thought of them, to the kitchen to dispose of. As he was returning to the front room, the telephone in the hall rang.

Gideon stood for a moment before lifting the receiver, not to try to guess who the caller was — he knew from of old the uselessness of that — but to recollect himself from the varied memories and intense musings that the letter from his daughter and the sight of the box had evoked.

"Hello!"

Gideon never followed the normal practice of repeating his telephone number when taking a call. There was a pause, then the voice at the far end asked him his name.

"Who's speaking?"

"Klotz."

Despite his apparent tendency to what seemed day-dreaming, when it came a crisis, Gideon reacted swiftly as if, he imagined, an elixir was secreted into his bloodstream.

"Good afternoon, Colonel. I've been thinking of you."

"Who hasn't? Tell me that, Sir!"

Gideon laughed, yes, his greeting had had a comic side to it.

"But you weren't expecting to hear from me?"

"Well, no. I didn't think you'd have time for private calls."

"This isn't a private call, Sir."

Gideon's heart sank slightly as Klotz went on: "Anymore than was the one you told me about Stalin making to the Russian poet."

"Pasternak."

"Yes. The name had slipped me. Do you imagine yourself as a local Pasternak?"

There were times for caution and times for daring. Not being quite sure which of these this was, Gideon said: "Yes and no."

"Do you and your magazine not claim to tell the truth that is everywhere else suppressed?"

"That's right, Colonel."

Yes, Gideon perceived that he would have to take risks.

"When has the truth ever been told? Neither by you nor anyone else, because people would take such offence at it that you'd be silenced with the full support of almost everyone. People don't want to be told that they must be controlled for their own good. Only a handful of citizens know what is to their advantage and that the masses always use too much freedom to put themselves — oh, completely voluntarily, that's the irony — under the domination of governments composed of characters more corrupt than the average voter."

"Maybe, Colonel. All the same, the artists and prophets manage better even under corrupt administrations than in dictatorships."

A slight pause. Gideon knew that he'd pronounced words that Klotz didn't like to hear.

"You think your magazine will be remembered when the name of Klotz is seldom mentioned and then with amused contempt?"

A more lengthy pause. Had Klotz laid down the receiver without replacing it on its cradle while he radioed his nearest mobile squad to Gideon's apartment to arrest him?

But no, he was still there at the end of the line.

"Do you intend, Sir, to try to continue with the publication of your weekly?"

"That is something we haven't yet decided."

There it was: the fatal words spoken, and, for all he knew, also recorded in the Colonel's office.

Klotz: "You're like this Pasternak character in one way at least, a prevaricator!"

And there it was: the click, followed by the dialling tone.

Gideon stood with the receiver still in his hand in the hallway. A shiver went through him with the knowledge of the enormity of his failure to win over Klotz. Not the kind of shiver that could be banished by Kathy.

He had been given a unique opportunity of bearing witness before the highest tribunal in the land to what he believed — give or take a few uncertainties — was an intimation of truth and hope infiltrating the fabric in which the community was shrouded, and had, if not quite denied it, made a poor show.

Like all those civic and spiritual authorities he despised, he had hesitated, hedged, and in Klotz's own word, prevaricated. Of course, Klotz hadn't been taken in. But that afforded Gideon no comfort.

What now? Klotz might still send a mobile militia squad for him, and this seemed the more likely after what Gideon had said to him, almost threatened him with, in his final words.

Should he wait here to be picked up, or take the lift down to the basement — where he had deposited the heavy biscuit tin — and hope to make his way out the back and across the couple of yards into a street?

At that moment he thought of Pieta. What would she wish? That he escape and, from his hiding place at the clinic, carry on with editing *Faillandia*?

He put back the receiver, returned to the front room, and started to read the letter from Laura.

His daughter wrote to him seldom and she began shyly and somewhat awkwardly, mentioning first the weather and then telling him of her fears for him because of what she called 'the apparently unsettled state of things where you are'. Perhaps she expected a letter addressed to him to be censored. But as he read on and came to what he guessed was the reason for her having written, that seemed unlikely.

She told him, also in rather hesitant style, as if embarrassed to acknowledge her emotion, how moved she had been by *Faillandia*.

She didn't particularise or say much about the articles, stories or poems — or quotations from dead poets — that had so affected her, though she did mention the last verse or two of Pasternak's — there he was again to haunt Gideon — poem: *The Hospital*.

What so pleased Gideon was her conclusion, more hinted at than actually said, that her former distrust of, and hostility to him, had been overcome — that was the rather cumbersome word she used — and she had an inkling of the star (her word too) he'd been following all along. She no longer blamed him solely for the breakup of the marriage, in fact she seemed to see him and his actions in a new light.

All this was good news to Gideon, though he couldn't, especially at this crucial moment, but think she'd swung too far in the other direction in her judgement. In particular, the 'star' that she wrote of as shining from some of the pages of the magazine, he certainly hadn't set in the night sky, and had only followed intermittently.

Nevertheless, it was a weight off his spirit, one greater than he'd acknowledged, as he saw now that it was lifted. For, although Laura didn't go as far as that, her change of heart — if he could call it that — was one that her mother might also have had had she been alive. For mother and daughter were, he knew, very much alike in their psyches. But what he was getting at in his own secret mind was that the baby, Sabina, had she lived would, far from feeling alienated from him because of his desertion, have come to realise a bond between them, 'strong as the trunk between leaves and root', were the words that came to him from he didn't know where.

# TWENTY FIVE

When Kathy came into his room at the clinic in nurse's uniform, it was to him like their first encounter, except for the uncertainty at that time as to its outcome.

The heart of the sensational mystery lay, for him, as he indulged momentarily in this thought, that what she was going to bestow on him she would become ever more acutely aware of as part of her own body.

"Shall I undress or keep this on?"

Gideon knew that she meant: 'won't it heighten the shock, the sensation, if we do it like this?'

"It's something I'll never get over."

Gideon was lying beside her, both dressed, reflecting on what had just taken place.

"If you ever did, you couldn't do it."

"No."

"It starts up there . . . " her fingers pressed the sides of his forehead and then moved to the back of his neck " . . . and travels down the spine . . . ", her hand followed the route " . . . Ah, it's there again already!"

Gideon was awoken later, still in Kathy's arms, by the sound of sobbing.

After they both listened for a while to what appeared to come from down the passage, she got up and went to investigate.

She seemed to Gideon to be away a long time during which the sobbing did not cease for a moment.

At last Kathy returned. Her face had shed the glow of sleep, sex and well-being, and even her hair, through which she had pulled a comb, seemed lack-lustre.

"It's a man a couple of rooms away, lying face downwards on his cot and sobbing his heart out."

She said she had gone to the sister on duty in the general ward for the night nurse — Kathy passed as being privately engaged — who told her that the patient whose condition had been diagnosed as one of 'acute melancholia' usually wept all night long, refusing the morphine injections prescribed.

"Didn't she say what he's grieving over?"

Kathy shook her head.

It struck Gideon that once the patient had been examined and questioned, his past history noted and perhaps entered in his dossier which might then be filed in its correct category, a treatment prescribed, then nobody had personal responsibility.

But then, recalling his talk with Dr. Roggan, Gideon felt he might well be indulging his own bias in regard to institutions.

"Should we not try to find out?"

This was as much a musing to himself as a question to Kathy.

"The Sister said he sleeps most of the day and after the evening meal sometimes walks up and down the corridor."

Kathy had got back into bed, but the world to whose fringe they'd been brought, and from whose wasteland the sobbing was wafted to them, was so far from that in which they'd fallen asleep, that Gideon was now almost as chilled by the thought of love-making as a short time before the thought of it had enflamed him.

Another realm, another life, another mode of being, which neither his and Kathy's, nor Leo's, nor that of any of their associates touched at any point. Except, that is, Pieta's, and he couldn't tell precisely what kind hers was or felt like. All he knew was some of its signs, or 'symptoms': her wounds, her care for the sick bird, her preoccupation with the Gospels, the understanding that she shared with Frère Emanuel.

Ah, he had still to tell her of the telephone talk with Klotz and its near fatal ending. What did he mean by "near fatal"?

Not for the magazine, whose survival it hadn't affected one way or the other but for what he thought of as his self-respect, or more exactly, psychic well-being. And this depended on learning from Pieta, even at times following her against his rational, self-preserving judgement. Left to himself, he tended to prevaricate, to tell Klotz: "we haven't decided", in order not to rupture relations with him which he prized for what he knew in his heart were base motives.

The truth was that nothing could now stop the next number from appearing. Various people, all important in a strange manner, some dead, seemed now vitally involved. Apart from Pieta and her friar, based here under the same roof as her, it had suddenly come under the patronage, so to speak, of Paul, his deceased wife, Judith, and — if he had grasped the implications — Lydia.

Kathy said she'd go and make them tea in the room she'd noticed where there was a stove and utensils.

While they were drinking it, she wondered whether he shouldn't try to change his room.

"I slept through it the previous nights and tonight we only heard it because of our late love-making."

"But from now on you'll be listening for it."

"I can't just move out of earshot."

"It's what we do all the time, Gideon. Mostly we don't even have to move, it's so arranged that we're safely out of hearing and sight of all the heartbreak."

"How do you know about that, Dove?"

He was somewhat surprised by her comment.

"A healthy young woman with a comfortable job in her father's hotel hasn't the chance that nurses have, especially in a psychiatric clinic, of experiencing that side of life."

"That's what I thought."

"So did I for a time. But I was curious, at least on and off, about what was round the corners where I never looked."

Had she been trying to take a look the night they met? Had that been her rather inept attempt to look down one of the

215

dark alleys that led off her well-lit street?

But he didn't ask. If so, it surely hadn't been her first, and she could have told him about her explorations had she wanted.

No matter how close they were, there were areas hard to define, psychic or numinous, too intimate and even more private than the realm of sexuality, into which he could not probe.

Next day Gideon found Pieta dressed and waiting for him to accompany her on a walk in the hospital grounds. Once outside, she suggested that he take her to his room in the clinic.

What on earth was going on? Gideon, though unsure whether it was a gift or a curse, had a facility for finding himself suddenly cut off from a scene in which he was participating. He felt as if struck by a bout of amnesia, unable to connect with the present. Was this what was meant by the rather hackneyed and tiresome expression: 'from the outside looking in?' But he wasn't looking in. 'On the outside looking out?', was more like it. Did schizophrenics experience states such as this? Or certain manic natures?

He took stock of the bedroom as if seeing it for the first time. He might be in a spartan hotel such as he used to stay at in a back street of one of those then mysterious foreign towns, and to which (the amnesia didn't reach that far) he'd taken back Lydia at their first encounter.

What, though, about this young woman taking typed sheets from a briefcase and placing them on her knee? What, above all, was his and her relationship?

The aberration passed, but he had been given a terrifying taste of the ambiguity that underlay even what he cherished as most secure. He was sure he'd been momentarily immersed in the kingdom of darkness, something far more negative and evil than what he'd come to identify with State and Church leaders, institutional liberals and dictators alike.

This might possibly be what Pieta and the friar had to contend with. Was this what she was sometimes up against in her secret life with its afflictions that Kathy called neurotic or

216

imaginary, and what he himself had, at times of uncertainty, supposed were self-induced 'wounds'?

What he showed Pieta was the map of the New Jerusalem that he had brought back from the apartment and a couple of articles he wanted her opinion on.

"But where are the shops?"

She had only looked at the plan for less than a minute and had discovered the omission that, in his poring over it, Gideon had failed to see.

"Perhaps the heavenly architect didn't bother with such practicalities," she added "or else he left it up to us."

Pieta bent over the map, a pencil between her teeth and a frown on her forehead, as if a decision was urgent and a start on the new city was being made in the morning.

His relationship to her was several-sided. He felt tenderness for her at this moment to the point of wanting to draw a finger across her brow, down her cheek to the slight indentation at the corner of her lips, and let it rest there a moment without risking a kind of sacrilege by inserting so much as the tip into her mouth. It was one of dependency too, in that she was the source of clarity in the doubts, dangers and confusions that beset him. But she was also a source of mystification and ambiguity in what she'd let him glimpse of her secret life.

Pieta put aside the plan and looked at Gideon.

"Judith Weissmann died in this clinic."

"Why, did you know her?"

"Only in her last days when I was a patient here for the first time."

At first Gideon didn't want to go into this new surprise she'd sprung on him. He'd enough to unravel already, but then he changed his mind.

"What was wrong with her?"

"She didn't have the will to live."

"I thought she was in an accident."

"Yes. But she was recovering from that. Her husband, Captain Weissmann, used to spend the last nights at her side. It

217

wasn't a private room like this, and I was a couple of beds away. When she wanted to drink, and the night nurse was busy, she'd call me over because I knew my way about and was a mobile case. In the daytime, when her husband who was an army officer couldn't be with her, I sometimes came and sat by her bed."

"She wanted to die?"

"No, she didn't, but she hadn't a strong hold on life. You see, she didn't like it here, she didn't like the job Captain Weissmann had, and, above all, she wanted to return to Israel."

"She had come from there?"

"So it seemed. She told me of the bright hopes they both had for making a life there better than it was almost anywhere else, and certainly better than here. Though at first she was reluctant to speak of her dislike of living in Failland in case she'd hurt me."

"Isn't that something shameful, Pieta, that a foreigner, a Jewess, because her husband gets a job in the army, comes to live in this country known for the Christian commitment of the majority of its people, and is so unhappy that she dies of it!"

# TWENTY SIX

When next Gideon saw the figure pacing the corridor, he approached him with trepidation and asked if he'd care to have a cup of coffee. The man stopped rather jerkily, as if brought up short by seeing at the last moment an obstruction in his path. He raised his ravaged face to Gideon and regarded him.

"Or a glass of wine."

There was a pause which Gideon knew better than to break — or thought he did, believing that a wrong word could scare off the hunted creature — as the other looked over his shoulder back along the passage towards his own room, deciding, it struck Gideon, whether to try to escape by flight or by an assault on his tormentor.

Then, turning his head again, his eyes met Gideon's.

Now, whatever Gideon had found out about himself in latter times — it was nearly all shameful, and he thought he hadn't come to the final dregs — there was one thing that, though not exactly a virtue, he needn't hang his head over. He had learnt that when a situation became sufficiently critical there were almost no principles, which normally he believed in, that he mightn't betray. But he'd also learnt, or perhaps always known, that when it came to the bruised reed (he liked to put these matters to himself in biblical terms) he could never break it. (He'd heard of murderers who went to great pain to free trapped animals or transfer a caterpillar to another leaf before trimming a rose bush).

So when the man, who seemed to be around forty, after looking him in the eye, nodded, Gideon wasn't all that surprised. Indeed, had he not guessed that there was in him a subtle air of being himself one of the last and the least — as he thought of it — that might well be wordlessly communicated to someone in distress, he wouldn't have spoken in the first place.

Gideon stood by the door of his room that he'd left open to usher the other in, but the man held back and Gideon understood that he should lead the way and risk the other following him or returning to pacing the corridor.

Gideon entered the room, crossed it without looking back, and when he was sitting on the bed he saw that the other was inside.

"In case you're wondering who I am, my name is Gideon Spokane."

Wondering, bemused, distressed, the other might be, but Gideon didn't suppose it had much to do with him or his identity. However, his introducing himself might bridge a critical moment and, he felt could do no harm.

"Thank you, Mr. Spokane, for . . . "

The first words the other had uttered trailed off into silence.

"Sit down, if you'd care to."

The man sat down, his long legs curled round each other, a hand resting on the arm of the chair each side of him, ready for instant flight, despite his apparently entangled legs.

" . . . for your hospitality."

He finished what he'd begun to say, which Gideon recognised as being a considerable effort.

There was another silence, this time less fraught, according to Gideon's now finely registering inner scale.

"Those adrift in a lifeboat after a shipwreck aren't in a position to offer each other hospitality."

Gideon saw he had caught the other's attention which was something. However, he made no comment, but took a visiting card from his inside pocket and handed it to Gideon. On it was printed 'Professor M.E. Ellis', followed by the name of a provincial university, but the 'Professor' had been crossed out.

"You gave up your post, Mr. Ellis?"

"You could say I had problems."

A pause. Gideon waited, not wanting to put another question so soon after the first.

"Some had the presence of mind to bring with them extra garments or a loaf of bread."

This belated comment on the earlier lifeboat remark didn't take Gideon by surprise. Indeed his own thoughts tended at times to lag behind in a conversation lingering over the last-but-one remark.

"The lucky ones."

"My classes were poorly attended, sometimes no more than two or three turned up; one morning the lecture room was empty except for the cleaner with whom the last two students had left a message that they wouldn't be attending any more."

"That's something that must haunt many people, and not just lecturers and academics: the fear that nobody is going to turn up for the appointment. Oh, I've been through that in a private capacity, Mr. Ellis. The waiting in vain, that one can't come to terms with and wonders whether one hasn't mistaken the hour or the place, except that in your case the shock came at once with the cleaner's message, and wasn't broken more gently through being grasped gradually. And various reasons for the non-appearance can be reflected on, I don't say, in leisure or relaxation, the situation is too tense for that, but at least with a better chance of finding a tolerable one."

"Oh, in my case the reason was no secret, Mr. Spokane. It was common knowledge. You see, I couldn't get through a lecture without a hitch, that's to say: without breaking off and being unable to finish, and this inability was getting worse."

His visitor was taking a direction which Gideon found it hard to follow, though he knew he mustn't drop too far behind. Best be patient.

"Earlier I'd been able to banish it from the classroom, to bottle it up."

A pause. No, Gideon decided, this wasn't the kind of one in which to risk a word.

"Then it got so that I couldn't hide it from them."

"Your distress?"

"My knowledge, which was hidden from them, of not just the uselessness of what I was teaching them, but the cruel travesty of it."

"What was your subject?"

"Physics, as it happened, but that's irrelevant. They're all a mockery and a delusion."

"Yes, I see."

Gideon didn't mean that he had even been as far along this fatal path, but that Mr. Ellis could go on.

"It overcame me so violently that I couldn't hide it."

Gideon was once more falling behind, but this time not that far that he couldn't follow from a considerable distance. There were the times when he was overcome by a dizzy nausea as he looked down over the solid parapet of daily life, which normally he never did, into nothingness. This happened when he was forced up against the ornamental wall along the edge in places where it was crumbling and the masonry slipping outwards.

This couldn't have happened to him in a lecture room, or when his mind was fully occupied, but say, when watching a particularly misleading TV commercial or glancing through a particularly complacent newspaper editorial.

The spectacle of these people selling their shoddy wares in places where the true gifts were spurned, (did he dare number *Faillandia* among these?) made him aware of how fragile the protective fabric was between himself and the brink of surrender.

Gideon could just about imagine that the people in the streets, intent on their various business and oblivious of the huge farces in which, to Ellis, they were all involved, was a sight he'd fled to pace these drab corridors.

"Did I hear you say you'd prefer coffee to wine?"

Gideon put the question formally, supposing a casual query would hardly penetrate the other's inner darkness.

"Ah, no, I don't think you did. Preferences are luxuries I can't afford. But it's very considerate of you. I'm quite unused to anything like that. Here they wouldn't dream of asking me anything."

"But you're here of your own volition?"

Gideon understood that those in this part of the clinic were voluntary patients.

"Volition?"

Gideon for a moment mistook the repetition of the word for a sign that his visitor was quite unfamiliar with it and was about to substitute 'wish', when he realised he wasn't sure if the other had been a professor of philosophy or physics.

"Under Dr. Roggan you're in good hands," he added, to expunge the perhaps tactless question.

"He tries out drugs on such as me, and some must be partially effective. At first when I came I used to cry out at night, which they called screaming. But now, though I still have the fevers, I sleep the night through."

What about the weeping? Gideon wondered. A nurse had told him that the pillowslip was soaked every morning. Did the sobbing take place in Ellis's sleep? But such probings led nowhere, or to places from which Gideon drew back.

"According to the Gospels account, Jesus Christ, on the night before his cruxifixion, was beset with a similar nausea."

Gideon came out with this remark for his own sake rather than his visitor's. For, as far as he could see, which he admitted might not be far, this was finally the only source of comfort. His temperament didn't allow him to avoid contemplation of the abyss by the common distractions such as sex, money-making, drink, drugs, sport, but at least he could look over the edge in the belief that this other had done so with far greater awareness, and been, as Frère Emanuel had put it, all but overwhelmed by what he had had to contemplate.

Not that Gideon supposed he was never distracted from glimpses of a universal devastation. Kathy was his dove in the cleft of the rock-face that fell away into nothingness.

223

It was easier, as the visitor had no preference, to pour the wine than to make coffee.

"Ah, claret! That reminds me of days gone by."

As if the memory was too painful to let him take his ease over the wine, soon after recalling it, Ellis, with half his glass undrunk, rose and took his leave.

A few minutes after his departure, when Gideon had composed his shocked system into a state in which its nervous reactions could operate, he went to the basement to discuss the layout of the next issue of *Faillandia* with the printer.

When he returned to his room, Paul Weissmann, wearing his Staff Captain's uniform, was awaiting him.

The wine glasses, both now half-full, were on the table and Paul was drinking the claret, which he commented on favourably. Beside the wine bottle was a thick book on whose cover Gideon read: *The Life of Fyodor Dostoyevsky.*

Gideon had been expecting the visit, but certainly not one that had anything to do with literary matters. He'd understood that Paul meant to appraise him of the situation. He'd been cut off from events since coming to the clinic and wasn't sure what Paul, who was cautious on the phone, had meant.

Now it seemed it was the military situation that was critical. Another surprise to Gideon who'd supposed that the fighting, that had never been more than street skirmishing, was over, with the city firmly under the control of the Klotz Provisional Committee.

"Aphrin, yes, but not the whole country. There's an armoured division commanded by a general loyal to the former government advancing on the city."

"To engage in the third battle of Alphraburg?" Gideon suggested, before he had time to consider if the remark was appropriate. He was about to explain it, but Paul interrupted him.

"You've been studying Faillish history."

"With the old gardener here, who goes on tending the grounds, oblivious of any such threat."

"Which he has good reason to be, though I daresay, he doesn't base his tranquillity on reason. General Dorff's lot were mobilised hurriedly as a rather desperate attempt to dislodge Klotz. It might just succeed if the people here open the city gates, as they did in the battle you mention, a manner of speaking, but you know what I mean, Gideon."

"Is there a chance of that?"

"Hardly. I've just had a long talk with Klotz. I found him in bed — you know, his apartment is next to mine — and he's not worried."

"Did he mention a talk he had with me on the phone?"

"No."

"Nor the magazine?"

"No. But he asked me my opinion of you."

"He's one for getting informed opinion."

Gideon didn't ask what Paul had told Klotz, nor did Paul inform him. Instead, he opened the book he had brought at one of the marked pages and read out:

*It was in Florence that he* (Dostoyesvsky, that is) *first thought of a great novel in which he would challenge the progressive movements in Russia and proclaim his faith in the regeneration of his native land . . . through a return to the tenets of Christianity.'*

"Just a minute, Paul. We're on another battleground."

"Yes, the vital one to us and equally bitterly fought over. Listen to this:"

*He wrote to the poet, Maykov, from Dresden in 1880: "What I am writing now is a tendentious thing. I feel like saying everything as passionately as possible." And to his journalist friend, Strakhov: "I am relying a great deal on what I am writing for the* Russian Messenger *now, but from the tendentious rather than the artistic point of view . . . for I am entirely carried away by the things that have accumulated in my heart and mind."'*

"I've been reading some copies of *The Russian Messenger* for those years in the Faillandian Library with the help of one of our Russian interpreters. In some ways it has a remarkable similarity with *Faillandia.*"

"Surely our magazine is not reactionary."

Gideon, though he'd never read anything that had appeared in the Russian monthly apart from Dostoyevsky's novels, had always understood its outlook to have been ultra conservative.

"Depends on the viewpoint. For the old-style Marxists-Leninists it's pure opium. So was Dostoyevsky's vision of an ideal Russia that he expressed in his novel serialised in *The Russian Messenger.*"

"Which, of course, was never realised there or anywhere else."

"Never finally realised, no. But there have been times when it seemed about to be as I was telling you. Substitute the Torah for the New Testament and the state of Israel in the early years after its foundation was very close to Dostoyevsky's Holy Russia."

Gideon pondered this news for a few moments. *The Russian Messenger,* Holy Russia, the State of Israel under Ben Gurion, *Faillandia,* the State of Failland, as its sons who had fought in the two battles of Aphraburg had dreamed of it, and as it could still become.

"And when your hopes came to nothing there, Klotz persuaded you to come and help found the Promised Land here."

"He didn't put it like that. I came here on two years leave from the Israeli army when I was offered a temporary post by Klotz in Military Intelligence. I'd always a deep admiration for Failland and its history, many of us had in Israel at the time. Besides, Judith's brother had this job here and wanted us to come."

"Are you sorry you came?"

"Judith never liked it here, she was homesick and after the accident she might have recovered had she been at home. But there's Sarah to think of; as you know, these things mean a lot to a child. We must have imbued her with our ideas of a haven where all of us, including children and animals, would live in a miraculous harmony. And though it is all in the balance, perhaps, Gideon, she won't be completely let down?"

Strangely and disturbingly, Gideon interpreted what Paul had said as an appeal to him personally.

## TWENTY SEVEN

Gideon was touched and also frightened when he saw that Paul, that independent spirit, was so reliant on him, and through him, on the magazine.

After his talk with Ellis, when he had a glimpse of an area of consciousness from which he was insulated, Gideon was anxious to hear from Paul, who was now the closest to him of all men, not excluding Leo, some of what he had gone through to have come to the point of transferring his trust from Klotz to *Faillandia*.

Without his having to ask more than a simple question about how much time Paul was able to spend with his wife here at the Olive Tree Clinic, Paul himself went into her illness and its consequences in more detail.

"I hadn't realised how much she would miss our flat in Jerusalem with its view towards the Dead Sea and the Jordan Valley, still part, to her, of the Promised Land. Her father had been a friend of Martin Buber, whom, as a young girl, she remembered coming to the house, and she'd been influenced by his teachings based, I think, on Hasidism. She was also a great admirer of Isaac Bashevis Singer, and, I remember how glad I was one day to see a copy of his novel *The Penitent,* that had just come out in translation from Hebrew, in an Aphrin bookshop. It was a small sharp joy, with a bitter side to it, Gideon, to have something special to bring her on my visits.

"Her father, like mine, and many who first emigrated to Israel, had been born in Germany, though her mother came from Russia, and he belonged to the Talmud Jude of whom

228

Isaac Singer wrote that they had never served any king, prince or dictator, but were driven to their death for their personal God."

These figures and their teachings were either new to Gideon or at best no more than names. Was Martin Buber's personal Hebrew God and the Christian God who communed with Frère Emanuel and Pieta, each a different aspect of ultimate reality? And what about his own very private vision of the Silent Defector? Was the model of reality that Ellis had made and that he wept over nightly a less faithful representation? Gideon had no way of answering such questions, and he did not pretend to himself that he had.

"Sustained by your loving care, looked after medically by her brother who was so close to her, and with her favourite book beside her, your wife can't have felt herself forsaken."

'De-orientated', was the word that Gideon recalled hearing Dr. Roggan use about her, which he thought to mean: 'set on a different course.'

"Loving care, yes, Gideon. But if one can't follow that loved one into the place she's been brought, it's hard to communicate. It's like the difference between a visitor trying to get across to a prisoner with a barrier between, and the same two people at home together, hardly having to speak in the quiet evening, their faith in each other undisturbed.

"I don't imagine you've any such problem when you visit Pieta, Gideon. You two seem to understand each other instinctively and wordlessly."

"Not always."

Gideon was thinking of how he had hurried to her with what he'd supposed to be good news.

"It was you she chose to edit the magazine that meant so much to her, although, if you'll forgive me, Gideon, the selection wasn't that obvious to anyone else."

That was just what Gideon had felt himself, but he wasn't going to let his friend get away with his complete agreement.

"The old monk had the same idea."

"I've heard of him, though I don't suppose we shall meet. Did I tell you that one of my most consoling memories is of Judith taking me to see Martin Buber in a Jerusalem suburb?"

'Consoling', Gideon noted the word that Paul had used.

"You see, Paul, it's in the pages of *Faillandia,* or some of them, that we come closest, Pieta and I."

This idea had come to him of late and he was glad to express it.

"I can see that. If Judith were here, how she'd have welcomed it! It might have made all the difference.

"What's going to happen next?" Paul surprisingly asked him.

"You know more about that than I do."

"Militarily speaking, Klotz will consolidate his grip on the whole country, after some resistance here and there, particularly in the central mountains.

"What I meant was: what is happening in the minds of that minority of the citizens who are already, if unconsciously, shaping the next vital year or two in Failland's history? Or to put it plainly, Gideon: How far can *Faillandia* influence them?"

Gideon hesitated. Not, he thought, with the near-fatal hesitation that had been his first reaction to Klotz's question, but because, and again all the indications to the contrary crossed his mind, he wasn't sure of its impact. This, he saw, was evident to Paul who went on: "In the early years of the modern State of Israel there were several periodicals, to one of which Buber contributed, advocating anything from a liberal Zionism, through a prophetic Messiahism, to adherence to the Old Law, none of them with the authority and following of yours."

Of mine? Gideon wondered at the way Paul attributed what he saw as the whole complex, risky, by no means safely established, operation to him.

"Have you any copies of these periodicals? Of the one with Martin Buber's contributions?"

"No, we left them behind, as well as the small library that Judith had collected and that was precious to her, and that had a magazine section with a rare copy of *The Russian Messenger*

230

for May 1871, that had belonged to her great grandmother, and a very tattered copy of *Epoch* of a few years later."

Epoch? Gideon waited, knowing that it wasn't Paul's way to make mysteries or to show off his erudition.

"That Dostoyevsky edited until it was suppressed or went bankrupt, I'm not sure which."

"Should we print something from this Buber of yours, Paul? If he meant so much to Judith."

"That's different. We were conservatives of a different kind, not revolutionary ones, hoping to re-establish our Kingdom of Zion by endless patience, great endurance and the secret promise, which has always been all we had.

"While a minority kept the ancient observances, chanted and prostrated ourselves each day before the 'Wailing Wall' the others were setting up a business community based on a healthy economy."

"We have our promise too."

This was half a boast, although for brief moments Gideon had inklings that a faith in such a promise, signified for the more credulous perhaps by the sprig of Fael, and for others, like Pieta, by a spiritual belief in Failland being destined to become a latter-day ark, persisted in the minds and hearts of a surprising number of people. As was being attested to by the response to the magazine.

"You, Gideon, do you believe in it?"

When he looked into himself for an answer he was conscious of shifting instincts, of an impulse to rely on Pieta and the Friar, in some of the pieces in *Faillandia* from poets and prophets, even in certain passages from the big tome of the Dutch theologian's he'd first seen in the fortress-library, and, in the end, no firm commitment. What he'd never for a moment believed in were the brash promises of an economically flourishing Failland within a community of socially equitable, mutually trusting nations.

Kathy arrived soon after Paul had left and went to the kitchen to bring his evening meal on a tray, an arrangement she

231

had come to with the matron whom she thought was aware of the reasons for Gideon's stay at the clinic, and also of Kathy's own role.

After they had eaten she took off her nurse's uniform and they got into bed, so that there would be time for love-making before they were reminded of the despair of the patient down the corridor.

Tonight, either grief overtook Ellis earlier or their desire was more persistent. Kathy had stretched on the bed, not waiting to take off all her clothes, in an urgently inviting posture and he had entered her without preliminaries, which resulted in a quick, strenuous bout of sex.

They finished undressing, got into bed and were about to enter a more subtly sensual phase of love-making when the low, convulsive, heart-rending sobs started.

"For Christ's sweet sake!"

Gideon substituted the exclamation for an explicit comment on what he was doing to her that he'd been about to murmur into her ear.

He was for the first time in his life confronted with the two extremes of sensation between which most experiences lie. His mind was flooded by signals from his nerves convincing him that what Kathy and he were doing was life's ultimate purpose and fulfilment, while the sounds from the other room suggested that it was the deception of deceptions.

"It's no use," Kathy said.

"It bloody is use, and more than ever," he said.

He wouldn't give in to the chill breath of a doom imagined by neurotics and madmen. He was pulling her, heavy and reluctant-seeming, onto him. But her body of itself took the posture that, given his state of frozen rigidity that was far from tender, buried him deep in her while they were too distracted to quite take it in.

But in no time the old fleshy machine was at work and there was no mistaking how wonderfully effective it was in taking their attention away from everything else. Gideon concluded

232

afterwards that no doubts could enter the mind when even a loveless couple were copulating.

He told her this to comfort her, when later she said she couldn't help feeling guilty at reaching a peak of delight with the sounds of another's distress constantly in her ears. But it only made her feel worse.

"A wonderful little machine that can be wound up or turned on, come what may, and it whirrs away inside you till it explodes, and the orgiastic waves ripple out from the centre to the toes," he added in an equally futile attempt to distract her.

Kathy got up, and dressed, then went off to make a cup of tea, including one for the patient two rooms away which she'd leave beside his bed, and, she told Gideon, find had been drunk when she looked in toward morning.

"Commandant Paulhen drove up to the hotel with a lorry-load of armed toughs this afternoon loooking for you," Kathy said when they were drinking theirs.

"Did he say what for?"

"Oh, a friendly visit. I didn't recognise him in some kind of battle-dress at first."

"Not an emissary from the Colonel?"

"I don't know, but I think not. He seemed to be on his own, with his armed squad, that is."

Gideon had no idea about whom or what she was talking. Then it dawned on him.

"Oh, you mean Frank!"

"I'd a drink with him at the bar; it's better to keep in with someone like that these days. He said to tell you he'd just sailed in with the arms and gave me a number to call if you needed his support, that's how he put it."

Gideon supposed he had bought them with money from his wealthy American woman. Strange what women will do to keep a vigorous sex-mate on hand, which was perhaps understandable in the light of his and Kathy's recent experience.

Even stranger, the risks men take for ideals that cannot profit them personally! On the only occasion Gideon had met

Frank since the finding of the biscuit tin, nothing had been said about it.

Next morning Gideon rang the number Kathy had given him and, instead of hearing some conspiratorial talk about the role he, Frank — alias Commandant Paulhen — was playing in the 'revolution', Gideon was invited to lunch on the yacht.

Taken aback, he didn't at once reply, and Frank went on: "You'll be well looked after, the harbour's under the control of my militia and you'll be fetched and brought back with a bodyguard."

Militia? Surely Frank wasn't claiming to be in charge of the quite numerous but more-or-less unofficial force that the media sometimes referred to by that name, and sometimes as the guerillas?

"Who'll be there?"

"Just ourselves, Boss."

"Ourselves?"

"Lilo, naturally. It's she who's giving the party, and Gerhard, my second-in-command, big, blond, East German Marxist, you know the type. I think her ladyship has her eye on him, but that's neither here nor there. And, oh yes, somebody I think you know, Nolla."

"Not Miss Grimmick?"

"Who else!"

"Where did you pick that one up?"

" 'That one', Boss? Don't you like her? She said she'd started as your receptionist at the *Faillandia* offices. That's where I met her one day I called round and you weren't there. She's on the editorial staff now, isn't she? Oh, perhaps I should't mention that on the phone, I'm not certain whether the magazine is approved of or not at the moment by his Nibs."

Gideon accepted the invitation, largely out of curiosity. It might be instructive to see the report Nolla would no doubt give Paul of the lunch-party, for transmission, if sufficiently interesting, to Klotz. He told Frank, whom he had not yet ventured to call Karel — he'd have had to laugh — to fetch him from the Hotel Aphra.

He decided to tell nobody, except Kathy, about the lunch party. He had other things to discuss with Pieta and as for Paul, let it come as a surprise when he received the report from Nolla.

## TWENTY EIGHT

The car was driven by Frank in what Kathy had described as 'battle dress' but was more like an old Faillandian officer's army uniform with the insignia removed and a black-and-red shield-shaped emblem on the shoulders of the tunic. These, Frank told Gideon, were the old Faelish colours, which as soon as the revolutionary committee was firmly established, would be those of the national flag.

"What revolutionary committee, for heaven's sake?"

Gideon, already half-regretting having accepted the invitation, was impatient at what struck him as boastful posturing. In the rear mirror he saw a car following them that also had a uniformed driver.

"Surely you've heard, Boss, placed as you are at the nerve-centre of events."

"Not a word." (Let Frank do the talking).

"It's no more than a rumour, but I thought you might be able to tell us which of the names mentioned as making up the five members, under chairman Klotz of course, have already been selected."

"Let's hear them."

"The Archbishop of Aphrin heads all the lists, Tolling isn't it? Then there's the ex-prime minister, Nording, and another politician, Lucius Canavan, and, let's see, oh yes, somebody you must know, a writer called Kimm. Something to appeal to everyone, that's how I've heard it described."

At first Gideon was silent from disbelief, then from astonishment, finally from nausea — a faint taste perhaps of what Ellis experienced all the time.

"I don't believe it."

If only two of these people had been selected as even interim administrators in the new regime, it meant Klotz had lost out. Or that he had never had the daring and resolution that Gideon had credited him for and admired.

Even the corrupt old system of 'elected representatives' hadn't come up with a more notable lot of first-class mediocrities.

Gideon had woken up with a shock to a realisation that perhaps he, Pieta, Paul (with his talk about Ben Gurion, Martin Buber, an 'Israel of the spirit') and Leo, had been indulging in a kind of collective egoism in which they thought they could turn history in their direction, whereas neither Klotz nor the former government, for all their self-satisfaction, indulged in such fantasies. He went through the names again to himself, and for each substituted what he thought of as a true promoter of their 'dream' for Failland.

For Archbishop of Aphrin — Frère Emanuel.

For Lucius Canavan — Leo Gadbally.

For ex-Premier Nording — Paul Weissmann.

For Mario Kimm, what about himself?

There he was, wasting time day-dreaming. Going, it might be, to the other extreme, he resolved there and then to ask for an appointment with Klotz and, perhaps accompanied by Paul, to put to him as persuasively as he could, something like the following proposition:

That unless he turned for guidance to the finest spirits available, who were neither power-seekers nor flatterers, he would be one of the undistinguished leaders whose courage had been exhausted by the first daring throw, and had afterwards taken the easy way. Such men crowded the fringes of history, without place or trace at its fiery centre.

Frank drove more slowly along the quay to which several yachts were moored by their sterns. At one of the more luxurious, the car stopped, they got out and crossed a white-railed gangway that rose only gently to the shiny, scrubbed after-deck, where, under an awning, Gideon, his senses now very alert, took in the elegantly-laid table and the middle-aged woman who rose from it to greet them, whose name was Elizabeth Simnel, or Simmel (he didn't quite catch it), and whom Frank told him to call Lilo.

A cabin boy in a white jacket appeared through a door with a tray of bottles, glasses and a silver urn tinkling with ice. The drinks were distributed by Frank in his semi-military attire and it only needed Nolla Grimmick's theatrical stepping over the high lintel onto the deck as if it were a stage in close-fitting jeans and bikini top to transform Gideon into the tiny world of drawingroom or bedroom farce. But when, through the humid autumn heat of the harbour, he caught a scent of leaves burning in suburban gardens, and imagined a whiff from the hospital grounds, he regained his own perspective.

The next arrival was the driver of the car he'd noticed behind them. A blond figure with a bunch of tall, white lilies in his arms, sprang (it seemed to Gideon the *mot juste*) up the gang-way. Kissing her hand, he presented the bouquet to the American woman. He then bowed to Gideon and introduced himself.

*"Kapitaan Gerhard Kellner aus der DDR."*

Gideon wasn't sure what the muscular young man was doing here or where he'd sprung from. It wasn't until the guests had sat down at the table and he was wondering what the bowl placed in front of him contained, that their hostess made a little speech both mystifying and enlightening him.

"For me, dear friends, this lunch is a historic occasion. What a joyful privilege it is to have at this table some of the leading spirits of the great Faillandian intellectual revolution. And that a prominent Marxist-Leninist from Eastern Europe has joined us with so appropriate and touching a gift makes it completely memorable."

Gideon took a quick glance to assure himself that the 'leading spirits' could only be Frank and Nolla, besides himself, the latter whom he had on one side and their hostess on the other. Nolla asked why he hadn't brought Kathy.

"I know she was asked as I sent out the invitations."

Somebody responsible had to be in the office at the top floor of the Hotel Aphra. But having left Klotz in doubt about *Faillandia*'s future, he couldn't tell her this or it would go into the report that he supposed she would make of the lunch party.

To change the subject he asked about her weekend with Kemp.

"He wanted to see how a girl spent every moment of her Saturdays and Sundays, and you wouldn't believe, Gideon, what he paid me."

"Did he get a kick out of it?"

"Oh, yes, though, by our agreement, there was no question of pawing me, just looking on."

"At everything you normally do?"

"That, and a bit more. I had to give him his money's worth."

"Did you get anything out of it besides the money?"

Gideon didn't expect her to tell him she'd learnt where the magazine was being printed, but put the question to see how she'd react. She took it in her stride.

"I learnt as much about old men as he about girls. Oh, I drove the old fool crazy!"

Lilo took advantage of the pause after this remark to ask Gideon whether he didn't agree with what she'd been saying to Gerhard about history repeating itself in very queer ways.

"What I've been reading in your magazine made me very conscious of that."

"Oh, you're thinking of *The Russian Messenger*, Lilo."

"And what Russian messenger are you thinking of?"

"No, of course it wasn't the right-wing Russian periodical you had in mind. You've some influential publications of your own."

He meant in America, but saw at once that this remark was equally inept in the circumstances.

"Have we? No, I didn't mean anything literary. What I'm

interested in is the deeper level of psychic history. I wonder, Gideon, have you been struck by the similarities between the present situation here and some of the chief actors in it, and those in Judea at the time of Christ?"

Christ once again! and this time in a quite new guise.

Better be careful or he'd make another stupid remark. He gave the question his full attention, and couldn't see a connection. But she went on, evidently taken by an idea she had perhaps already made use of at other lunch parties.

"Colonel Klotz is so very like Pilate. He acts in the same shilly-shallying fashion towards your wonderful magazine as Pilate did to Christ, first removing the ban on it, and then suppressing it again."

"He's in awe of it," Frank rather surprised Gideon by remarking.

"Just as Pilate was of the Saviour," Lilo went on "so he wanted to release him instead of the gangster, Barabbas, whose part is being taken by Karel."

"I don't see . . . " Gideon began.

"It was when the Colonel was persuaded that your magazine was a threat to law and order that he banned it and gave Karel's gang, who'd been roaming the streets, raping and looting, his official recognition as militia."

"Lilo, you're exaggerating," the young German told her.

"That was before you joined them, darling."

Gideon glanced into his hostess' pale face under the large straw hat, to see what he could make of it. She had surprised him with this fantasy that, for all its extravagances, she hadn't plucked from the nearest tree, as the saying goes.

Her greenish eyes looked back at him, and if Gideon had put words to what they seemed to signal, they would have gone something like: 'Oh, you didn't suppose I'd any idea of what was going on in this uneasy country of yours. This rich, globe-trotting, foreign divorcée, who stopped over because she had temporarily taken up with one of your barbarous fellow-countrymen, could tell you things that would surprise you even

240

more if she had the opportunity.'

Isn't it I who's fantasising now? Gideon asked himself. But he wasn't completely sure of the answer.

"Have you met Klotz, then?" Gideon asked Frank.

"At your apartment, don't you remember?"

What Gideon had wanted to know was had there really been some arrangement by which Klotz tolerated Frank's armed followers in return for him carrying out certain assignments for him. Why not ask Nolla when he had a chance?

"Then there are the holy women," Lilo went on "I believe a virgin too. As well as a Mary Magdalen."

She was looking again at Gideon. Did she mean Kathy?

"And Paul of Tarsus."

Who could have told her about Paul Weissmann? Who but Nolla. But did the parallel mean she had heard of his having been won over by *Faillandia*?

"But it's the sanctified virgin, who is the inspiration behind your magazine, whom I'd really like to meet. Will you introduce me to her, Gideon?"

He was silent, and Lilo, taking in the expression that must have briefly touched his face, went on quickly:

"Don't take that request to heart, I ask right out for whatever I want at the moment, don't I, Karel, even if it's the moon. But I have an idea that might be possible without embarrassing anybody. What about sailing over to the island of Dominicus, just you and your wife, Gideon, with me, to call on the Prior at the monastery?"

At least she hadn't asked to see Frère Emanuel and probably hadn't heard of him, as nor, Gideon surmised, had Nolla.

"Bearing a gift, of course."

"They don't accept presents."

"Oh, not a personal one, a donation to the priory."

What on earth had she in mind? Something she'd thought up on the spur of the moment, that's how, Gideon thought, her vivid imagination functioned, a jump ahead of the previous fancy, which itself had been improvised.

241

"Lilo possesses a Russian abbot's pectoral cross set with emeralds, said to contain a holy relic."

Frank's announcement seemed to rivet the attention of Gerhard who till then had looked bored. Gideon tried to recall whether such an ornament had been among the treasures presented by Nicholas II to the English King displayed in the showcase at the geological museum, but couldn't. In the discussion that followed between Lilo and the two men, he had an opportunity to ask Nolla if she thought there was really some understanding between Klotz and Frank.

She answered at once, without showing surprise at Gideon supposing she might know.

"Of course not. Karel, or Frank, or whoever he is, is far too much a security risk. He himself doesn't seem to be sure whose side he's on."

"You know him that well?"

"He came to my flat with two of his thugs, pretending he'd been sent to search it by Klotz for contributions to the magazine."

"Did he find any?"

"He didn't even look. What he'd come for was in the hope of getting me to have sex with him."

"Did you?"

"He persuaded me to let him rape me."

"What does that mean, Nolla?"

"That I hinted that if he sent his bodyguard away, I wouldn't put up a violent resistence."

"You don't hold it against him?"

"Can't afford to, Gideon."

Because, through him, she'd got friendly with Lilo, and through Lilo and her parties could hear all sorts of interesting rumours, gossip and speculation, as she had this afternoon?

What a very strange girl, you are, Gideon was going to express this thought to her, but changed his mind. Instead he asked: "I wonder whom Lilo sees as your counterpart in the New Testament."

"Judas, I wouldn't be surprised."

Gideon didn't show any astonishment or ask her why. It was almost as if by now there was an understanding between them. Though why she risked admitting her secret role to him, if that was what she was doing, he had no inkling.

From his place at the table Gideon had a view of the quayside. There were families strolling by, looking at the yachts, though there were not as many as formerly and, indeed, the really big ones were few compared to the number from various countries he recalled long ago when he brought Lydia and Laura to the city for the afternoon.

What struck him in particular was one of the vehicles that had been off the streets for weeks being driven slowly past with its flashing electric advertisements, a harbinger of the fragile stability.

Might not the new 'Committee of Five' have sanctioned a return to mobile commercials as one of their first decrees? But, of course, Gideon was letting apprehension run away with him — this first glimpse of returned normality disturbed him. So that Frank's next remark to the company seemed altogether ironic.

"To think that only twelve months ago, when we were night-watchmen at the Geological Museum in London, Gideon and I used to deplore the mess that this country of ours was in, and discuss for hours what could be done to rally a handful of dissidents. Isn't that right, Boss?"

"The usual exiles' bravado."

Let him, and whoever is interested, take this as they wished. Yet, was he not being negative and ungrateful to harbour this sense of depression? Wasn't it a miracle — a far more considerable, if not so startling a one — than the flight of the fledgling from the friar's hands? Gideon was immediately ashamed of his previous thoughts, and added, before anyone else could make a comment: "A great deal has happened since then to be grateful for."

He turned his attention to the dish that had been placed

before him a minute or two earlier and which he had hardly tasted. And as he did so, as if such a presentiment could not have come to him when his thoughts were concentrated on the subject, he, for no rational reason, foresaw that under Klotz Failland might well return, not to its former state of subjection to international business concerns, a worldly Church and un-distinguished power-hungry politicians, but to domination by some foreign and equally deadly condominium. And their last state would be worse than their first. And, terrifying thought, all that stood between them and this disaster was *Faillandia*!

## TWENTY NINE

When Frank left him back, Gideon asked him in for a drink at the hotel. The first thing he saw was Pieta, about to take a couple up in the lift, wave to him as the doors closed.

Although he'd known she was coming out of hospital, he hadn't expected her back today, still less that she'd be at her job.

Yet there she was at her ordinary work, unnoticed and quite unremarked. He was touched at the glimpse he'd had of her and her quick raising of her hand above the prosperous bulk of the two women who'd stepped into the elevator.

After ordering drinks at the bar, Gideon excused himself and went to meet her as she brought the lift down again. This time she was alone. He stepped into it and Pieta brought it up to an intermediate floor where they could be alone together for at least a few moments.

"Oh, my dove, are you really all right?"

Yes, she was his dove, too, if of a wilder species to the one to which he likened Kathy. One who flew further and returned from far places, as now, shy, and just out of reach.

"Ah, how glad I am, Gideon, to be here in my small, mobile cell again."

"In spite of its being invaded every few minutes?"

Scent from the last two occupants still lingered.

"To have a small task and be a little bit of use, that's all I need. Sometimes I imagine I'm drawing water from a deep well up to a parched place."

"As Rachel was doing for her father's flocks when Jacob

first saw her."

"I never thought of that."

And Gideon knew she hadn't. Unlike him, who imagined himself in various roles, most of them flattering, she never, he believed, in all her meditation, saw herself as anything but one of the last and least outstanding.

"The wounds, are they quite healed?"

She nodded.

He would have liked to know whether they had left any trace in the way of a scar, but he didn't ask.

"Won't you be leaving too, now?"

"The clinic? Yes, I'll check with Paul first, but I think the situation has changed."

Now that meeting her for consultation about the magazine could be held here, and, as he'd heard by ringing the concierge, there had been no attempts to find him at his apartment, Gideon decided to move. It would relieve Kathy of the fulltime jobs, as well as, and this came into it, free him of the presence of Ellis a couple of rooms away or in the corridor. Apart from the first time, Ellis hadn't accepted Gideon's invitations to his room, and the only other slight contact with him was the cup of tea left by his bedside around midnight, which Kathy could get the general night-nurse to continue.

"You and Kathy could stay here for a bit before going home. The place isn't full, so you wouldn't be taking up a room that might be let for forty pounds a night."

"Is that what it costs to stay at the Aphra?"

"Double or single, it's the same. And a single person doesn't get any reduction for the one less breakfast."

"You know all about it, dove."

"I hear it all at work. Some of them talk as if they were alone in the lift."

"As if you were part of the machinery."

"I don't mind being overlooked. Alone with men it can be a nuisance."

"What happens?"

246

"It's mostly talk to start with, with perhaps a tentative touch, and that gives me time to put them off at the next stop."

Should he ask her more? She wasn't Nolla who would have liked to tell him more about what Kemp had wanted and what he'd got for his 'money's worth'.

There was a short pause.

"I'd better get going again," she said.

She didn't press a button, though, and they were looking at each other, with Gideon aware that all hadn't been said. He tried to think what it was that he (she?) hadn't got around to saying to the other. But racking his brain was no good. How much longer could they stand there in silence? Should he have expressed more concern over what she'd just told him? But he didn't think that that was what she had wanted.

He was aware of the stillness in the confined place that wasn't a mutual relaxation.

"Ah, what strength you have, Gideon, without knowing it! That's what I rely on."

What did she mean? Had this been what he'd sensed still had to be said? Surely not. He mustn't ask her or say another word until he could think it over calmly and meditatively.

When he came to himself, the elevator's doors were opening into the foyer. There were three of four people to be taken up, but they couldn't have been waiting or a bell would have rung. How lucky they were not to have been interrupted, Gideon thought. Not that their conversation was that important. Indeed, hadn't it been for that moment of, to him, awkward silence, followed by her words which, however much of a misunderstanding they were on her part, he took as an expression of hope that now he must live up to, he might have supposed they'd wasted the precious minutes.

He told Frank he was sorry for leaving him on his own so long.

"I couldn't have made it quicker myself, and I'm a pretty smart pisser!"

247

What had seemed to him a long talk that had changed direction several times, with pauses betweeen, was to Frank no longer than it took to go to the toilet!

Frank was telling him of arms purchased in East Germany with the help of Gerhard, when Gideon's attention was diverted, not by any occurrence in the vicinity, but by the realisation of why during the last minute or so with Pieta in the elevator he'd had the feeling that there was something that hadn't been said.

He hadn't told her what had been at the back of his mind ever since the drive from the hotel to the harbour: that is the rumoured setting-up of a 'Committee of Five' with the names of the proposed members.

He had been so moved to see her out of hospital and back at her job, an emotion that had persisted during their secluded talk in what she called her mobile cell, that he'd forgotten all about it.

Hadn't the magazine been an excuse for his visits to her in hospital? What if his involvement in *Faillandia* was because it meant an involvement with her? He'd asked himself these questions before, because he believed in an inner clarity of thought and conscience, however much he might go in for prevarication and evasion when outside pressures increased.

"One more glass of the *Aphra Beaune* that my father-in-law brought a few barrels of with him when he came here to lay down in the hotel cellar, and when I've work to do, and I'm sure you have your duties to get back to." (Whatever on earth they are.)

Gideon didn't add the last few words aloud, but wondered to himself what Frank was up to with his followers, with Russian small arms, and this phoney from East Germany, posing as a Marxist. No more, perhaps, than one of the mercenaries, normally at a loose end, who in wartime join whatever outfit promises most risk and prestige, who have a longing, and need, to be sent on dangerous missions, where the usual moral and social restrictions no longer hold, who even revel in close combat and relish the sight and feel of blood. And in between strut around in battle dress and their paratrooper berets with the distinctive badge consisting of notorious initials, calculated to be stared at with awe by the crowd, and in excitement by sensual women — he thought of Nolla among others — while striking a chill into the more humane and faint-hearted citizens.

Gideon himself was half intrigued by this kind of pathology and half-repelled by it.

As soon as he had taken leave of Frank, still walking steadily after all the wine at lunch, and the several glasses afterwards, Gideon crossed the foyer to the lift which he saw from the indicator was at an upper floor. As he was the only one waiting, he hesitated to summon it, not sure how Pieta would look on his reappearance so soon.

It wasn't in Gideon's nature to take her declaration to heart and rely on it, being slow to suppose a woman, any woman, could find in him the qualities that most appealed to her. This, as he reviewed his past, was perhaps what had so often prevented warm and promising friendships with women becoming what he thought of as 'relationships'. He'd hung back when he might have carried the day, or the night.

It had happened that first evening with Kathy, in spite of her consenting to his taking her to his flat, and perhaps even Lydia, had he not so readily seemed to concur in her cold and 'out-of-reach' moods, would have welcomed an expressive lover. This last surmise, though, he was inclined to reject. Had she not, if only once or twice over the years, told him that there was something about the sexual act that disgusted her.

Finally Gideon pressed the 'down button' and watched, quite apprehensively, the floor numbers light in succession.

He heard the lift descend from above and then looked away at the moment it stopped and the doors began to open. He glanced back when he had rallied his failing nerves and on Pieta's brow was neither the frown he'd feared, nor surprise in her eyes, nor irritation in the line of her lips.

"Come."

He entered the lift and she took it up a couple of floors before either spoke. Then Gideon, with his tendency not to leave well alone, asked: "Am I not a nuisance?"

"I was expecting you. Each time the lift was summoned down I thought: It's Gideon. But it wasn't. Everybody else, people having eaten and drunk themselves silly going up to their rooms to lie down till dinner."

Now that he was with her, had indeed hurried to her with the intention of telling her what he'd heard about the Committee of Five, he saw that that was of no importance. Nor had she been expecting him to bring her any reports from outside, but simply, he realised, so that they could be alone together for a few minutes as they hadn't been since before she'd gone to hospital. But if it wasn't news of these outside events that they wanted to hear of each other, then what did they want, he asked himself. It was something that he could only approach circumspectly and see how she reacted as he went along.

"Did Kathy tell you how many hotel guests asked where 'the little lift-girl' was when you were away?"

"Yes."

"You have this mysterious fascination such as is attributed to the figure whose sex is indeterminate in the Song of Songs: 'Draw me, we will run after the odour of thy ointments.' "

"I surprise them by being polite and saying: 'Good morning' and 'goodnight', and the *Song of Solomon* doesn't come into it except in your fantasy."

He tried again.

"Do you remember the tree outside the window of your ward?"

"I only noticed it the last couple of days when I was out of bed, and all the birds. What about it"

"According to another of my fantasies, when Frère Emanuel released your fledgling from the open window, after perching a few moments on one of the plain branches above the avenue, it took flight in what, after studying a map of the city, I saw was the direction of the Olive Tree Hospital."

A bell buzzed and a light went on in the panel. Gideon thought of asking her to let him out at the floor at which the lift was stopped and to pick him up again after she'd finished transporting those waiting below, but then supposed that this time he'd taken things far enough.

Instead, he had her take him to the top floor before descending. And there in the small room where much of the editorial work of the magazine was carried on, he found Kathy busy typing.

To her he could talk of the lunch party and evoke an interesting response, in particular in regard to Nolla's weekend with Kemp, something that would surely have bewildered her sister.

Kemp, it turned out, had given his version, a rather different one, to her father, and this she related.

What pure gossip they were indulging in, he reflected, a shared curiosity about the private lives of others that brought them together in an added intimacy.

Kemp had told Leo — they were old and trusted friends — that his only reason for wanting to spend the weekend with the girl was to be allowed to sleep at night with his head in the hollow between her shoulder and upper arm, after swallowing the sedative tablets that he had to take against insomnia.

"But when the old man woke in the night, he was alone in the bed and haunted by the thought of death, a fear that always overcame him just before dawn when the drug wore off, which was why he longed for a companion at that dreaded hour.

"He waited, thinking Nolla had only slipped to the toilet and that in a minute he'd feel again a comforting pillow of bodily life under his head that was heavy with the darkest of thoughts."

Kathy paused, to tease Gideon.

"So what happened?"

"He heard voices from the other room where she was entertaining a boyfriend."

"The sly bitch!"

251

Kathy laughed and he joined her, recognising how comic his spur-of-the-moment indignation must have struck her. After all, this was only one side of the piece of gossip, and quite different from Nolla's account.

Kathy asked whether he couldn't move out of the clinic to the hotel, if it still wasn't safe at home. She had discussed it with Pieta too, and there were rooms empty at the moment.

"Oh yes, as soon as possible."

The return from the hotel where was all manner of living going on, in the foyer, the bar, the restaurant, even the lift, not to mention the bedrooms, to his room in the clinic off the corridor that led to where Ellis lay sobbing, beyond which he'd never ventured, was like descending to the nether regions from the world above.

"When I get back this evening I'll speak to Dr. Roggan, thank him for his kindness, and say I'll be leaving tomorrow morning."

It required considerable resolution to contemplate a return there, but he was helped by the thought of all those whose habitations were similar places, asylums, hostels for the incurable, refugee camps, prisons and, perhaps even more commonly, squalid dwellings in grey, grassless, treeless, permanent-disaster areas, where no amount of determination, no patient striving, no goodwill or readiness to accept, could ever create a small private haven or the most primitive home.

A brief, imaginary glimpse of such habitations of hopelessness sufficed to shame Gideon at his weakness in face of one more night at the clinic.

"But you're not planning to return there alone?"

He'd supposed that Kathy would remain at the hotel, sharing their old room with Pieta.

He had listened· in the course of the long day to so many points of view, heard such stories, rumours, gossip and, from Pieta, had heard the expression of such an astonishing faith in him, that by now he was disorientated, conscious of doubt and isolation.

"Would you really come too?"

She laughed: "You sound as if I was accompanying you to the scaffold."

This lightly-meant remark of hers was what came back to Gideon when, shortly after they had returned to the clinic, there was a knock on the door of his room and Dr. Roggan entered.

In his extreme nervous state, Gideon waited in apprehension, and it was Kathy who asked the doctor to sit down, which he did on the side of the bed. He took an envelope from the pocket of the white coat he was wearing and leant it against the vase of autumn flowers that Kathy, on her first night shift, had arranged on the bedside table.

From where he stood Gideon could read his own name on the envelope: Another message, on top of all the other communications of the day.

He made no move to pick up the letter, unable to put aside Kathy's references to a scaffold in connection with their return here. It was Kathy, who had never met the doctor, who was left to ask him if he would like her to fetch them a pot of tea.

The doctor evidently agreed, though Gideon, trying to see through the envelope, or at least intent on guessing the signature, hadn't noticed a sign from him, before she left the room.

"Professor Ellis left this for you."

The doctor indicated the letter.

"He has been discharged?"

In the brief silence following his question, Gideon realised its stupidity.

"He killed himself this morning with the drugs which he'd been secretly hoarding."

Another pause. Then, hardly conscious of what he did — because a few minutes later on Kathy's return he was surprised that it had disappeared from the table which she was clearing for the tea things — he took the letter and placed it in his inside breast pocket.

A place of execution, if a self-imposed one, after all.

"What time did it happen?"

On the one day that he had been away! While he was at lunch on the yacht, or earlier? Had Ellis knocked at his door and got no answer?

"The nurse found him on his bed when she looked in around eleven, not having seen him as usual in the corridor."

"What a disaster!"

For Gideon that is what it was, and he thought Pieta would see it so too.

"Hardly that, Mr. Spokane, so much as another realisation of my failure. Each time I lose one of my patients my ignorance is borne in to me with increased force."

Ignorance of what? But Gideon didn't ask, instead he took and held Kathy's hand.

# THIRTY

Gideon read the letter that Ellis had written to him after Dr. Roggan had left. There were parts of it he couldn't follow because they were in the language of advanced physics, others because, he supposed, they were in a language which, though using common enough expressions, he had never had to learn.

Up to a point he could follow what Ellis called the glimpse of reality he had been given. This had been 'revealed' to him, as he put it, in terms used in his own particular subject, the study of sub-atomic particles.

*'Concepts of good and evil do not reflect anything in the cosmic order. This order has no purpose. "Purpose" is one of the words unknown in the small corner of universal reality that we are able to probe. The ordering spirit, though that term too is misleading, shows every manifestation of basic evil, to use another word with a purely localised meaning.'*

Then came a passage about the quantum, the energy and the behaviour-structure of photons, protons, neutrons and of what Gideon believed to be basic units of matter. Without knowledge of the terminology, he could do no more than recognise that the initial theme was being proposed in these terms.

*'Art, religion, philosophy and science itself, are merely ways of what has been known since Copernicus as 'Saving the Appearance', that is to say: creating a model, not of reality, but of something sufficiently human to live with.'*

Towards the end, Ellis addressed Gideon by name, as at the start, to tell him that he thought that Gideon too had at least *'an inkling of the truth, though in your case you have the stoicism and the personal responsibility that I lacked.'*

*'The myths that you have had the courage to live by, great literature and the Gospels, based as they are on the concept of a struggle between good and evil, which we like to see as the battleground of the human spirit, have no doubt often failed you. There must have been times, as you hinted, when "the Appearance" wasn't saved for you either. "The triumph of evil"; what a comfort that would be if it accorded with the facts. But it doesn't because there is no moral clash in the real Cosmos, only that of forces imperceptible to man.'*

What about Ivan Karamazov's little sticky leaves? Are they not there for us to see and touch each spring, Gideon reflected, without trying to examine the logic of this thought as an objection to 'the letter'.

But he was already reading the passage in which Ellis seemed to be summing up what had gone before and directing the whole to an inevitable conclusion.

As Gideon understood this extended conclusion, there was first a rejection of man-made models of reality, including those which used theories of space and time. These were 'information-gathering devices of the human nervous system.'

*'Space and time are figments necessary for man to imagine he has a foothold "out there", but he has none. Not only are good and evil an attempt to gain some shelter and comfort, but logic and reason are extinguished in that darkness. There is neither a "yes" nor a "no" to our importunate question, not even a "maybe".*

*Perhaps at the very most there is in the ordering of the Cosmos a reflection of our sense of beauty and simplicity. All is one. Our minds can only deal with distinct entities, not with complete unity. We propound matter and energy which, in so far as our model corresponds to reality, are not separate entities but lie along a continuum.'*

Which seemed to bring Ellis to his intolerable conclusion:

*'At certain spacial interstices, which we call stars, there*

*takes place thermo-dynamic explosions which create new universes and new waves of energy destructive, over and over again, of our cherished beliefs in signs of tenderness, divine or natural, including "The Little Sticky Leaves" you once mentioned in our conversation.'*

"What does he say?" Kathy asked. She had waited patiently while he had been reading.

"I'm not sure. I'll have to think about it, perhaps even then I won't really know."

"Come to bed."

She was already there and, he thought, had probably dozed off once or twice.

Ah, how weary he was! Not just of the day that had gone, but of the prospect of the coming one, a herald of which was the bluish-grey tinge caught between the almost bare branches of the trees in the hospital grounds.

Next morning, however, back at the hotel with a room of their own for the moment, Gideon had regained much of the one thing he had in abundance: a zest for living.

He showed the letter first to Kathy who commented that: "As far as I can make out, poor Ellis was haunted by an idea that everything was about to be destroyed by an atomic war."

When, later, Pieta read it, she said nothing, until Gideon asked her.

"The temptation had become too strong."

"What temptation?"

"Oh, the oldest, most disastrous one: to despair."

Oldest! What about disobedience and the Adam and Eve story, or come to that, pride and Lucifer? But her theological theories and other pecularities, he had to respect as an integral part of her.

"I'll ask Frère Emanuel."

"About what?"

"If there is not a kind of retraction at the very last of what went on before. I think he knew, if only at the last moment, that your little uncurling leaves are out of reach of the cosmic

257

explosions."

That lunchtime Leo, with the two girls and Gideon, dined together in the corner of the restaurant reserved for the management. Gideon kept thinking he was taking part in a quiet celebration, both of Pieta's recovery and of his and Kathy's return. And each time he dismissed the feeling of this being out-of-place on the day after Ellis's suicide. But on the third or fourth creeping back of his secretly festive mood, he wondered whether the emotion of shock and compassion (he hadn't known Ellis well enough to feel a great loss) were not sufficiently close to the surprise and gratitude that 'all is well, in spite of all' to turn the little meal to be both a memorial one and a thanksgiving.

Ellis, of whom Leo had never heard, was not mentioned. Nor was *Faillandia*. What was mentioned were the various versions of what happened during the weekend that Kemp spent with Nolla.

Leo, who had only heard Kemp's own account, asked: "Who do you think the boyfriend was that Leonard heard talking to Nolla in the middle of the night?"

Pieta, who hadn't heard any of the versions, shook her head, not so much as if she couldn't guess, and was impatiently awaiting the revelation, as to indicate her indifference. Despite which, or, as Gideon thought, more likely in order to tease her, her father announced: "No other than our brave Colonel!"

"Klotz!" Gideon exclaimed, unnecessarily.

"I don't believe it," was Kathy's response.

As for Pieta, she appeared to be thinking of something else, though as it turned out, from her next remark, not all that unconnected.

"Marriages like the Kemps are doomed from the start."

"What makes you say that, you weren't there at the start?" Leo asked her.

"One doesn't have to be everywhere to get an inkling."

"Come on, then, and let's hear what our little high priestess would have prophesied had she been at the wedding ceremony."

258

"You can laugh, Daddy, and it may seem funny that some-one like me thinks she knows things about what goes on between men and women that all of you are too close to to have any clear view of."

Gideon felt like clapping but waited in suspense as if much depended on what was coming.

"I'd have thought your little sister has an inkling or two," Leo said.

"I'm not talking about love or sex, which may be the corner-stones of marriage, but about what's in between."

"Come on, then, let's hear about that."

If only, Gideon thought, her father's semi-mocking tone didn't deter her.

"It's the nervous system. We live on our nerves more than people realise, or want to, perhaps. For any sort of close relationship, but for marriage especially, the nerves of two people must respond. In the relationship of a man and woman that's what makes the harmony of their days and nights."

God be praised, she's hit on something there! Gideon was recalling his own nervous dependence on Kathy, his fits of shivering when he needed her so badly.

"Nights too?" This was Kathy putting in a word.

The sisters smiled at each other.

"Tell us about the nights," Leo suggested, though Gideon wasn't sure to which girl. It was Kathy who went on.

"You're quite right about all the small irritations of daily living which I'm sure often end in complete incompatibility, but the nights are for obliterating them."

"Maybe, for the lucky ones and in the early days. But it can come to a conflict between dislike of each other and sexual desire."

How did Pieta know all this, which Gideon himself hadn't been all that aware of?

"It's the dislike that usually gets the upper hand," she went on. "But the desire doesn't just disappear, even if, in old age, it retreats into the mind. Some men at least are still obsessed with what seems the mystery of women and want to probe it even without sleeping with them in the technical sense. Mr. Kemp *did* sleep with Nolla in the ordinary sense and, who knows, perhaps got more out of it than he did with Mrs. Kemp."

"A marriage of true minds," Leo quoted Shakespeare, rather sententiously and inappropriately, which made Gideon put in a remark to get Pieta back where she had been.

"That was wonderfully clarifying, Pieta! You might have been analysing my own first marriage."

"Did you know, Gideon, that shortly before her death your first wife spent some time in the Olive Tree Hospital?"

"I wasn't here."

He'd been in London with Kathy when he'd heard from Laura that Lydia had gone to hospital, and hadn't returned to Failland to visit her.

Not that at the moment these old griefs and guilts had a hold on him. Pieta's surprising comments had gone to his head — or nervous system? — and, yes, he was actually shivering, however slightly. He even had to refrain from lifting his glass in case he gave himself away, if not to Leo, to the sisters. His attention was withdrawn from the conversation and focussed on Kathy. With a great effort he brought himself back to what Pieta had just told him.

"How do you know?"

"The matron mentioned it one day when Kathy visited me and I introduced her. She asked if she was related to a Mrs. Spokane who'd been in one of her wards not so long ago."

Lydia could still haunt him making herself present unexpectedly. Now he recalled the dream he had had the previous night. He was staying at the Hotel Aphra, but it seemed to be contained in a larger building so that the rooms and corridors opened into unfamiliar ones. At the reception desk he met her booking in or out, he didn't dare ask which.

"Lydia!"

He was astonished and excited, as if somebody he'd waited for and given up hope of meeting, had turned up at the last minute.

"Hello, darling!"

She didn't seem surprised at all.

"Let's go to your room."

Did she have one, or had she just given it up? Or, perhaps, more importantly, would she pretend to have given it up? Or, having given it up, would she go back to the desk and ask for the key, saying she had forgotten something?

However it came about, they were in somebody's room. Should he make a move? 'A move'? What a way to put it! he reflected. She seemed to expect it, which, come to think of it, was most unlike her.

It was like long, long ago, only better. They were close as, in fact, they'd never, or seldom, been.

She was saying something about a ticket she'd purchased and asking whether she should get another.

It didn't cross his mind to enquire where she was going. Other things seemed more urgent. For one, it worried him that she was not wearing a wedding ring.

Without Gideon knowing how it came about, the mood altered, and they began to have the old suspicions of each other, He saw her expression change from one of warmth, even, he'd imagined, of invitation, to the half-contemptuous look he thought he remembered. (Wasn't he making the past worse than it had really been? He was too downcast and confused to be sure).

He framed sentences with the deliberate intention of hurting her and uttered them. He knew she was trying to do the same, but she hadn't his command of words, of instinctively finding the ones that would re-open old wounds, or inflict new ones. He knew that if Lydia were to get up and leave the room, that would be the end. They would have parted forever.

And so she might at any moment, unless he humbled himself and without exactly asking her forgiveness, reach out and take

261

her hand. How cold it was! Had he already taken it? — say a tender word, and then — the hardest of all, but also the most sublime — convince her that what he'd been saying had come from his own sense of being bereft, of misery, and that he wished, above all else in the world, to revive and sustain their marriage at the deepest level.

Her eyes shone, and they kissed. Gideon was afraid that she'd return to the subject of the ticket. How could he accompany her, or she him? But she said no more of it, as if she too knew the limitations of the situation in which they now met.

Gideon had woken beside Kathy with a lightness of heart he hadn't known, and therefore not missed, for a long time.

## THIRTY ONE

At last they escaped from the hotel dining room. Because of what seemed to him the long delay after the first pang of desire — which Kathy later confessed had excited her too — before they were alone together, Gideon thought he'd never wanted her so much.

Kathy went about it simply and sensibly, drawing the curtains as soon as they were up in their room, while he locked the door. Then she waited until he was back from the bathroom before, standing at the window in the half-light of the afternoon, she undid her blouse.

He knew that she liked him watching her undress, partly because it both increased her own sense of shock and plunged him into deeper degrees of desire at each unveiling.

It was a reminder of the sensual ceremonial at which Pieta had attended after their wedding and which he, and, he thought, she had just been reminded of. When she bared her breasts, she seemed to wait a moment to see if he could resist the magnetic attraction of these orbs in order to go on watching her. Indeed, he took it as a kind of game between them, her lingering over disrobing to make it the harder for him to see it out without interrupting.

"Don't you think I'm distraught enough as it is?"

"Whatever you are, it's all right with me."

Lydia had told him, probably in a moment of irritation, that he was debauched.

When Kathy was fully naked she announced: "There! we're all set."

263

It was an expression he commonly associated with her having got herself ready to go out with him, or having buckled her car seat-belt, so that, in the present context it was the more provocative.

At that moment the bedside telephone rang, startling them both in their faraway pleasure-garden of sensual delights. Looking back later, Gideon thought he recalled that, along with the slight shock, he had felt a dread out of proportion to any of the likely reasons for the unwelcome interruption.

Perhaps this was a transference by him of the shadow of later events onto the moment of their heralding, but what made him believe in his presentiment was that he hadn't hesitated in taking up the receiver, as though he knew there was no escape, in spite of Kathy's natural exclamation: "Don't answer."

Paul Weissmann was downstairs and wanted to see him urgently. Gideon, who was still dressed, went to where Kathy was standing by the curtained window. She had covered her breasts, as if, he thought, instinctively feeling the sudden fear that had pressed on his heart, extinguishing in a moment the excitement there.

He didn't kiss her mouth. 'That will have to wait', the thought came to him rather ridiculously. He put his cheek to hers.

"Will you be gone long?"

"We're seeing Klotz."

She didn't ask: 'What about?'

That, he knew, wasn't her way, but neither was the long look she gave him.

"We'll go home when I get back."

Why, when they'd decided to stay at the hotel? Because they'd be out of harm's way there now was how he put it to himself.

Paul, in uniform, was in the foyer. He hadn't sat down. Gideon took him to the bar, not because he wanted a drink, but because it was the best place to talk in private. He showed Gideon an evening paper with the headlines: 'Biscuit-tin Horror'.

264

Skimming the columns very quickly, as he'd learnt to do, he read that biscuit-tins had exploded in several official buildings in various parts of the city, causing a number of deaths and, as yet, an unknown amount of damage. A couple of the innocent-looking containers, one in the General Post Office and one at the control tower of the airport, that had not exploded, were being defused and examined. They had both appeared to be unopened tins of a well-known foreign brand of confectionery, whose presence, at least in most of the places where they'd been left, would not have caused any immediate suspicion.

Gideon folded the sheet and laid it on the bar counter with the headlines underneath.

"Is that how you heard of it?"

"No. Klotz rang me, and I picked up the paper on the way here."

The thought came to Gideon that Klotz wanted to see him because of the suspect biscuit-tin placed at the door of his apartment which he might think must have a connection with these. But Klotz hadn't telephoned Paul primarily about the bomb explosions which he'd only mentioned after telling him he had had an urgent request from the British Ambassador for an interview.

His involvement with *Faillandia* had brought Gideon to the fringe of the world of political power. Because of it he'd met people he would never have otherwise, Klotz himself, above all, as well as Lucius Canavan, the Archbishop of Aphrin and, of course, Paul himself. But these, the latter in a very special sense, were his 'own lot', fellow countrymen, and he had never considered these contacts as anything out of the way.

The British Ambassador was another matter. Gideon was not sure what he represented, but it was something quite beyond the fantasies in which he sometimes saw himself as, perhaps, mediator in a strife-torn Failland.

"What can he want? What have the explosions to do with him?"

265

"Oh, it's not that."

No, nothing was what Gideon supposed. He waited: "There had been a call to a foreign power from members of the former Government to intervene here."

"To the U.K.?"

"Oh, no, of course not. To one of the super-powers."

No, Gideon wasn't going to ask which. He wasn't going to ask any further questions, or put forward, even to himself, any more suppositions. Possibly Paul hadn't himself been told what country it was that had been invited in, if it had been a request for military help, and not just, as on second thoughts he thought more likely, political or diplomatic pressure.

"What does Klotz want with me?"

That, finally, was what really concerned Gideon.

"He wants you to be there with Cusack."

Gideon's first impulse was to refuse. Not only did the prospect of meeting Klotz again after what had happened appal him, and he didn't think the British, or any other Ambassador, had anything of benefit to offer him, Pieta or the magazine. Perhaps he would be asked about the big jewel haul at the Geographical Museum. This supposition didn't lessen his reluctance.

"He's been an admirer of *Faillandia* since the first number, and no doubt the Colonel thinks of you as an asset in an interview that he doesn't seem to relish."

Bewilderment and relief.

"Is that all it is?"

"All? Isn't that enough for you?"

By now they were in Paul's car and driving. Not to either airforce headquarters or the old Government building, in both of which Klotz had offices, but to the big block where both Paul and Klotz had their apartments.

But even of this Gideon couldn't be sure, because there were diversions at several junctions with military manning the barriers.

"There were rumours that the tins contained nuclear

material."

Rumours? Gideon said nothing. He hadn't seen any actual damage. Could so small a nuclear bomb be constructed?

"Sarah asked to be remembered to you."

Who on earth was that? In the midst of mysteries, threats and a national crisis, here was Paul introducing somebody else to add to the confusion.

"That was thoughtful, especially at such a moment."

"Oh, I don't worry her with these matters, and she doesn't see the papers."

Ah, Gideon felt guilty at not at once recalling the little girl who had welcomed him with such grace at his first visit to Paul's dwelling. The other time he'd called, she hadn't been there.

"You made a good impression on her, which seldom happens."

Yes, it had been mutual, even if Gideon had hardly given her a thought since.

"What a blessing she must be to you."

Gideon meant, but didn't add: 'In your loneliness.'

Paul struck him as lonely, as having few friends, indeed, no friend at all apart from himself. He had too many reserves, by which Gideon meant areas of interest in which he wouldn't have trusted anyone, like his Zionism, if that's what it was, his intelligence work, his abiding preoccupation with memories of his dead wife.

What had Gideon in the way of friends apart from Paul? Leo, yes. Frank, not really. But he had not one but two great blessings. He pulled himself out of these idle reflections, surprised at how he could drift into them while driving through a city in the grip of invasion fever — was it? — to a meeting with a dictator and the representative of a foreign power.

Gideon knew the answer: love, friendship, the blessings bestowed by women, or young children, by memories that survived death, these all concerned him more than any public event whatever.

267

"Tell me, Paul, as simply as you can, what's happening?"

"A variation on Hitler's trick of instigating violence in a neighbouring state as an excuse to invade and annex it. In this case, it's the old gang causing well-planned internal incidents and then inviting a foreign regime that shares their principles of government to restore order, and in doing so to put them back where they were."

When they arrived at 'the Cedars' — Gideon noticed some of these trees along the drive and began to enumerate to himself the buildings in Aphrin named after trees, including the hospital, but quickly desisted — Paul led the way down the wide, bare corridor past his own front-door.

Gideon had managed to gain a precarious and calm inner state of mind, and therefore didn't allow himself to speculate on the coming meeting. Though his state of mind was not all that orientated towards public affairs because of the memory of his thrill at Kathy undressing by the window, and the even more exciting thought of Kathy's enjoyment of it.

Just before pressing the bell, Paul said to him: "Don't let Klotz down by letting the Ambassador know that the two last numbers of *Faillandia* were clandestine.

"All right."

But it was far from all right. Gideon still not being at all clear on why he was being brought along.

Having resolved not to be distracted by whatever minor shocks were in store — such as being searched — before reaching Klotz's office, he took in as little as possible of the exchange between Paul and the commissionaire who opened the door to them.

He followed Paul, who himself was following the broad back and thick neck above a stiff tunic collar across a large room — in Paul's similarly designed apartment, the living room — and through a door that Gideon didn't remember in the latter.

Instead of the breathing space of an ante-room that he'd been expecting, there in a smaller one than they'd just traversed sat the Dictator, as Gideon now thought of him, behind a desk. Nolla Grimmick was at a table in a corner, somewhat reassuringly, but Gideon felt he was grasping at straws.

His bearing, Gideon reassured himself, as he went through the handshaking and greeting, was natural, and didn't betray his extreme shifts of mood which left him disgusted with himself.

"You know my secretary: Nolla Grimmick."

He was actually thinking of denying it but pulled himself together in time. He quickly made his distracted thoughts focus on an easy affirmative and an affable, with a touch of reserve, greeting to the girl.

When they were seated, Klotz looked first at Paul and then at Gideon, reminding the latter of how a conductor regards his orchestra before the first beat of his baton.

"I shall ask in the British Ambassador in a moment, but first here is a short resumé of the situation. The ex-chairman of the National Assembly, Nording, and the ex-deputy leader of the parliamentary opposition, Lucius Canavan — both acquaintances of yours, I think — with a couple of minor fry, have sent a Memorandum on what they call the unconstitutional and undemocratic seizure of power by disloyal elements of the Failland armed forces under my command, to the Government of the United Kingdom."

In the pause that followed Gideon noticed that the curtains were drawn across the long window and recalled the steel shutters attached to the windows in Paul's living room, and also — with a painful wrench of his attention — the other curtained window in their room at the hotel.

"The British Ambassador" Klotz went on, after seemingly waiting to let what he'd said sink in, "informed me of what these traitors are planning a couple of days ago. At the same time, he assured me that his Government had no intention of agreeing to a request to intervene and that he personally had given the foreign minister an account of the situation here, which, and I believe him, he'd put in a favourable light.

"He told them of your magazine, Sir, which he greatly

enjoys reading for its liberal views and how large its sales are since I lifted the ban imposed by the Nording Government."

What did the 'Sir' denote in this context? Not, Gideon thought the irony that he'd detected in its use on their first meeting. There might even be a hint of respect now discernible. And, indeed, why not? Hadn't *Faillandia* come to Klotz's rescue, or at least helped him out of a nasty situation? But hadn't there been something more than respect? A faint but, to Gideon, unmistakable, hint of entreaty. As in the 'Sirs' lavishly bestowed on prospective benefactors by those — in old-fashioned scenes — seeking favours? Hadn't Klotz slipped it in to let Gideon know that he was begging him for his (Klotz's) sake but also for the sake of their country, not to contradict the fiction (the despicable lies, as in another mood Gideon might have thought) when the subject came up with the Ambassador.

"I'm really glad, Colonel, that our little magazine has helped give an enlightened image of Failland to the British Government. Incidentally, we have a number of subscribers in London."

"It's also on sale in Tel-Aviv," Paul announced, putting in a word for the first time: "presumably because the quite extraordinary commentaries on the Old Testament, the Psalms in particular, appeal to the more traditional Israelis."

"And fanatics everywhere."

This remark from Klotz cast a slight chill on the talk. Gideon understood it as an expression of irritation when it came to the foreign readership of the magazine. In England, well and good: it helped matters at the moment. But when it came to Tel-Aviv and God knew where else, it made a more drastic imposition of the ban — such as Klotz had decided on before this new crisis occurred — more difficult.

The Colonel had meanwhile told Nolla to usher in the Ambassador. As she passed Gideon she glanced at him from what he thought of as 'under her lashes', a phrase he had read many times and dismissed as romantic fiction.

He took it as a suggestion that because she had a close professional relationship to the other two men in the room, and to one of them an intimate one — though, even if true, she couldn't know that he knew of it — that didn't mean he need feel out of it.

This Gideon didn't take as anything more than a further indication that the girl liked to be 'where the action was' (these clichés were coming back to him thick and fast!) and of course she knew he wouldn't be here at this crucial meeting if he wasn't somebody of importance in the present situation, in spite of what she must consider his air of incompetence.

The Ambassador preceded Nolla into the room, wearing what Gideon guessed was a morning suit, though he didn't recall having come nearer to one than through the glass window of a man's outfitter.

As for his air, Gideon couldn't categorise it so easily: It contained gravity and what might be poise, though not suavity to any marked degree.

After he and the Dictator (Gideon was now dramatising the scene for his own satisfaction) had shaken hands, Klotz introduced him to 'His Excellency, Alexander Cusack O.B.E.' adding the initials of the order in what seemed to Gideon an excess of formality, and possibily not even required by protocol.

Klotz referred to Paul as his aide-de-camp, and a former citizen of Israel, which latter piece of information, as with the O.B.E., Gideon thought might well have been omitted, unless that is that the Ambassador was himself a Jew, which neither his name nor appearance suggested.

In Gideon's case it was 'Editor of *Faillandia*', nice and simple, and, evidently a more impressive designation than that applied to Paul, because the Ambassador expressed what seemed more than a polite interest in the fact — even allowing for what Gideon took to be the niceties of diplomatic usage.

He was now congratulating him, and Nolla appeared to be taking shorthand notes, on the panel of contributors who, "at least in those fields in which I and my friends are competent to

271

judge, have a deep knowledge of their subject."

"And what's more, Mr. Spokane, are original thinkers."

So far, so good, reflected Gideon, if a little diffuse. But what came next both surprised him and raised his spirits.

"You achieve a political and social equilibrium rare in such a progressive publication, if I may so so."

"Thank you, Your Excellency."

Would 'Sir' have been sufficient? Well, no matter, Gideon was waiting to hear more, and for Klotz to hear more, and for Nolla not to miss recording a word.

"For instance, last week you balanced extracts from Dostoyevsky's anti-revolutionary novel, *The Devils*, with a radical essay called 'Beyond Marxism'. "

Gideon glanced at Klotz, who, according to Paul, after seeing this very number, had instructed him to discover the whereabouts of the underground press and have the ban, already in operation, immediately enforced by seizing it, as well as any copies of the issue he could lay his hands on.

The Colonel was looking down, appearing strangely tranquil, almost contemplative, reminding Gideon of a photograph of Stalin, though the actual features had little in common, except for the moustaches that, unlike Hitler's, covered their mouths. He raised his eyes, meeting Gideon's as if he sensed his regard. They were dark, and had a glitter, in spite of seeming not more than half open.

"Written, I think, by my old friend and your father-in-law, Leo Gadbally."

From whom (Nolla via Kemp?) had he heard this? No good denying it, but at least Gideon could share responsibility.

"It was a matter of collaboration, which we find usually works best. I did the research at the National Library."

But Klotz didn't seem to be listening. He was glancing through what Gideon saw was the new clandestine number of the magazine.

"Our imaginative writers are the conscience of the nation," he announced, looking directly at Gideon with that light in his small eyes that was not so much malicious as amusedly brazen.

"You have given a good example to some elected governments I could name by the way you have established press freedom at the start of your administration, Colonel," the Ambassador told Klotz.

"Our revolution, Ambassador, is broadly enough based to give expression to the more critical minds within it, such as Gideon Spokane's. When its history is written, he and his magazine will have an important place in the story."

"Excellent!" exclaimed Cusack.

Nolla was scribbling away on her pad, interpolating, Gideon fantasised, an occasional erotic thought, to be included in the final document and given to Klotz.

He had heard of a British Prime Minister — Gladstone or Disraeli — whose female private secretary had a habit of inserting obscenities into the middle of some boring confidential report she was typing for him.

So momentarily intrigued was Gideon by this idea that he almost missed a sign from Paul indicating the time had come for them to withdraw.

Apprehensive as he'd been at the outset of the conference — if that's what it was — he was now in no hurry to leave. He was quite ready to listen a bit longer to the Ambassador's views on *Faillandia* which both pleased him and took him as much by surprise as had the fledgling's flight out of the friar's hands.

The analogy seemed fitting, because he thought he could trace the operation of, to him, unknown and powerful interests in both events. 'Interests' in the one case intent on the bird's, and in the other, *Faillandia*'s survival.

On their way back to the hotel, Paul stopped at what had been a travel agency run by the country to which the appeal for intervention had gone after it had been turned down by the British Government, though the latter fact had not got into the news media.

When Paul returned to the car where Gideon was waiting, he

273

told him that the other explosions had been at buildings occupied by agencies of the same foreign power, including the embassy.

"What do you make of that?"

"What do *you* is more to the point?"

"I suppose you know who left the other biscuit tin at your door?"

"Somebody who, as Nolla said, doesn't know which side he's on."

Or who changed sides because of my rejection, Gideon reflected.

"I imagine it's meant to make it the easier for the foreign government in question to intervene with the excuse of the safety of its nationals."

They called at another of the bombed buildings before returning to the Aphra, where Gideon sought out Leo to tell him about the meeting with Klotz and the diplomat, and arrange about the transference of the printing press and office furnishing back to the top floor.

He had decided on this during the drive, for he believed that Klotz was so ironically prevented from enforcing the ban that the magazine could safely come out of hiding.

He had seen a headline in a late edition of an evening paper with news of a curfew being imposed on the city.

"So it's just as well to have it all centralised again, and for Kathy and I to stay here with you. We've a busy few days getting the magazine out by Friday."

"Shall you print anything about the role it played in convincing the Brits that things weren't so bad here as was being made out by some of their media?"

"No."

He would go on as if he had believed the little act of liberalism that Klotz had put on for Cusack. Otherwise, he would be a party in a secret understanding with Klotz and that was dangerous.

Indeed, to make up for what he saw as his connivance with

Klotz at the interview, he would publish certain pieces he had been holding back because of their anarchist leanings.

"But I'd like to have the second part of your 'Beyond Marxism' piece, especially as Cusack was so impressed by the first instalment."

This, in Gideon's view, had nothing to do with polemics, being in the nature of a thesis that could be a tentative sketch for some later philosopher to base a theory on, which might (here Gideon's imagination was in flight again) in turn inspire a new social reformer, as Hegel had Marx.

Before, however, finally making up his mind about the main contents of the first openly-published number for some time, Gideon wanted to consult Pieta and tell her about the interview at Klotz's.

She was lying on her bed with a pile of typescript sheets beside her.

"Anything new in the way of a revelation?"

"Stale . . . stale . . . stale, dried-out hearts and clever little minds."

Gideon laughed.

"Don't look so woebegone, Dove, the precious pearl isn't buried under every pile of rubbish."

"Where have you been?"

"Why, what makes you think I've been anywhere?"

"Kathy told me about the phone call. She was anxious. Does she know you're back?"

Because of all that had happened, it hadn't struck Gideon that a sudden summons to see Klotz might indeed have presented a threat, or that the longer his absence the more worried Kathy could have been.

He took up the telephone from the bedside table and on the intercom dialled her office.

"For Christ's sake, where are you?"

"Here."

He'd been negligent. Hadn't he almost dragged himself out of her, if not quite, to answer a summons that could have

275

meant arrest and incarceration? And here he was on the edge of Pieta's bed, and, if it hadn't been for her, mightn't have announced his safe return for an hour or so.

"Where, for heaven's sake?"

"Up in Pieta's room."

It was too much for Kathy. He heard the line go dead as she put the receiver down.

"How can you be so callous to somebody for whom you're the whole world!"

Gideon gave Pieta's question the same consideration that he had to the several serious ones that had been put to him in the last few hours, including Paul's about who he thought was responsible for the bombings. But no intuitive answer came to illuminate his understanding. Was the way his mind worked, and what for a more precise definition, he thought of as the affections of his heart, all a less-known area to him than the communal consciousness which he prided himself on being able to interpret in a way that made him such a good editor?

"I don't know."

"Don't you love her as she loves you?"

"Of course, I love her too."

"I know you love her too. But leave out the 'too'. Think over in all gravity, because it's a grave matter, as to whether it's her sharing your sexual instincts that appeals to you or if you've discovered in her something that makes you aware, for the first time, of another human being with all the same sensitivities, vulnerabilities, hopes and fears as yourself."

There was a pause while Gideon took this in. This was what Pieta meant by love, and it was not for him to find fault with it, though he noted, with regret, the 'for the first time'. How could she say that after what she had told him yesterday. He recalled her words verbatim: 'Ah, what strength you have, Gideon, that's what I rely on'."

"You thought better of me in the lift."

"You've great qualities and great vices, and you don't seem aware of either."

Gideon found Kathy weeping in her office and, if he hadn't loved her before (in Pieta's sense), he surely, he reflected, loved her at that moment.

Whether this was the love of which Pieta had spoken, Gideon didn't know. Whatever it was, it was something that he couldn't express verbally. Seldom at a loss for words to describe all kinds of feelings and relationships, he was now dumb.

"What's the matter?"

It was *her* asking *him*, not, as it should have been had he not been tongue-tied, the other way round.

"Why?"

"You're so pale."

He put his arms around her, as she added: "And not a trace of a shiver."

"Oh, no, Kathy."

He meant that he'd never shiver again in the sense that she meant, when the other, subtler links with her were swept away in the obliterating tide of desire.

They embraced motionlessly for the space of what seemed to him the biblical half-an-hour in which the tide turned and the moon changed its colour.

It was a relief to Gideon when, after a knock at the door, Paul entered, as it seemed impossible to endure more than a small quantity of such blessed intensity before it turned to pain. And when he asked them back to his apartment for dinner, that was welcome to Gideon too, who saw him as a go-between or mediator, somebody whose presence, while in no way impinging, would allow them gradually to accustom themselves to this strange new phase in their relationship.

"What about eating out with us?" Gideon suggested. He wasn't sure if the sudden addition of two people for Paul's evening meal might not be burdensome.

"That would mean a rush to keep within the curfew, that's why I suggested my place where you could stay the night. I'll phone my housekeeper if you're free."

'Curfew', 'housekeeper', 'free', words that took Gideon by

277

surprise. He looked at Kathy for her response.

"It'll be our very first outing for I don't know how long."

Another surprise word: 'outing'. Her coming to the clinic as a night-nurse could hardly be called an 'outing', that was true, and nor could a meal in the hotel restaurant when they were staying there.

By the time Kathy had put some things for the night in a bag and come down again, Paul had joined Gideon in the hall and was telling him that he had the impression when calling his home that the phone was tapped.

Another surprise: Gideon thought that if there was eavesdropping it would be on the instructions of Paul himself.

As they drove off it was the hour in a city, almost any city, that he loved best, when the street lights were just coming on and causing the clear sky of evening to descend and cover the tall buildings with a dark canopy.

From the back seat he saw the streets that traversed not only Aphrin but his own being, imprinted there as a temporal as well as a spacial record, so that in certain of them he was in another time, in a consciousness aware of other long-past events.

The route that they took on the first part of the drive was the one that led to the hospital and, further on, to the Northern station, past the garage where he had worked, and on into the suburbs where one road forked towards the racecourse and the other towards the mountains where he had driven with Kathy on their first ever outing, and she'd plucked the sprig of Fael.

At the junction where they'd have turned left, if he and Kathy had been going home, there was some congestion as the traffic lights were not functioning.

Paul had slowed down, keeping some yards behind the car in front and as the whole line came to a stop he suddenly pulled out from the lane and accelerated into a U-turn.

Gideon was used to drivers like Paul and Frank with sharper reactions than his who, forseeing a long hold-up, made a quick getaway onto another route, while he'd have remained in line in apparent patience, but inwardly tense.

The windscreen shattered soundlessly, or so it seemed, perhaps because his attention was absorbed by the other sound: two overlapping shots, not particularly loud but silencing for a moment all other noises.

Kathy! Paul was driving dangerously fast into a side street and out again. Kathy!

## THIRTY TWO

Gideon never learnt the extent of Kathy's internal injuries though Cadjella, who had operated on her, and Dr. Roggan who had also been present, told him that the single bullet had entered through the ribcage and emerged from the small of her back.

Between these two points, no more than a dozen or so inches apart, a destruction had swiftly and secretly taken place, turning his world to a desert in which he was alone and directionless, with none of his familiar landmarks by which to become orientated. As in the mythical, opposite or heavenly condition, there were no more questions to be asked. An end to all seeking and curiosity, that was one of the thoughts, all strangely inconsequential, that struck him.

He would have remained in their room at the hotel for most of each twenty-four hour period that formed the interminable days that followed, had it not been for the funeral arrangements and his work on the magazine. Others would have taken on these tasks, but Gideon had an instinct to act as though his responsibilities were important although he was no longer convinced that they, or indeed anything else, was.

He decided that Kathy should be buried in the small cemetery belonging to the hospital, the entrance to which he had often noticed in the wall of the park, though he had never been through it. Most of the graves there belonged to people who had died in the hospital without relatives or close friends, as in the case of Ellis, but, Dr. Roggan told him, there was also a small ruined chapel dating from perhaps the tenth century around which were some tombstones, worn thin as blades, with inscriptions just discernible as faint indentations on the smooth stone, belonging to monks and, it was said, ancient kings of Failland.

Pieta asked if he would like Frère Emanuel to conduct the burial service and, because she was the one person from whom he didn't hide the sense of indifference that had overcome him, he asked what the point of bothering to get him all the way from the island was, and no doubt obtain the Prior's permission, when the hospital chaplain was at hand.

"Because he married you and her."

"What's that to do with it?"

"More than you now think."

So he left her to telephone the Priory, and met Paul by appointment in a small café round the corner — how useless all these precautions that Paul took seemed to him.

Paul had obtained from Nolla a copy of the typescript of the shorthand notes she'd made of the conversation between Klotz and the Ambassador after Paul's and Gideon's departure.

"What's the point?" Gideon enquired, using almost the same phrase that he'd put to Pieta in reference to her suggestion.

"Something was said by the Ambassador that made Klotz decide that if the ban on the magazine couldn't now be strictly enforced, its guiding spirit must be removed."

"Kathy?"

"Gideon, however painful this is, it is better we know where we are, if only for later. Life will go on, though it's hard for you to contemplate."

"What had she to do with it?"

"It was you who were the target. I caught sight of the sniper at the window as we were coming to a stop and by the sudden U-turn made him miss."

Gideon read the two sheets of typescript without taking them in, and then was starting to re-read them when Paul interrupted.

"Leave them."

"Are they important?"

"In the sense that the transcript is for me clear enough evidence that Klotz listened to the telephone message to my housekeeper, then posted his marksmen, after having the traffic lights at the junction — perhaps others too — disconnected.

"I see."

Gideon didn't really follow, but he trusted Paul in his role of intelligence officer to unravel the intricacies of this plot which he said he'd uncovered.

Kathy's funeral took place on a late autumn morning with the smell of smoke from a heap of smouldering leaves in the air, and was attended by a couple of dozen or so mourners. Besides Gideon, there was her father and sister, Gideon's daughter, Laura, Frank and his American friend, Lilo, as well as — but of these Gideon was hardly aware — the Canavans and Kemps, besides the two doctors and a couple of nurses from the hospital.

Gideon, Paul, Leo and Dr. Roggan carried the coffin across a corner of the park, passing close to the tree that Gideon had first noticed through the window while keeping watch beside Pieta, and Frank and the other doctor carried a number of wreaths.

When the coffin had been put down beside the grave and the old friar was about to start saying the prayers for the dead, preceded by some words of his own that nobody — or at least not the chief mourner — were expecting, Paul showed Gideon the card on a large wreath of chrysanthemums and asked what he wished done with it.

"Colonel Klotz, in deepest sympathy and regret," Gideon read.

At that moment he noticed the park-keeper, on the outskirts of the little group, and went to shake hands with him.

On his return to the graveside, he saw that the wreath had been laid with the others beside the coffin and that thus there was no need to answer a question that he remembered Paul putting to him.

Frère Emanuel, who had been reading prayers from the liturgy, took a few steps onto the fresh earth at the edge of the grave. In the same monotone, so that it was a moment or two before Gideon realised that he had slipped the missal into the pocket of his white habit and was no longer reading, he started to speak to the little group.

"At first there was death and there was love, in isolation, and each a lonely and terrifying experience, as is confirmed in the ancient legends where pain and sorrow is the lot of the lovers as well as the warriors.

"Then the two became one in the Person of Jesus. What was unimaginable, because it was completely contrary to our instincts, was made real, and we saw the two most opposing and far-apart of our experiences as completing and enhancing each other. That happened, Sisters and Brothers, when His risen body bore the signs of death which were also the imprint of His love and compassion.

"*Kinder*, it is within the shadow of death that love was transformed and gained a new depth. And death too had taken on a new dimension, because Jesus descended into the pit and came out of it with His love made visible and perfect.

"When I celebrated the union of our daughter, Kathy, and her loved one, it was, as such must be on earth, as well as a foretaste of joys and exaltations, also a forecasting of the pain that the true union of man and woman involves them in."

Gideon's attention wandered. He took in the words and knew that he would remember them later, but now his heart was closed and nothing from outside entered it, whereas his surface mind was occupied with comparative trivialities.

What, for instance, was the meaning of the 'and regret' in Klotz's handwriting on the card? Was he expressing his regret that Kathy had been killed instead of Gideon? He would ask Paul later what he made of it, if he remembered or, by then, attached importance to it.

Gideon spent the next two days in the room at the Aphra

that had been his and Kathy's. This was partly on Paul's advice, who thought that he would be at risk if he moved about freely while Klotz was making up his mind whether to complete the failed attempt to eliminate him, and risk what was now no more than a suspicion becoming public knowledge of his determination to stop the magazine.

His first visitor was Pieta in the early evening, in the jeans, shirt and denim jacket she wore when on the elevator, for the same reason, as she'd said, that Joan of Arc dressed herself as a man. Besides some typescript for his final approval, she brought a tray with sandwiches and a bottle of wine.

"I don't think you've had anything to eat since yesterday's lunch."

Whether or not, and he wasn't sure, he was glad of the respite, as he thought of it.

Of all the meals, from banquets to light repasts, that he recalled, some partaken in strange conditions and circumstances among them, this was perhaps the most memorable. Not that there was anything outwardly remarkable about it. Pieta was restarting him living again after the hiatus since Kathy's death.

"With Daddy's compliments," she added, setting down the tray on which there were two plates and two wine glasses.

When the wine was poured and each had taken a bite of salmon and cucumber sandwich, Gideon asked her what she thought — meaning what her father might have told her *he* thought — was going to happen.

"On the six o'clock news it said that diplomatic relations were being broken off and a couple of foreign warships were coming to evacuate their nationals. There was also something about the funeral of. the wife of the editor of *Faillandia*, killed on Friday, in a car accident. Why do you think it said that?"

"Because the news is now being manipulated to suit the state authorities, and only *Faillandia* is left to tell the truth."

"Yes. There's a copy of Frère Emanuel's notes for his graveside oration.

Pieta pointed to the sheaf of typescript, and though this wasn't what Gideon had meant by 'the truth', he nodded.

"You remember, Pieta, the harsh things you said to me in your bedroom?"

"Of course."

"That too was truth, and it came just in time, revealing me to myself, and making my last hour together with Kathy more perfect than ever before."

"That's the kind of truth that *Faillandia* has to tell, about love, sex, death, books, and even your horses — but we must leave the blind to lead the blind."

"The politicians?"

"If we start taking off the lids of pots in that devils' kitchen, we'll end up sick from the fumes."

"But people keep writing in to ask how we think society should be administered, and we've got to give some kind of answer. That's why I got your father to write the essay 'Beyond Marxism'."

"Which seemed to say that real democracy would give people the right to take things into their own hands in matters that seriously effected them and not wait for bureaucratic half-measures."

"He says that either it's going to happen, or the whole thing will come to a nasty end. I thought that Klotz would agree, but it turns out that this was one of the pieces he took most exception to, though when the Ambassador expressed interest in it, he was silent."

"They're all in the same power-business, only the politicians work a more popular system than the dictators to keep themselves on top."

He thought this was the first time he'd heard her make a political remark.

They talked until it was time for Pieta's shift. Gideon had wondered why she kept this job when she could have been occupied full-time on the magazine and earned more at the same time. Now he saw that she didn't want to become a

285

professional journalist, preferring to be a 'lift-girl' who sometimes helped with the editorial tasks of a weekly magazine.

He understood it was part of her disbelief in professionalism. In her view, anyone all of whose time and attention was devoted to one subject became dehumanised and, thus unfitted even for their own particular tasks. Besides politicians, this went for scientists, doctors, lawyers and, perhaps especially, writers and critics.

Writers like Mario Kimm lived in an isolated literary world and turned out something called 'literature', which in turn fashionable critics pronounced on, these pronouncements reflecting their own limitations when it came to non-literary instincts and emotions.

"Yes," said Gideon, speaking for the first time since Kathy's death from the heart, "the Sunday Supplement critic sees his small mental world reassuringly reflected in the highly-thought of so-and-so's new novel, and in his/her review reflects the writer's image back to him, each gazing happily at himself in the mirror held up by the other."

Whether Pieta grasped the connection between what they'd been talking about and this unexpected response wasn't clear. All she said was: "You may as well take the last sandwich."

When she left, taking the tray with her, Gideon had emerged from the state in which all thinking had turned to feeling and feeling to the single awareness of a throbbing wound.

When Leo rang from downstairs to ask if he and Paul, who had just arrived at the hotel, could come up and see him, Gideon was able to say he'd come down. Once with them, though, in Leo's office, their company was an infringement of the solitude he'd entered, and he realised he could only share it with Pieta. Not that he had to do more than listen to what Paul had come to tell him.

As for Leo, Gideon felt he was looking at him in resentment mingled with shock, as at somebody who shouldn't have been there, was only there at the cost of the loss of his daughter. But he might well be confusing his own feelings with those of his father-in-law. 'It should be Pieta coming to tell you about what happened', he said half aloud, but Leo didn't appear to hear.

He had got the transcript of the notes that Nolla had gone on taking after Gideon and Paul had left.

Gideon looked through it without coming on anything which struck him as justifying this apparently urgent visit, until Paul pointed to a piece of dialogue towards the end.

*Colonel Klotz:* "How did Spokane strike you?"

*Ambassador Cusack:* "Not at all as a fanatic, whether of the right or the left. Someone likely to go far."

*Colonel Klotz:* "In what way?"

*Ambassador Cusack:* "In his chosen field."

*Colonel Klotz:* "As editor of a popular weekly?"

*Ambassador Cusack:* "I'm sure you realise he aspires to something more than that, which is all the more reason for congratulating you, Colonel, in giving him and his paper such freedom. My Government would be prepared to take the same risk in the cause of free speech and a free press, but, as you know, there aren't many other countries where he wouldn't have been prosecuted before now."

*Colonel Klotz:* "There is still France."

*Ambassador Cusack:* "French liberalism went so far that before World War II society was being demoralised by publications like *L'Action Francaise,* which resulted in the Vichy Government and a host of collaborators."

Paul's finger was pointing further down the page, but Gideon's concentration lapsed and he read no further.

"Is that what you came to show me?"

"And to see about you taking a holiday abroad."

The suggestion was unexpected, but Gideon considered it. One of the few sentences that he'd just read without immediately forgetting was the reference to France and French society.

"I could go to Paris for a week."

He was thinking of the *Hotel des Sources* at Enghien run by

Marthe's friend, the ex-jockey, without really seeing the necessity for the move.

These few words were what were needed to set off a series of pre-arrangements, culminating in a plane from that part of the Failland airforce loyal to Paul, landing that night at Orly airport and Gideon's arrival around midnight at the small hotel — three stories over a bar-restaurant — at Enghien-les-Bains in the Paris Banlieux.

He awoke in his room on the top floor and went to the window. Instead of the courtyard with the palm in wooden tubs that he had looked down at from their room in the Aphra — the view that Kathy had drawn the curtains on that other day as she undressed — he saw a small station across the street, and several single-deck dark green buses lined up outside it.

What on earth was he doing here? Even if he went, with his still packed bag, and boarded one of the auto-buses, it wouldn't take him far. He lingered in the room after he had dressed until the house-phone, that he hadn't noticed, buzzed, and it was Marthe Delaunay for whom he'd left a message the previous night.

Down in the restaurant she was drinking coffee at a marble-topped table where he joined her.

"How nice to see you over for the 'Arc'."

For what? But he wasn't going to ask. The time for questions was over, and as he shook hands and she called over to the bar for a café-au-lait and croissants, Gideon watched for a glimpse of pink tongue between her grey lips when she opened her mouth.

"You've been having trouble."

Nothing! only the white gleam of teeth.

"How did you know?"

"It's in the papers here."

"No."

"Oh yes, about your Colonel — what's he called — proclaiming a state of emergency and bombs exploding at embassies. Wasn't that who they were looking for when we were held up coming from the racecourse."

"Was it? He must have slipped in in spite of them."

He'd intended this as a joke, to keep the conversation on a lighter note, but he saw it hadn't come off.

"We can go together into Paris. I usually get the nine-twenty train."

To Paris? This had to be considered. Try as he might, he could think of no business he had to contract there. Of course, there were the sights to see, the streets to be strolled through, the cafés to be visited. None of which prospects had any appeal for him. Still, it was better than remaining in his room, which might well seem strange and draw attention which he certainly wanted to avoid. And from Paris he could telephone Pieta, as he'd promised.

A stream was flowing at this hour winter and summer, wherever morning had dawned. In cities all over the earth, millions of men and women were being transported, their nerves and senses, still under the spell of night, after a brief transition for ablutions, dressings, breakfastings, to the realities of the daily grind.

"You'd best buy a book of tickets."

They were on the platform of the station at Enghien-les-Bains in the exterior-active dimension, but in Gideon's interior-intuitive one it was deep night in the countless bedrooms of the huge global apartment-block where, steeped in various textures and temperatures of darkness, sleep slowed the heartbeat and stilled the brain cells of these mythical millions, causing a current other than that of daytime to flow through them in a different direction, revealing to the sleeper alternative experiences, inexplicable disasters, but also the finding of the lost out of all likelihood, even the joyful, beyond all mere imaginings, resurrection of the dead.

This was the stream — to return to where Gideon's fantasy had started — that was now carrying him, in its continual flow of staggered hours around the globe, into one of the great centres of activity where he alone, of all the thousand millions, would have nothing whatsoever to do.

He kept up a flow of quite irrelevant musings for as long as he could to postpone the confrontation with present reality.

"St. Denis, already! Having someone to talk to does shorten the journey!"

Marthe had been talking most of the twenty minutes or so it had taken from Enghien, and Gideon had put in a word where instinct had told him it was needed, without having to interrupt the interior scenario.

At the Gare du Nord, when he heard that Marthe was going to Republique, Gideon, after a glance at the metro chart, said goodbye until the evening, saying he was bound for Odeon on another line.

He then went back again to the large hall of the terminus at which they had arrived.

# THIRTY THREE

The idea of going out into the autumn streets of the foreign city with nowhere to head for, appalled him. The only destination he could think of as one that could draw him to it was the small cemetery reached through the hospital grounds, the only welcome landmarks on the way being the ancient olive-tree and the mound of perhaps still-smouldering leaves.

He went into a café that opened onto the main hall of the station and sat at a table which, like an island in the middle of a current, was continually being passed by travellers with luggage, children, and even animals on leads or in their arms.

From this traffic he was largely insulated by the nature of his reflections, or rather by the atmosphere evoked by them. It was dense enough to blot out the coming and going in a fog out of which emerged briefly a dark figure with a white apron to whom he automatically gave his order for a beer.

The surfaces and objects immediately under his gaze were as strange and threatening to him as the rocks he is stranded on are to the castaway. When his hand rested on the formica of the table-top, he quickly returned it to his pocket.

Ah, how he longed for the feel and sight of that holy ground, where the weeds grew in silence and shade under the old wall! He smelt the damp earth where the park-keeper had turned some sods close to the wall to clear it of the thick roots of ivy that clung in heavy, dark-leaved tufts to the loosened stones at the top. Wafted to him with the scent came some lines from a poem of Christina Rosetti's:

*'Safe from the frost and the snow,*
*Safe from the storm and the sun,*
*Safe where the seeds wait to grow one by one,*
*And to come back in blow.'*
He lingered over each line, almost each word, wondering at
some, and questioning others that did not seem to be in tune
with his meditation.

'Safe'. How desperate must have been the fear, to come to
the point where the grave becomes a refuge!

'Where the seeds wait to grow'. They waited, and the thought
of their 'waiting' illuminated the darkness. 'One by one', he
rejected, as being no more than a stylistic device for the sake
of rhyme. And 'to come back in blow' he wasn't sure about,
he'd have, in his present state, preferred the verse to end with
the 'waiting'.

These reflections restored a little of his faith as against the
despairing conclusion that Ellis, whose grave was within his
range of interior vision, had come face to face with.

Ah, were I back there listening to the sobs from down the
passage!

He thought of *Faillandia* that had gone underground, and like
the seeds, (was he being carried off on imaginary paths leading
nowhere?) was waiting. Thinking of it thus, perhaps for the
first time, he saw it as also illuminating the darkness that had
fallen on his land.

When he telephoned Pieta, which was the only thing he had
to do during the hours until evening, he would ask her to put
these lines into the coming issue. He had to remember which
shift she'd been working at the start of the week, so as to time
the call when she was likely to be free.

On his way to the telephone booth with enough coins to
ensure they weren't cut off in the middle of the conversation,
he saw a familiar caption amidst the display of periodicals.

There, between a German and a glossy Italian magazine, was
a two-week old copy of *Faillandia*, which he bought and took
with him into the booth where it helped to transform the small

glass cell into a halfway house between the noisy, crowded station and the afternoon quiet of Pieta's room.

So many digits to dial, each one bringing her a degree nearer! Threads that formed a fragile net cast with a series of clicks against the muted background roar to fall around her. And the low, distant ringing summoning her from so far away, though Kathy was still further! And yet, despite the intense expectation, her voice startled him. She was beside him here, as in the lift, and, at the same time, the distance between was greater than ever before.

"My dove!"

"Yes."

"I shouldn't have been persuaded to leave."

"I've been talking to Frère Emanuel about you."

"Why about me?"

"He thinks you should go to the island which, by an ancient charter, is under ecclesiastic jurisdiction."

"Do you remember that day in the fortress how we both imagined a dungeon below?"

"Like John the Baptist's."

"That's where I'm calling you from."

"You're self-dramatising, as usual."

"Don't tell me off, not on the phone where I can't watch your face."

"If you're in a dungeon, where do you think *I* am?"

"In your quiet haven of a room at the Aphra."

"Yes, I'm the one who is sheltered, that's true."

" *'Safe from the frost and snow'*, though it wasn't of you I was thinking when I recalled that poem just now."

"You were thinking of the hospital cemetery."

"In spite of my callousness, she was my companion and bride."

"You achieved it with her, Gideon, perhaps only finally at the last moment. But that is something rare, more miraculous than my resurrected fledgling."

"Yes, it was more than sex, though the sex was perfect, and

**293**

I remember it too and always shall. Not just our love-making in general. But the one or two special occasions when we had the same urgent desire at the same moment, especially at the times when it was immoderate and out of all proportion, like where she came to see me one morning when I was working in the top gallery at the museum. It became a memory of a shared aberration and that had its own secret bond which you shouldn't dismiss as just trivial."

"Oh, I don't. Wasn't I there after your marriage ceremony, taking part as best I could in the preparation for its consummation! That's a memory that I too cherish, and so it's not beyond me to understand how you and Kathy treasured other less ceremonial sensual secrets."

"Let us always share our memories of her, Pieta, even if, as time goes on, we think and talk of her less urgently, but never without the sense of what she was that we have now. I don't know how I'd bear the loneliness, keeping her in my heart all on my own."

"All sorts of once-precious things fade — how hard that is! — but no, you and I will never let Kathy, sister and bride, slip out of our thoughts and prayers."

Now Gideon could tell her about seeing the copy of the magazine which before hadn't seemed worth mentioning.

"*Faillandia*, yes, we have to keep faith in that too," Pieta said, "all the more because it was the indirect cause of her death."

Although Gideon wasn't sure that he followed her completely, he nodded, forgetting momentarily that she couldn't see him.

"The first outing we ever had was to the mountains where she found a sprig of Fael which she brought back and dried and is still in a vase in our flat."

"That reminds me: Are you going to keep it on or shall I give the concierge notice and have your things brought here?"

Yes, he could talk about such practical matters again, thanks to Pieta.

"What should I do?"

"Come back to the island as soon as Frère Emanuel has talked it over with the Prior."

Gideon's coins were running out, but he told her he would ring her again before her evening shift.

His heart was lighter as he made his way back through the station hall to the café, but he still would not venture out into the streets.

He bought a copy of *Paris Turf,* but found nothing in it to interest him and, instead, re-read some parts of the old copy of *Faillandia* and was glad to see how little out of date it seemed. Perhaps this was because many of the articles were on subjects vital to the authors who wrestled with them, as Jacob with the angel, to win from them a meaning, instead, as was common elsewhere, making statements which, if reversed, could still have passed as serious comment.

Families of travellers flowed past him — it was not yet time for the homing commuters — and well before the evening rush-hour when there would be queues outside the telephone boxes, Gideon telephoned Pieta again.

There were things he had forgotten to say on the first occasion about love and sex and how they can fuse in moments of passion, not forgetting other moments when sex is laughter, delight and shared extravagance, like the time coming back from the island on the Prior's boat. That was an occasion of even more shared excess, and disproportion in relation to time and place, than had been that in the Geological Museum.

But, to his surprise, what Pieta started talking about was Lydia.

"She shouldn't be forgotten, Gideon."

"Memories of her are mostly painful, but in a quite different way to those of Kathy. Anyhow, there are others to remember her, like our daughter, Laura."

Mention of his daughter made Gideon recall her saying that her mother would have been delighted by some of what appeared in *Faillandia* and that this had caused him to reflect

295

on how little he had done to delight her, but, on the contrary, sometimes used his intimate knowledge of her to irritate and even hurt her.

"It isn't for Lydia I'm concerned, it's for you, Gideon. If you banish her from your thoughts, it's because you want to forget a period of your life, years and years that, good or bad, the good with the bad, you can't be indifferent to."

He wanted to ask Pieta what it was all about, his life, where there was a beginning or an end to take hold of and unravel a little to see where the thread might come from, if it came from anywhere. But he understood that even if she knew she couldn't tell him, because it wasn't a matter of an ancient lore, even less a piece of knowledge, to communicate, but rather a matter of his having a sense of his own destiny, regardless of how obscure as it might well turn out to be. His coming on the poem again, followed by his talk with Pieta, was restoring this to him.

Pieta was so simple, so at one with her wisdom. She was so reliable that she took even quite menial tasks seriously and seemed convinced that everything mattered, and even that she was responsible for it. Not only for him and Kathy, but even, just now, for his first marriage.

Gideon felt a need to tell her how he thought of her, which, as far as he recalled, he'd never done before. It was not enough to call her 'dove' or even 'my dove', which had also been one of his names for Kathy, but in her case the association was with the *Song of Solomon* while in Pieta's it was with the sick bird — which, however, had had nothing dove-like about it — that had recovered and flown away.

"There's endless time these days for thinking, and you may be sure that I'll spend a lot of it reflecting on everything you've been saying. As for you, Pieta, you're never indifferent to anything that comes your way."

This hadn't come out as he'd hoped, having nothing of the emotion he wanted to convey to her. He felt inhibited by the convention that recognised only fixed categories of love:

296

mother-love, filial love, brotherly love and the sexual love between a man and woman which was deemed to include affection.

He was aware of the flow of people past the booth increasing as he stood with his mouth and ear to the instrument, while there was silence between them.

Was Pieta disappointed at his last remark which he thought sounded like an approbation bestowed on a good pupil by a teacher.

It was time to end the conversation and meet Marthe as they'd arranged (without her guessing, of course, that he'd never left the station) for the journey back to Enghien.

How could he ring off on this false note? And why be inhibited by the conventions of a banal society with its hard-and-fast categories and no time for relationships that didn't fit the tribal pattern.

Gideon hesitated. How impoverished was language! There was only the one hackneyed, sullied and over-used word for all the extraordinary and complex responses of the mind, heart and senses to another being.

So be it, he said to himself, she won't take it amiss, knowing how to reflect on it and, in her wisdom, give it a new meaning.

"Pieta, my love."

"Au revoir till tomorrow."

Gideon had dinner with Marthe at the table where they'd breakfasted in the small bar-restaurant. When she had asked him how he'd spent the day, he came out with the Louvre and the Orangerie, which left her somewhat at a loss and the subject was dropped.

Bernard, the ex-jockey, brought over a bottle of red wine that he presented formally with his compliments, leaving Gideon with an uneasy feeling that this was the *patron*'s way of bestowing his blessing on what he took to be the two about-to-become lovers. Perhaps it was also to indicate that he himself had no claim to the girl, if Gideon had supposed there was something between them.

Whatever Marthe talked about, which was mostly horse-racing, it seemed to suggest an intimacy with him, either already present or to come.

"When I was fifteen and just arrived from Martinique, my father, who was a great gambler, took me to the races and when he'd backed one of the horses in a close finish, instead of shouting the first name of the jockey like the others, I'd cry: *Oui . . . oui . . .* between ecstasy and anguish, though I was still a virgin."

He didn't ask what that had to do with it, because he didn't want her to go further into it. But she talked of other things, or other aspects of racing, without any hints of eroticism, and he relaxed and yet experienced a sense of let-down.

"Luckily, I don't have to be at the office till noon tomorrow."

They had lingered over the meal and it was quite late, but not, he thought, so late as to make normally early rising a problem.

In the narrow hallway she didn't pause for him to bid her goodnight but, without looking back, started up the steep stairs.

Gideon saw the back of her legs as he followed, dark through the semi-transparency of her tights. The hollow at one knee was covered when the other was revealed as the skirt slid high on that side when she took an upward step.

Whom would he harm if he let himself go with the dark waves that washed over him at every upward step? He remembered thinking that night with Kathy at the clinic how even a loveless coupling could shut out all painful thoughts. Would not a respite from them restore his balance?

But how could he be sure of that? When he telephoned Pieta again in the morning would there not be a very recent memory to come between those he shared with her, and — something of which he could even be less sure — could he let himself be swept away like this without being carried somewhere where Kathy would be less present, though she would be the last to blame him.

He stopped on the first floor landing and Marthe continued

her ascent. He heard her call down to him from above, but he remained standing and did not answer.

Next morning he took an early train into the Gare du Nord and breakfasted in the big station café. Afterwards, sitting alone at the table — the place was almost empty at this hour — he felt an unexpected return of some of his old self-composure.

He no longer shrank from going out into Paris, although the idea hadn't any great attraction, nor was he impatient for the hour when he could ring up Pieta.

He had emerged from a nightmare, not, of course, to a realisation that he'd been dreaming, but at least in possession of his waking faculties, such as they were. And what they were intimating was something like this:

The events of your life don't make much sense to you, nor, as you realised yesterday, is there any use asking Pieta, or anyone else, to make things clearer.

Clarity of mind is not a condition necessary for you to fulfill your vocation, the nature of which for the time being, and perhaps to the end of your life, you won't be able to discover, nor even believe in.

What you will come to understand — you've already been given inklings which you've tried to dismiss — is that in your case loss and failure is part of the story.

Well, Gideon mused, I didn't need one of my subconscious 'voices' to tell me that. They are the vital part of many of the world's greatest stories, from the Gospels, through fiction, to obscure and squalid personal ones.

But while that was one thing, to accept gratefully — or even gracelessly — that his own story was being woven to this pattern, was another.

He knew well that such musing was pointless, and also enervating. It was a matter of acting on whatever renewed insight was granted him. That meant returning whence he'd come as soon as possible.

When Gideon telephoned Pieta, he told her he'd decided to return.

"And don't try to persuade me not to, Dove."

"Me? I'd never have consented to your leaving, if you'd asked me in the first place."

He hadn't asked her, that was true. He'd supposed she agreed with what she'd heard from Paul and Leo about the danger he was in from Klotz's assassination squad.

Pieta told him to return as soon as possible, stay a day or two at the hotel, and then take up residence on the island of Dominicus, "where Daddy also has a hotel."

He'd better get used to Pieta taking more of a hand in events.

"Of course, the magazine will go with you."

"Yes, of course."

But it hadn't been 'of course' a few minutes ago. Now he was letting himself go with the shape of things were taking, or Pieta was directing them, and behind whom was perhaps Frère Emanuel, and behind the friar?

Once Gideon came to the conclusion that to try to mould the situation to his own ideas of what would make it turn out well, what was prudent, what must be avoided, would be fatal to his own well-being (he didn't define this more exactly), to the future of *Faillandia,* to the bond between himself and Pieta, and, more obscurely, to that between him and Kathy, he became at peace with himself and, as the saying goes, with the rest of the world. So much so, that, instead of hurrying back to Failland immediately, he decided to stay where he was over the weekend and to accompany Marthe to the big race on Sunday.

In his present state of mind, or neurological system — as he thought of it — he had no sense of awkwardness with Marthe when meeting her on the Saturday evening at the Hotel des Sources. He greeted her with a kiss that she seemed about to draw back from but at the last minute thrust her face forward to receive on the lips.

This didn't surprise him. He felt unusually sure of himself as being in harmony with the course of events, as he imagined it. And besides, the girl was too excited by the prospect of the race, for which she was to write articles for both *Paris Turf* and *Faillandia,* to harbour a grudge. When he told her he would take it back with him next evening and translate it on the journey — that he was making by surface transport — he knew they were fully reconciled.

## THIRTY FOUR

Gideon travelled by train and ship to have more time to adapt to whatever was in store, though aware that his arrival back in Failland would be as much a second leave-taking as a home-coming.

Not that he hadn't come a long way to adjusting to a more solitary life in these few days. How quiet it would be, he reflected, for much of its former eventfulness had come from living with Kathy. But he no longer dreaded the future as he had on the outer journey, and he could now think of her, recall some of their times together and even address her in thought without being overcome by the loss.

He bought a bottle of wine at the ship's bar, even selecting a 'Bordeau Cadet' from the wine list as if such choices could be made to matter again. He took it with him to his cabin, as he would, had Kathy been with him. And there, with an impulse to continue an old habit, he thought over all that had happ-ened since the funeral, as he would in words, had she been there. And, indeed, coming to certain incidents that he thought of particular importance, he did verbalise them in his mind.

'Telling' her of the events helped him understand them better himself. In this manner he now thought that what had stopped him following Marthe beyond the first floor of the hotel had been a fear that if he ever made love to another woman it might diminish the precious memory of the unique sexuality he had shared with her.

Half addressing himself, but not leaving her out, he con-sidered it carefully.

"You see, the fact of the hotel patron presenting us with a celebratory bottle of wine precluded the sense of committing a misdemeanour that I had with you. It may sound ridiculous, but with you it was more like a conspiratorial act, something hidden between us that mustn't be found out, and I could never think of it as licensed, legal and fully approved, could you, my lost one?

"It wasn't only in these ways that you had a delinquent air. It went back to that evening when we first met and you stepped out of the queue and into my car which, when I heard where you worked and who your father was, seemed like a piece of daring perversity."

The days and nights will be much emptier, he reflected, and then, not to leave her out, told himself if this applied to him, how was it for Kathy? Could death be said to be pure emptiness, in which, with time no longer ticking away, there is nothing to look forward to? Ah, the interminable afternoons and evenings! But he felt he wasn't capable of probing into this and doubted whether anyone, Ellis on the one hand or Frère Emanuel on the other, was either.

"Let it be as it may," he said to himself as he finished the wine, content to think that it rested with him to leave the mystery undisturbed.

Gideon spent most of the next morning in his cabin translating Marthe's piece about the big race at Longchamp. She had made it into a little drama, full of tension, starting quietly with a reference to the warm autumn afternoon with the leaves in the Bois de Boulogne just beginning to turn, the presence of the French President, looking 'untroubled and relaxed', despite the public scandal in which he had become involved the week before.

She gave brief, but extraordinarily visual, descriptions of the more notable horses in the parade, the favourite, like the President, looking relaxed and unruffled to the extent of appearing to yawn.

When he got to 'at the start Manibeau lost five lengths,

303

*and with Floridor setting a strong pace . . .* ' although he knew the outcome, Gideon felt the release of tension, and may even have unconsciously breathed the sigh, half of relief and half of apprehension, there in his small cabin that was drawn from many breasts at that moment.

Around noon he went on deck and to the ship's café situated forward. Out of habit, or, rather, out of an unexpected nostalgia for his days spent at the Gare du Nord where he felt he'd received assurances and even blessings without which he could hardly have survived, he ordered a 'demi'.

Drinking slowly from the large glass of cold beer, which was not, of course, the best way of breaking his fast, he got into conversation with a middle-aged French couple next to him at the bar.

They were members of a party on a package tour of Faill-and for which they had booked and put down a deposit some months before. Hearing that Gideon was a citizen of Aphrin, they wanted to know whether life there was normal again since the recent disturbances they'd read about.

"You've no need to worry, Madame. Aphrin isn't Paris, *bien entendu,* but nor is it Beirut, despite the more sensational reports."

It turned out that they came from the Midi, didn't know Paris, and seemed not have heard of Beirut, for she shook her head despondently.

Gideon next saw them that evening with the rest of their party, to whom a courier was pointing out the island of Dominicus and its famous priory, having purposely shepherded them, Gideon supposed, away from the side of the ship from which several warships, including an aircraft carrier, flying the flags of the super-power to which the deposed Faillandian Government had appealed, were visible, anchored in the bay.

More reassuring to him was the sight of the Boston-registered yacht moored with the others, though there were now several gaps in the row, stern-on to the quay.

After the vessel from Le Harve had docked, Gideon let most

of the passengers precede him into the shed where they were checked. There were few people passing through the checkpoint marked 'Faillandian Passports', while at that for foreigners he saw the group on the package tour queueing up under the eye of the guide.

Gideon instinctively disliked checkpoints, even harmless ones such as reception-desks or checkout counters in supermarkets, but he wasn't at all apprehensive as his nerves weren't registering any danger signals. Not that he was completely relying on such inner and subjective signs. Pieta's ready agreement to his return had made him deduce she'd consulted Paul, and, anyhow, whatever danger he was in wasn't of arrest, but assassination.

Sure enough, his passport was handed back with hardly a glance inside. Too quickly, he thought, because no doubt he'd been recognised by one of the military policemen standing beside the security officers.

He took a taxi, and as he was paying the driver at the door of the Aphra, he noticed a coach draw up and some of the French tourists emerge.

Inside the hotel he caught sight of Pieta busy in the elevator, and went into the kitchen where Leo was supervising some of the dishes on the menu for dinner, and who took him into his office to welcome him.

Not that Gideon made more of his trip than a long Paris weekend, taking in the big race at Longchamp. The real report would only be given to Pieta, or rather the details filled in, for she already knew the course of (interior) events. And Leo seemed to accept the superficial account because he was waiting with more important news of his own.

"Yesterday we had a visit from the Secretary of State," and Leo mentioned a name that didn't give Gideon any clue as to what he was talking about. He didn't, however, want to admit this, in case his father-in-law guessed how much the experiences of the last few days were affecting him.

"I recorded the little ceremony from last night's television

305

news to show you."

For a moment or two Leo was busy with the video recorder, cassette, and the television set that stood on his desk. Then the scene from the previous afternoon, after a couple of startlingly coloured flickers, broke through the cloud on the screen.

A motor launch with the flag that he'd seen flying from the warships, and which evidently had crossed the bay from one of them, was moored at the pier from which the small white ferries sailed to the island, and a figure in a civilian suit stepped, or half-sprang with a too obvious attempt at a sprightly air, onto the quayside. Assembly ex-chairman, Nording, stepped forward but not too close to the visitor in order, it seemed, to allow for a deferential forward curve of his torso while shaking his hand and holding it just a little longer than natural, even for the cameras that turned away before Nording had released it.

With a start of painful surprise he recognised the old man beside Nording as Lydia's father, and then Gideon watched Lucius Canavan take over where the leader of the previous Government had left off and grasp the foreign dignatory's hand before it could fall to his side. But more astonishingly to Gideon was the next little scene as Mamine Canavan, looking matronly, even portly, and suggesting to Gideon's alerted imagination a *madame* welcoming a valued client to her establishment, threw her arms around the visitor and kissed him on both his tanned cheeks.

"Where was Klotz?" Gideon asked. "What possessed him to allow that farce?"

"Under house arrest, that's where he is, shut up in his fortress flat with some of General Dorff's men guarding him."

"Where's Paul?"

It was of him Gideon instinctively thought as the person to save them from the degradation that he had just witnessed.

"At home when I last had a phone call from him."

Gideon listened to Leo's account of events after some vessels

306

of the Super Power's Fleet had appeared in the bay the day that Gideon had seen them from the air on his flight to Paris.

The army, apart from his small militia, never firmly in the control of Klotz, had rallied to an appeal by the former regime and, on an order from General Dorff, were mostly confined to their barracks. Negotiations were going on — between whom wasn't certain — for the peaceful establishment of an all-party administration, presumably headed by Nording. Cardinal Archbishop Cornelius Tolling had issued a pastoral letter calling on the populace to 'remain loyal to their elected representatives' and had also forbidden them reading 'the prohibited propaganda publication, *Faillandia*.'

"And life goes on."

Gideon was thinking of the busy hotel kitchen where he'd found Leo, and of the smaller kitchens all over Aphrin where men and women were intent on their evening meal and the quality and cost of the ingredients.

Their world wouldn't come to an end, no matter who administered the affairs of the State. And yet, he reflected, among all those who had flocked to buy *Faillandia* there must be some to whom it had brought hope of a community where all public dealings and transactions between the members were informed by compassion, patience, and a conscience of unity in this now aborted revolution.

When Pieta was free she and Gideon had a late meal in the almost empty hotel restaurant. Recollecting his initial surprise that such matters as choosing from a menu, let alone a lively discussion about whether to add nutmeg to the spinach soup, should retain their immemorial importance in the face of what he thought of as the public humiliation of the nation, he asked Pieta if she had seen the Secretary of State welcome on television.

"No, but Daddy did and felt shamed."

He waited, but instead of going on, she was saying she hadn't eaten since breakfast. So perhaps all his imagined families around the dinner tables were right in attending to their immediate concerns and appetites, instead of brooding over the news bulletins or deploring the situation they would probably never again have a chance to alter.

All the same, he was a little disappointed at her equanimity.

"What's going to happen?" he asked.

"If the old lot manage to re-establish themselves, and Daddy says they will, you'll have to take the magazine to the island and set it up there, as I explained to you on the telephone."

"What about you?"

She regarded him, and turned her eyes back to the menu card without answering.

"If they end, all our aspirations, in a quiet take-over by whichever of the old political parties, or a coalition of them all, without the people coming out into the streets in protest, it won't say much for the influence the magazine has had. So that we've got to consider whether it's worth keeping going, especially if we're going to have difficulties," Gideon told her.

"It may have failed, in spite of the huge sales of recent issues. Who knows?"

"What a strange mood you're in, Dove! Nothing seems to perturb you."

She laughed, and regarded him again as she had a moment ago.

"Why are you looking at me like that? I'm the same old Gideon."

"Not quite the same."

"You're not thinking of Marthe?"

"Marthe?"

"The girl at the hotel whom I told you about, didn't I? You don't think I slept with her?"

"Gideon, does it matter?"

"I thought . . . "

"If the urge was strong, I suppose you might have, but that couldn't make any difference. You'd be just the same in the morning, minus the urge. It's that you're not so set on your own ways."

He was astonished by first her dismissal of the possibility of his having made love to Marthe as of little consequence, and then her intuitive grasp of something that had happened to him that he hadn't himself been aware of.

It was true that during the two days spent at the Gare du Nord and the long telephone talks to Pieta, he'd experienced a change of heart so subtle that nobody else would have noticed. It was even hard to put into words, but he thought had to do with becoming more reconciled to whatever would happen. And this included failure, though what form it might take he hadn't speculated on.

He was curious about her airy remark expressing unconcern over what he'd prided himself — quite a lot if the truth were known — on foregoing.

"I'd have felt guilty about going to bed with a woman on a passing sexual urge."

"Well, you know best, Gideon. But I'd have thought two passing sexual obsessions can be killed with one stone, and it's not the end of the world, as long as there's no third person to be deceived or hurt."

"You always astonish me, Dove."

She laughed, but he wanted to get to the bottom of it.

"If desire, or lust, affords a passing relief is it so unforgive-able — though discipline is better — to embrace the first woman who takes it in the same spirit?"

Pieta was drawing with a prong of her fork an indentated pattern on the tablecloth and for a moment he thought she was imitating Christ in the scene called 'the woman taken in adultery', but immediately dismissed the idea. He knew she was utterly incapable of acting, though, for all he knew, she might have so absorbed the various Gospel stories as to be uncon-sciously guided by them.

He repeated the question in a somewhat different form.

" 'Right' and 'wrong' are words that belong to the law and the last thing I'd dream of is laying it down."

He had to leave it at that and they spoke instead of the

309

future of *Faillandia* which he'd heard from Leo that the former Government, if re-established, would be sure to keep out of the bookshops and paper stalls, because of its large sales under the Klotz regime despite the formal ban.

"It'll have to really go underground this time, and that means on the island."

The way she stressed 'underground' reminded Gideon of their visit to the old fort and how they had both had the same thought of a dungeon underneath.

"Do you remember how we both thought of John the Baptist on our visit to the friar?"

"It seemed an unlikely idea to come into both our heads at the same time, but now it looks like a shared premonition."

"Of what?"

"Of where we'll end up with our magazine."

"Isn't that taking rather extreme precautions? I thought you said the island had ancient rights of sanctuary or was it your father?"

"It won't stop the drastic measures the new Government — or the old one re-established with increased powers and vindictiveness — are going to take. Nording, in a broadcast, promised to hunt down the enemies of democracy. Which reminds me: Paul wants to see you."

"Why couldn't you have said sooner?"

She looked at him with such hurt in her eyes that he was bewildered.

"What's wrong, for Christ's sake?"

He was annoyed because she'd left it until he thought it was too late for a meeting that he attached special importance to, and, as well, at her reacting childishly to what he believed was a gentle remonstrance.

Pieta clenched her hands into fists and dug them into her eyes as if to quench tears. She let her head drop onto the tablecloth — to further hide her distress? — with her hair falling forward in untidy strands and veiling the whole little scene from him.

310

Gideon got up and with an arm under hers helped her rise from the table and led her from the restaurant into the foyer where they met Leo.

"Where are you two off to?"

Gideon hadn't thought beyond taking Pieta away from the curious glances of a couple of late-dining French tourists.

"Up to her room."

A pause as the misleading suggestion behind his answer dawned on him and, no doubt, Leo. There was no good him adding that he was accompanying her as far as the lift, but, to break the slight embarrassment he asked: "What about you?"

Leo was off to a warehouse near the harbour to clear a consignment of delicacies of some sort that he'd imported. Either the curfew had been lifted or Leo had a pass, Gideon didn't enquire, nor comment on the lateness of the hour for such a business appointment.

"Can you leave me out at Paul Weissmann's on the way?"

It wasn't strictly on his way to the harbour district if that was where Leo was really going. But if this meeting was providential or a strange coincidence, which came to the same — then Gideon thought he must avail of it.

The curfew had been put back to midnight, Leo explained, as they drove through streets which, though not deserted, were emptier than usual. There was then a silence between them until Leo remarked:

"Don't think I was . . . "

A pause, as evidently Leo rejected the words he had chosen after some thought.

"No," Gideon said to make it easier.

"You and Pieta have my blessing."

"Thanks."

If he had accompanied her to her room could the unthinkable have happened? It wasn't unthinkable if, because of Leo's remark, he was thinking about it. And, moreover, went on thinking about it, if in a somewhat general or academic manner.

"Am I really not delaying you so that you'll risk not getting back by midnight?"

Gideon stuck to his suspicion that Leo was spending the night with a woman in another part of the city. He and Kathy had discussed her father's apparent sexual continence and speculated as to which of his two daughters took after him. "If it's me, he's very discreet about it," she'd said.

Sarah opened the door of Paul's apartment to Gideon and struck him as taken aback at seeing him. But she brought him down the two or three steps and across the dark living room to a lit corner where she had left a picture book open on the couch. Only when they were seated, did she explain that she'd been expecting her father.

"What a let down when at last the bell rang and it wasn't him!"

Gideon spoke to the child from his heart, and she in turn responded openly.

"Yes, it was."

She composed herself sufficiently to show him the book she had been studying, so as to help keep her from worrying.

It had old-fashioned illustrations of what appeared to be biblical figures with captions and accompanying text in Hebrew.

"Mamma had it as a girl."

Sarah was turning the pages until Gideon, feeling that this wasn't helping him to grasp what the book was about, stopped her at a picture of a man and two women attired in what looked like costumes for a theatrical performance.

Sarah explained that the illustration was of Jacob and his wives: Leah and Rachel.

"It's one of my favourite stories, but I don't think I could tell you it just now."

He didn't say he knew it, but this he considered no deception because he wanted. when she was more composed, to hear it from her.

She was hurrying through the book at a rate geared to her own anxiety and impatience. Picture followed picture too rapidly for Gideon to do more than sketchily fit a face or figure to her identification. Jeremiah, Isaiah, Amos, Ezra, passed him by before he could put in a word to halt them.

"Just a minute, Sarah. These are all strangers to me, and I'd like to have them sorted out."

The child paused at the page she had reached.

"They are prophets."

She appeared for a moment or two to be considering if this was enough clarification, and then added: "prophets of the Lord."

"What about John the Baptist?"

Gideon enquired on a spontaneous impulse, such as he found came easily when talking to her.

She looked dismayed, and, without answering, started flicking through the pages from the beginning.

"Never mind," he told her, intent on slowing down the nervous tempo. At the same time he wondered whether another of the more-than-coincidences, with which the latter part of the evening had started, might not manifest itself, however unlikely in the context.

The rate at which the pages were being turned slowed down as the child seemed to realise that the name mentioned didn't belong to any of the patriarchs who had been the guardians of two generations of female Weissmanns.

When finally the bell rang, Gideon went to the door, sensing the child's reluctance to be faced with a second disappointment. Paul was in uniform, which confirmed Gideon's impression of the ambiguity of the political situation. After Sarah had gone happily to bed, Paul gave him more news than Leo had been able to.

Nording and Canavan had broadcast, though not from the Aphrin television station which had been off the air since the day before, a statement announcing the setting up of a provisional Government under their joint leadership, with the usual promise, as Paul put it, of elections when the country's main institutes and services were functioning normally.

"So it really is the end?" Gideon asked.

"Or the beginning, according to how you look at it."

"How *do* you look at it?"

"I've never been a believer in parliamentary democracy, not, that is, with the sort of politicians we get as the system operates here."

Not, Gideon thought, a particularly extreme or surprising remark in the circumstances, but he needed time to reflect on it. This Paul seemed to understand, as they looked at each other in a silence that was a mutual acknowledgement that something of vital importance to a lot of people, including both of them, was happening. Gideon had the idea — how it came into his head he didn't know — that it wasn't only the living it affected, because, as he put it to himself, the dead have their place in history.

'Their place in history'. He was musing on the phrase and giving it a new connotation, turning it into other phrases such as 'their history and their places', or 'the history they, and to a small degree, I too, have made of these various places'. To Gideon, certain spots were hallowed, all within this land: the hospital ward where he'd visited Pieta, the hospital grounds with the ancient olive tree where a battle had been fought, its cemetery, certain rooms in a city hotel, a house and yard in the country, another cemetery, an island and a ledge of rock.

Gideon knew that what the two of them — not even of the same race — had just experienced wasn't a sense of patriotism, nor, as far as he could define it, religion. It was, he thought, a clinging to the past in love, and also grief, and the hope of taking that love, and the grief too, with them into the future.

Did it really matter who was in Government? What was there to fear in the political events of the last days, or months? Was a new administration, or the old one re-constituted, going to raise any of the buildings, corners in which meant so much to him, or build new ones on what he saw as holy ground or disturb the graves, which even if that happened, couldn't erase the memories of loved ones?

Well, no.

Why did his heart sink at the thought of the return of Nording, Canavan and others, with loveless, mean minds, agitated by small greeds, and ambitions to retain the favour of the people who had chosen them, largely out of indifference or as, at best, a lesser evil?

Perhaps because there'd be an intensification, if only slight, of the stench that emanated from all places where power was publicly centred, and which could, on occasion, filter into his private haven.

Had he heard from Paul that Klotz stood a chance of being able to hang on, would his heart have risen? Could he have rejoiced at the triumph of Kathy's assassin, even though it had been by mistake?

## THIRTY FIVE

Paul accompanied Gideon out of the door of his apartment to where a lieutenant, a sergeant and a corporal, the latter two armed with automatic weapons, were strolling up and down the wide corridor.

After exchanging the officer's salute, Paul introduced Gideon as 'the distinguished journalist' who wished to interview Colonel Klotz. The lieutenant hesitated, but only, it appeared, about whether or not Gideon should be searched. When this was done rather perfunctorily by the corporal, Paul shook hands with Gideon, who was surprised by the ease and casualness of these events, and turned back to his own door while the lieutenant went with Gideon to that of Klotz and rang the bell. He then announced himself into a grilled mouthpiece that Gideon hadn't noticed on his previous visit. After a few moments, he heard a key turning and a bolt being drawn, and wondered whether what had been called house-arrest wasn't more like a retreat into a last shelter.

A young man, whose face Gideon recognised without at once being able to identify, opened the door and Gideon made his request. The blond youth held out his hand.

"Don't say you don't remember me, Mr. Spokane."

"For a second you took me by surprise."

They shook hands, Gideon still unable to place the other, while the lieutenant saluted and returned to his two men.

"You didn't expect to see me here, that's natural."

It was the young East German, Gerhard, whom Gideon had met at lunch on the yacht. Now, in a smart, pale civilian suit

316

and without the sunglasses that he'd worn on that occasion, it was his slight accent and rather red lips that recalled him to Gideon, who repeated his request to see Klotz, leaving out any mention of an interview.

Gerhard, whose other name if Gideon had ever heard he'd forgotten, indicated a door from the hall with a jerk of his head and a slight grimace that might have been a wink, had that not been so unlikely.

"He'll see you, don't worry, especially if he thinks you're an emissary from Captain Weissmann."

And so it was. Gideon was ushered into the room he remembered, where Klotz was at the same desk as on the day that Gideon, Paul and the British Ambassador had been present.

He greeted Gideon as a welcome visitor, indeed as if he had been waiting for him.

"You've come from Paul?"

"Yes."

"He couldn't get away?"

"Well . . . "

"What news? Excuse me, sit down, won't you?"

Gideon sought out and took the same chair he had sat on the last time, although there was another handier. His instinct, confronted with imponderables, was to grasp at whatever he saw even the slighest connection with. While he turned over the question that Klotz had put to him, the Colonel went on:

"Did he give you a message for me?"

"Nothing specific, Colonel."

Gideon, whose nervous system was on red alert — though the phrase wouldn't have appealed to him — wanted to avoid for as long as possible Klotz revising his first obvious welcome. He'd an idea that if the conversation could be sustained for the first few minutes without a hostile silence intervening, he might get through to Klotz as he had once or twice thought he'd been close to doing.

Now that the Colonel's reign was as good as over, Gideon thought he might win Klotz over to what he himself was just

317

beginning to understand: that failure, even a spectacular one, was necessary for any movement that was later to gain a historic importance.

It was an idea impossible for politicians to accept, and, indeed for a dictator either. But Gideon had come here, he only now clearly realised, with the faint hope of reversing this imperative. Then, if he — or rather, the friar and Pieta — were right, some surprising good would come of it.

He recalled an article that Pieta had asked him to print in *Faillandia*, though it wasn't signed and he didn't know who had written it. In a passage about the last days of Hitler in the bunker, the contributor had speculated about what would have happened if Hitler, in full consciousness of the calamity he had brought down on millions of people and on himself, (because at this mysterious level, the decisive events are personal) and accepting his utter humiliation, had bowed himself to the blood-soaked rubble and publicly proclaimed his guilt, like Raskolnikov in *Crime and Punishment*. He wouldn't have been 'saved' in a political or wordly sense, nor would the millions of his victims have been brought back to life, but Gideon believed, something would have happened to turn the blood-stained tide, and the peace that came to his part of the world would have been one nearer the hopes of the survivors.

Not that the victims of Klotz numbered millions nor, yet at least, even thousands, but among them was what had been for Gideon the one above all.

"What does that mean: 'nothing specific?' Has he the missiles ready to launch?"

"No, Colonel."

It had taken a little time for Gideon to understand that Klotz, like all such men who find themselves deprived of power and cornered, could not take the leap into the new reality. So, in their desperation, which they dare not acknowledge, they turn to hallucinations and conjure up phantom armies and machines of destruction to come to their aid.

Klotz's face was lowered as if he was reading, but there was nothing immediately on the desk in front of him. Nor were his heavy eyelids closed. Gideon had been asked — he was asking himself — how to describe the expression, and after hesitating, because of the evident incongruity, the word 'recollected' came to his mind. The last time Gideon recalled receiving a similar impression had been at Compline at the priory. Perhaps the very peaceful and the totally defeated have something in common.

"No, there aren't any."

Had Klotz really said this in a whisper as if to himself, or had Gideon, in the intensity of his wish, imagined it? Did he also only imagine the tensing of nerves at the back of his cranium and down the spine as an emanation of the other's anguish?

Klotz looked up and asked: "Do you mind what happens to *Faillandia*?"

For a moment Gideon resented the question as implying it was he, and not Klotz, who had been using the crisis for his own purposes, through the magazine. But then he recalled the times when his feeling had been ambiguous, when, in fact, he had seen Pieta's insistence on taking such an uncompromising line as unnecessarily inflexible.

"I don't think I ever felt very intensely about it while it was threatened from within. When I saw the warships in the bay, invited there by Nording, Canavan and the others, I understood for the first time the passion of the people who died before their executioners defiantly crying their love of their land."

"Who are you thinking of?"

Gideon, to his own surprise, could answer almost at once, mentioning names that had, it seemed, been stored away at the back of his mind.

"The writers and poets have been the ones who were most aware of what was happening to the place and the spirit of the people who meant most to them."

"You never get over Stalin and his purges, do you?"

"It isn't of his victims I'm thinking. There are plenty of

319

others to keep their memory alive, these days they have most of the publicity. It's others that I don't want to forget, like the young Breton poet, Robert Brassilach, shot by the French at Fort Valerien in 1944, crying, 'Vive la France', Boris Wildé and Benjamin Fondane, French poets executed by the Germans a few years earlier. There was the Irish poet Patrick Pearse shot by the British in Dublin in 1916, and the Japanese novelist Yukio Mishima, who committed ritual suicide in Tokyo in 1970 out of despair at what he saw as his country's degradation."

"Is there a writer here who will go to his death shouting 'Vive Failland!'? Aren't they a timid lot of bastards?"

"There are some who weren't too timid to contributing to the magazine after you'd banned it."

Klotz got up and, going over to one of the tall windows, drew back the curtains. Then, stooping, he wound the lever that raised the steel shutters and Gideon saw that the park outside was floodlit.

He stood looking out with his back to Gideon, who was thinking: he has only to open the window and step onto the lawn into the path of the bullets from the sentry-posts behind the bushes, and they'd be no time for any cry of defiance.

The door that led to the rest of the apartment opened and Nolla entered the study. She looked at once toward the window, having, Gideon surmised, heard the sound of the blind being wound up.

She went over and, without a word, let it down and pulled the curtains across, then turned to Klotz and spoke in what couldn't have been quite a whisper because Gideon just caught a couple of the words, and from them guessed that she'd said: "You'll keep your promise."

It sounded to Gideon more like a reminder than a question and he didn't interpret it as referring only to Klotz, but to an agreement in which she would share.

Gideon was surprised at how much smaller she was than he remembered. She was hardly taller than Sarah Weissmann and when he took her hand in greeting it was like a child's.

320

"How was your weekend in Paris?"

"I was staying out in a suburb."

"But you saw something of the Gare du Nord."

So she was still in touch with the network of agents that Klotz had set up, one of whom had kept track of Paul's drive through the city in the car in which he and Kathy had been passengers. Perhaps she had a record of his talks with Pieta, still having a tap on the Hotel Aphra telephones.

But why inform him like this of what she'd found out, and in a tone and with a glance from her dark eyes that seemed larger than ever in her narrow face, which far from being hostile, struck him as trying to convey to him, now that it was too late, an acknowledgement that he, Gideon, and perhaps Pieta was included too, was the lucky one after all. Of course Gideon realised how much he was weaving into her words, but they had been unnecessary ones if she hadn't wanted to tell him something about herself and also about how she saw him. No, 'lucky' wasn't quite the word. Instead, he thought of 'blessed' or 'chosen'.

She had listened in to him and Pieta and, in what surely must have been a very painful bit of self-revelation, had a glimpse of a world from which she was forever shut out.

"That's right. The best moments were at the Gare du Nord."

Let her ponder that. If he was right in his supposition — and as regards this girl nothing was too fantastic to be impossible — then she'd know that he had understood her and was confirming all that she had grasped.

"Shall I make coffee?"

Though neither the Colonel nor Gideon answered, each supposing perhaps that the question had been addressed to the other, Nolla left the room.

Klotz, again seated at his desk, said: "Speaking of victims" (had they been? Gideon wondered), "you don't know what that girl went through when she was a Government typist."

"Which Government?"

Not that it mattered to Gideon. His thoughts were elsewhere, somewhere between the Gare du Nord, Paris, the elevator at the Hotel Aphra, and the imagined kitchen where Nolla was brewing coffee.

"Canavan made her have an abortion just when his party had introduced the Adultery Referendum."

"That's a long time ago."

Gideon was only half-following and as he spoke he realised that on the seasonal time scale it was no more than from spring to autumn, or on the biological hardly long enough for the foetus to have been born.

"Wasn't he one of the early backers of your magazine?"

This struck Gideon as now irrelevant. It depressed him that at this moment of truth Klotz could still be concerned with these old rivalries.

"That's all old history, Colonel."

"You could publish it in your magazine which, as long as it's banned, couldn't be prosecuted."

Did he really, at this late date, misunderstand the whole tone and purpose of *Faillandia*, Gideon asked himself. Did he see it as some sort of gutter publication out to ruin the reputations of its opponents? He said nothing.

"I was joking. But what you might do is to print a short address by me to the citizens of Aphrin. I was going to give it to Paul for you, but you can take it now to submit to your editorial board."

Klotz took a couple of sheets of typescript from the desk and handed them to Gideon as Nolla returned with the coffee things.

"I'll make the decision myself."

Gideon was a little surprised at himself for saying this. Was it that he enjoyed the feeling of being the decision-taker and Klotz for once the supplicant? If so, wasn't that, in its own way, as petty an attitude as the Colonel's in relation to Canavan?

Assenting to Nolla's offer of coffee had been a mistake. It kept Gideon there after what he'd come to say or hear. Klotz became silent and was evidently waiting for him to go. He drained his cup in a hurry and stood up.

Klotz rose from behind his desk and said, without holding out his hand:

"We've this in common, Spokane, all that we worked and hoped for has collapsed."

Nolla accompanied him into the hallway where, catching his sleeve in a gesture like a child's or an importunate beggar's, made the appeal that Gideon sensed had been at the back of her mind when she'd confessed to having listened in to his phone talks to Pieta.

"You'll find it hard to believe, Gideon, but I know what it is to have a relationship that means more than anything in the rest of the world."

"Why shouldn't I believe you?"

"You despise me. And now even more for eavesdropping on you and Pieta. But I didn't do it to make any use of what I might have heard. All that is over. I did it on an impulse to hear what two people who had the kind of relation I once thought I had and that still haunts me, say to each other."

Not 'on an impulse', on several impulses, Gideon thought to himself. Should he correct her about Pieta and him, and remind her that his only love had been murdered by Klotz, possibly with her help and connivance? But all he said, recalling his initial shock at her appearance: "You too Nolla have been through a lot in the last few days."

"When he was training guerillas in Israel he went for a secretary and I got the job as a Jewess whose parents had settled there after their flight from Germany before the war."

A fellow countrywoman of Paul's! Below the very dissimilar surface Gideon thought there were traces of this passion that still smouldered on in members of the race long after it had first lit a narrow strip of land at the other end of the Mediterranean.

"When he had a short leave, not long enough for him to spend it back here, he took me with him to Eilat on the Red

323

Sea. It was the off-season and the big hotel was half empty. There were wide corridors, perhaps for better ventilation, though there was air-conditioning in the rooms, and the place, besides feeling deserted, was rather dark because of the window shades."

What was this? A tourist guide to the hotels in the State of Israel's most fashionable resort? But Gideon listened attentively, aware that if the girl wanted to convince him of her having fallen in love with Klotz, she had to evoke the setting. He knew, none better, that the atmosphere of the place was fixed forever in the mind by the intensity of the psychological experience that had happened there.

"Lev spent a lot of time learning Hebrew and seldom went to the beach."

"Lev?"

"That's what I call him when we're alone."

It surprised Gideon to realise he had never heard Klotz's first name. Just as members of royalty only used their christian names, there were leaders, among them some of the most famous, who were known by their patronymics.

"Short for what?"

Now that, unexpectedly, he was hearing intimate details about Klotz, Gideon thought he might as well get this clear too.

"Leo."

Hardly longer, but Gideon asked her to go on.

"When I came in out of the sun and walked to our room along the empty, dark corridor in my beach robe, I was a priestess on my way through the temple to the inner shrine."

The girl knew what she was talking about. But she mustn't leave it at that.

"Go on, Nolla."

"He'd be sitting at the window with his back to the door when I opened it, and I knew wouldn't at once look round. I stood there watching him close his books and tidy his papers while I slipped off my robe. There was nothing I wouldn't have given him or done for him, Gideon."

"Is that still so?"

"Yes."

"What can *I* do for him?"

She had not, Gideon knew, confided in him for nothing.

"Put the piece he gave you into the magazine."

"You know, it surprised me that he wrote it."

"With my help."

"I see."

"And you could ask Captain Weissmann about the possibility of flying him to Israel where he could get his old job back. I've already discussed it with Paul."

"But not with Klotz?"

"No."

"And you'd go with him?"

She looked at Gideon without answering, and he saw in her eyes that she didn't believe in the realisation of this dream.

## THIRTY SIX

When Gideon went next morning to Pieta's room she wasn't there. He hurried down to the reception desk but instead of the note he expected, the clerk told him that she and the boss (Leo) had left early with a lot of luggage (the presses and printing papers?). He said this casually as if Gideon knew where they'd gone and Gideon didn't let him suppose otherwise. Indeed, it could only be to the yacht en route for the island.

Gideon's first reaction was panic. Either because she thought he'd abandoned her last night in his hurry to go to Paul, or because of something he'd said to upset her earlier at dinner, or more likely, because she had at last seen through him for the broken reed he was, she'd persuaded Leo that it would be best if *Faillandia*, in its new hiding place, was carried on without him.

For a few moments Gideon was convinced that he had lost all that remained to him: Pieta, the magazine, and Leo's friendship.

This is what it is to be completely bereft, he told himself, something he hadn't experienced in its totality even at Kathy's death. This is what Klotz's state of mind was when I told him I had no message from Paul. And also Nolla's as I left the apartment.

Although it now seemed purposeless, for he really believed he'd been ditched as editor in his peremptory manner — Gideon wasn't so much nervously pessimistic by nature as incapable of judging dispassionately when it came to what concerned him deeply — he read the contribution from Klotz.

He thought he could detect the parts dictated by the Colonel and the substitutions or revisions made by Nolla.

The piece was neither as origianal nor as inspiring as Gideon hoped but he supposed he had always tended to overrate Klotz.

*'In ancient times outstanding individuals had dominated the world, there were giants of men who as conquerors, emperors, philosophers and poets, made early history. It was an heroic time in which in some communities the common people shared. But there were the others with their own non-vision, who resented anybody rising above their common level. Out of this negativity came the cult of the mediocre and a clinging to the norm, and fear of anything that hadn't the familiar about it and which couldn't be identified with ordinary people's lowest instincts.*

*When those with these credentials had been chosen by popular vote, they formed themselves into political parties, drawing the assurance from their numbers that they lacked as individuals.*

*This system was fortified by most of the media which gave excessive coverage to the most trivial and dishonest debates in the national assemblies, thus confirming the seriousness with which the parties and their leaders took themselves.*

*One way to reform the present system of government was to abolish political parties and elect administrators on their individual qualities and without any label, which is in itself a demeaning way of identifying a human being.*

*Another was revolution, for which was needed a person of vision with great resolution, who need not initially win over the populace, provided he took control of the armed forces. However, in countries where the people had been brain-washed into believing they were free to select who they were governed by — whereas, of course, once in power the politicians operated the system to suit themselves — it might be necessary for the revolutionaries to campaign first through the media, especially by diminishing the space given to the debates and speeches of the politicians, and substituting a build-up of sport with photos of sportsmen and naked girls, as was already happening in certain communities.*

*But against this there was the danger* (Gideon saw Nolla's hand here) *that a preoccupation with football pools, a constant reminder of the joys of sex (illustrated), and other like features, could produce a politically indifferent society.'*

Gideon was interrupted by Pieta — he hadn't heard her enter the room — announcing:

"Daddy and the printers have gone to the island and we'll join them later."

To be rescued from total rejection and loss — as he'd imagined it — into the very heart of the fold in this casual way was too much. It should have been heralded, preceded by at least a brief ceremony of re-instalment.

With an effort he managed not to ask questions that would have given him away and appraised her of his fatal weakness of flying to extreme conclusions on the flimsiest evidence.

Instead, probably overdoing the matter-of-factness, he asked her to sit down and have a look through the typed sheets on the table he'd drawn up to the bed.

"And I've two more contributions for us to consider," Pieta said, taking the folded typescript from her bag and smoothing out the sheets beside those already there.

So there we are together, Gideon reflected, and it's not a dream, sitting side by side on the edge of the bed, our heads bent over essays and articles dealing with matters that have nothing at all to do with the thoughts in our hearts, or, anyhow, in my head, or with the beating of my heart.

"What's this, Dove?"

The same words that he'd come out with, or had managed not to, a moment ago, but now in relation to the uppermost page on the pile.

It was a piece sent by Hymna from England with a note which said that it was written by a young friend of hers and that she hoped they would think it as original and remarkable as she did.

Gideon quickly leafed through it to get the drift.

It took two writers: the Irish James Joyce and the French Jean Genet and, in contrasting them, appeared to arrive at an important philosophical and literary conclusion which Gideon saw he would have to go back to the beginning and read through to grasp.

He made a start and was soon aware that what was being contrasted were the sexual attitudes of the two writers, and that, to do so, Hymna's friend was quoting passages from each which Gideon surmised had been written initially for the purpose of self-excitation.

Genet had indulged his pornographic fantasies in his cell at Frèsnes prison as other inmates would have contented themselves with scribbling graffiti on the walls. As for Joyce, his sexuality took expression in a rather adolescent curiosity about women and both their sexual and excremental functioning.

Although Pieta had already read the piece, she now went through it again with Gideon, sentence by shocking sentence of Molly Bloom's soliloquy, and the outrageous descriptions of the couplings of transvestites with names such as 'Divine', 'Darling' and 'Our Lady' in Genet's explicit evocations.

Did she know what she was doing? Or had she already decided — since they talked on the telephone — that it was something best left to providence? That is, if he hadn't completely misunderstood her.

She was his citadel and castle in which he was constantly discovering new wonders, but there was the one door that remained locked, and whenever he came to it he felt, as in the old fairytale, that this was not truly his home as long as it was closed on him.

Gideon was in a state of nervous tension for which he was ready to blame Pieta (there was nothing for which to blame himself because he was reacting in a perfectly normal and healthy manner, as anybody he cared to ask would agree). Was she really so oblivious as to think they could sit like this with their heads bent, reading together scenes from Genet of sexual perversions and Molly Bloom's sexy monologue, her hair brushing his cheek, as they compared the explicit evocations? He was about to exclaim: 'A pity there aren't illustrations,' but didn't, because he had still a precarious inner foothold from where the view was different, from where he could still believe in their established relationship as precious and unique. What also strengthened his resolve was the surprising little lecture, as he recalled it, she'd given them on marriage that evening in the restaurant, which showed she was no immature virgin, knowing nothing of sexual passions.

"Dove."

"What?"

"Should we not take a break?"

"But we've only just started."

"It raises questions."

"That's why I thought we should go through it together."

With heads lowered they continued, and Gideon, though his thoughts were hard to focus on the essay, soon grasped the main theme.

Joyce's sexual fantasies were those accompanying masturbation, and they intensify the isolation that characterises his loveless masterpiece, and which he himself evidently experienced. Genet records, for the most part, passionate responses, usually his own, of one partner to the other, no matter how degraded or perverse their characters.

Joyce's sexual acts take place in the private world of people who in their social life conform to the conventions. Genet's take place between impassioned, violent or debased couples, who live their lives in an underworld of their own, whose values contradict all the most cherished social ones.

"Yes, Pieta, it fits in to *Faillandia*'s general field of enquiry."

Would it be possible, he was thinking in a flight of sexual fantasy that struck him as, in its own way, rivalling Genet's, that Friar Emanuel would perform a kind of mini-marriage ceremony over Pieta and him which would give a blessing to a single act of sex between them.

Not that Gideon didn't keep in a far corner of his mind whose cells were isolated and not — as he imagined it — directly connected to the main nervous system, a narrow, neutral strip or no-man's land, from where to cast a cool, reflective look at his most impassioned feelings.

This helped him now in getting the situation into a perspective in which he saw that these pornographic passages pored over with other women besides Pieta — Hymna, say, or Marthe (or Nolla, but he didn't want to think of her), would have a similar effect on him. Which proved that he already knew: that he was capable of an automatic sexual response as well as the one he had had to Kathy.

Pieta had another surprise: three typescript pages submitted by Provisional Assembly Chairman Nording's secretary, as she called herself, which contained an announcement, or pronouncement, of the new regime's aims and policies. In the accompanying note the secretary as good as promised that if this was printed in the next issue the ban imposed by the former dictatorship would be lifted.

Gideon read it through, and nothing could have been a more effective antidote to his heightened sexual instincts.

For a moment he thought that he had already read it, though he could not recall where. It was written in the familiar jargon he'd grown accustomed to before the 'revolution', a vague background irritant to those normal days.

Nording re-iterated his adherence to the principles of democracy, promising the 'liberated people' a freedom of choice through the ballot box — between himself and Lucius Canavan? — within three months.

He announced that nobody who might have supported the 'nation's enemies' would be prosecuted, provided they dissociated themselves from any continuing criminal conspiracy.

There was to be a thanksgiving Mass in the Cathedral, celebrated by Archbishop Tolling, at which the members of the Provisional Government and those of the Diplomatic Corps would hear a Te Deum sung by . . .

Gideon gave the typescript back to Pieta.

"Well?" she asked.

He was weary, and overcome by a sense of let-down for which he was ready to blame Pieta.

"Do what you like about it."

He guessed that till now she'd been too absorbed in their joint editorial responsibilities to think of how he was taking it. Now she took his hand in hers and he grasped it as might a drowning man.

"We'll soon be out of their reach."

He tightened his hold on her hand as his response, without quite knowing what she referred to, or whether it was not just the coming trip to the island.

There was, after all, no need for his previous panic at the violence of his desire, because with a touch she could calm it. Knowing this was perhaps why she had no misgivings about their going through the article together. Not that the Nording address hadn't acted like a cold shower.

It seemed no further measures would be taken against *Faillandia* until the new authorities saw whether the next issue carried the official proclamation, and so Gideon and Pieta had plenty of time to complete the move to the island.

For him the next few days were strangely relaxed, with a lightness of heart that surprised him, that he felt not just subjectively, but out in the streets.

Pieta gave up her job on the elevator and, as they'd sent the layout of the magazine to the island and heard by phone from Leo that it would appear on time in the coming week, he felt they were on one of those brief holidays such as he'd seen advertised as mid-week breaks.

Life in the city was back to normal — at the realisation of which he felt a pang of grief — with the traffic flowing around the Commemorative Arch of Fael at one end of Aphra Avenue, each vehicle evidently on a journey of vital importance to a destination that must be reached at the exact hour in order to operate this complex schedule of coming and going.

They visited the hospital to which they took several cases of the review copies of books that had accumulated in the offices of the magazine. They walked through the grounds, stopping under the tree that was always full of birds, and entered the cemetery through the door in the wall where they visited the graves of Kathy, Professor Ellis and Judith Weissmann. There was a fresh grave being dug beyond the small ruin at the centre of the plot.

When they got back to the hotel, Paul was waiting for them with the news that he had received an official report that Colonel Klotz and his mistress, who wasn't named, had been shot during the night while trying to escape from his apartment where he was under arrest.

"I wasn't at home, but Sarah heard the shots and, just before them, a shout that might have come from one of the guards in the park."

"Or from Klotz," Gideon suggested.

"He'd have hardly drawn attention to himself if he was really trying to escape. What makes me doubt the official account is that I had told him yesterday of the arrangements I'd made to fly him and Nolla to Israel, to which the commander out at the airfield had agreed."

"Didn't she make out a word?"

"A word? No, I don't think so. In any case, what must have happened was that they went in and shot him at his desk and Nolla in her bed."

Gideon imagined a different scenario. He saw Klotz raise the steel blind, as he had the night he'd been there, open the French-type window and, with an arm around Nolla, step out onto the floodlit lawn with a cry of 'Vive Failland!'

"Will you and Sarah go home?"

"Home?"

Paul was out of touch with Gideon this morning.

"To Israel."

"I wouldn't fit in with the present lot there and Sarah would soon be disillusioned."

"What about the present lot *here*?"

"I'll go back to the airforce, which never was a hundred per cent pro-Klotz, although he didn't realise it."

Gideon wondered how Paul could serve again in the airforce after believing, for some months, that he was helping to bring about a new kind of community. But he didn't put the question.

He thought of asking about the missiles that Klotz had apparently been relying on as a last hope, but decided to put no more questions. He wanted to let Klotz be, an unimaginative, vindictive power-seeker like the others, and yet, though it distressed him to have to realise it, with a place in his heart.

## THIRTY SEVEN

"Before there's time for the briefest preparation, with not a second to turn and look death in the face . . . Nolla in her bed . . . "

Pieta mused aloud. Gideon guessed that the words were only the articulated end of a train of thought leading back to Kathy's violent death.

"She didn't die in her bed."

"How do you know?"

Gideon didn't want to relate the story of his visit to Klotz, the incident at the window and his talk with the girl.

"Klotz and Nolla looked death in the face, as you call it, on the flood-lit lawn outside their office."

"Ah . . . "

Pieta uttered an exclamation as though, he thought, she experienced the impact of the bullets into her own breast.

"Neither were the kind to die in their beds; they had that in common, just as the politicians and their wedded wives have self-preservation in common and die nowhere else, except a few, at a time of revolt, hiding under them."

But Gideon told himself it was time to say farewell, not only to Klotz, but to the rancour in his heart against these others too. The great good of failure was that it made him come to a state of truce with the world and of peace with himself.

Paul saw them off at the harbour and they landed at Dominicus on an autumn morning, a place which he had once thought of as an isolated monastic settlement.

This time he had no such impression. There were cars on the island, one of which, with Josephus the porter from the Aphra driving, met them and took them the mile or two to a small hotel.

On the way across by one of the ferries, Pieta had told him that her father had renovated an old hostelry and opened it to tourists a few years previously, and was now taking over the management and bringing with him some of the staff from the Aphra.

"Such a lot has been going on that I'd no idea of!"

"I did mention it, Gideon, in one of our phone talks, but you'd other things to think of."

"Yes, what a state I was in!"

Of late he had been in a turmoil, carried away by all sorts of frantic fears and longings. Ever since — if he wasn't still fantasising — he had gripped Pieta's hand, he felt he was on his way to grasping, however much it went against the grain, the necessity of all that had happened.

Leo welcomed them at his new hotel, which initially struck Gideon as a mini Aphra, though that may have been because he was carrying with him so haunting an image of the latter, and later he wasn't aware of much similarity.

If anything, in even higher spirits than usual, Leo showed them their rooms which, Gideon noted, without coming to any conclusion about his father-in-law's intention, were next door but one.

"There's a gentleman in no. 20 who keeps early hours, not that there's anything wrong with the sound-proofing, and the Kemps are on the top floor."

More information for Gideon to take in and interpret; even though it mightn't seem of much importance, he was now alert to all the new details, 20 was presumably the intervening room, although he hadn't looked at the numbers, and why the mention of 'early hours'? Surely not to suggest to him and Pieta that they moderate their late revels? Or was it one of Leo's subtle jokes, which, very often nobody else could share? And the Kemps? Their presence did not really concern him, but Leo seemed to be apologising for it.

Pieta stayed in her room to unpack and, though Gideon would have preferred to remain in his and a little later have joined her. Leo brought him to the bar and gave him a short history of the island.

"Once part of Failland, after the rebellion that led to in-dependence, the island of Dominicus became independent, or if you like, continued under its own charter, guaranteed among others, by the U.K."

Gideon hadn't known, although come to that, neither had he thought much about it. As for the 'if you like', he didn't see what his liking had to do with it.

"Quite so."

This remark could be taken as indicating that none of this was news to him, without actually his claiming to be well-informed historically.

"What I bet you didn't know is that even today there are a number of families living here on the island with dual pass-ports: Faillandian and British."

Gideon said nothing, not because he'd any thought of giving an impression of being taken aback at what in fact was, as far as he could see, of little importance, but because he wanted to shorten the conversation and return upstairs.

"Which is why," Leo went on "the previous Government never envisaged extending the Anti-Adultery Referendum here, and also why the present lot will think a long time before violating the ancient charter."

This did make an impact on Gideon.

"We're under U.N. protection?"

"I wouldn't say that."

Gideon waited patiently to hear what he *would* say.

"No?"

"There are marines on the foreign warships in the bay, you know. Which is where you come in, old soldier."

This mode of address Gideon had taken for an expression of

337

affection, mixed possibly, with a touch of irony, as when Gauguin had called van Gogh *'Brigardier'*. But its use in this context was something else.

Was his father-in-law predicting possible hostilities in which he, Gideon, might play a part? Hardly. He determined not to let the tranquil acceptance of, and detachment from, outward events, with which he had arrived here, be so soon dispelled.

"It was the Prior who suggested that I ask you to go to London to put our case to Robert Cusack."

About the last person of whom Gideon expected to hear again.

"The U.K. Ambassador?"

"Ex-Ambassador. He was recalled to London."

Leo had always been abreast of the inside news, political and social, which, Gideon supposed, he garnered from some of those who stayed or dined and drank at his hotel.

Gideon had a second question that was the important one.

"How can I be the best person to put our cause, when I'm by no means sure what it is?"

"We can safely let Prior Celestine be a judge of that, old son. He has been a faithful reader of your magazine from the first, and has made up his mind that its editor is the right intermediary."

"I'll have to ask Pieta."

"You can take her with you."

"That's not what I meant."

Did his father-in-law think they were inseparable?

"It seems that Cusack has been appointed Counsellor at the U.K. Foreign Office — I'm not sure if I've got the official title right — and has considerable influence with the British Government."

"That's the first bit of hopeful news, domestic or international, that I've heard for a long time."

"You never struck me, old son, as having what they call your ear to the ground."

It was now 'old son' and not 'old soldier', which Gideon took as a sign that he was fully back in his father-in-law's favour. Leo's sudden departure the other day without a word to him had left a doubt in Gideon's mind that hadn't been quite cleared up at the time of his reunion with Pieta.

"Which is why I'm doubtful about getting involved."

"According to the Prior, and as far as this island goes, he's the *de facto* arbiter, the case to be put is not basically political. He believes that politics and ideologies will soon no longer be what determines the lifestyle of communities."

"With the help of the magazine?"

"What is going to take their place?" Gideon enquired eagerly. This was the first time he felt concerned in the conversation.

"You'll have to ask the Prior. But I've an idea that it's a subject on which you've your own ideas."

"Maybe, but what will Councillor Cusack think of them?"

"From the talk I had with him on the phone, they will be of great interest to him."

"What Prior Celestine hopes for is an understanding with the British in which they could re-affirm their interest in the independence of the island?"

"You've put it beautifully, old son."

At lunch in the hotel at which Leo didn't join them, whether out of his own sense of tact or because he was kept busy overseeing the preparations and serving of the various dishes, he told Pieta about the proposal.

Whether she would reject it off-hand, welcome it, or want to talk it over, Gideon realised that, despite their closeness, he couldn't guess.

"It comes from Prior Celestine."

"So your father said."

Then, instead of saying anything further, she immersed herself in a study of the menu, and after a few moments announced: "It's the old Aphra one, almost dish for dish."

She smiled happily as if this pleased, or consoled, her and relegated the subject that he had just broached to a place further down the agenda.

Pieta asked for baked sardines, which Gideon recalled seeing on her plate in another restaurant when they were having a vital discussion. He remembered how the small fish with their bronzed, shrivelled skins — not at all scaly — had impressed their image on the back of the mind — like the icon beneath which a supplicant prays without consciously seeing, but afterwards remembers for the rest of his life — as he had hung on her words.

Gideon was content to let her take her time, and meanwhile ordered a bottle of local white wine to go with the fish, though he himself changed his choice to *'Galantine de Canard'*, an island speciality, according to the menu.

"We'll consult Frère Emanuel," Pieta said at last.

He might have known this would be her first reaction, and not any of the ones he'd imagined. Not that he supposed the old monk would take it on himself to advise them on a matter of international policies.

After lunch they walked across the island to the ancient fortress-like building, through some of the vineyards belonging to the priory where, Pieta told him, she and Kathy, before her expulsion from the convent, used, with some of the bolder girls, to come to gather themselves baskets of grapes.

They had been here, the two girls who, in their different ways, had revealed to him what living was about at the time when he had been incapable of making anything of it. When, indeed, he had been failing the two people closest to him, here on this island two others, who were the cause of what he hoped was his redemption, were lightheartedly raiding the vineyards.

Gideon entwined his fingers in hers and they continued to the shore where they were separated by fifty meters or so of sea from what Gideon now saw as the friar's hermitage.

"I once waded across and the water only came up to here," she touched her midriff, "and I was smaller then, but I suppose the tide was out."

It certainly looked deeper than that now to Gideon. What had she once told him about walking on the water? Had that been a later dream or fantasy inspired by a childhood one in which the figure of Christ had been substituted for that of Frère Emanuel for whom the girl must have waited at the edge of the waves until she could bear it no longer?

But what right had he to try to rationalise an experience of hers because it was beyond him?

They sat down to wait on the deep litter of dessicated seaweed between the rocks. And Gideon became aware that this largely silent wait at the shore wasn't an accidental inconvenience due to the old monk's having no means of being hailed, but an hour or so in which to come to himself in a tranquillity in which what he had to say to Cusack was being given him, although he wouldn't be conscious of the actual words till the time came.

Then when Gideon was wondering whether the failure to contact the monk wasn't a sign that they should come to their own decision, there he was in his boat rowing towards them.

"I expected you, Kinder. Indeed, I was waiting for you," was his greeting.

Gideon, who thought it was surely *they* who had done the waiting, smiled and received a firm shake of the old but, he knew, very capable hand.

"We've come to ask for your help and advice," Pieta said.

"But not to do with a sick pigeon this time?"

The talk lapsed while they stepped from the small boat onto the steps roughly hewn in the rock, and climbed the stone stairs to the big bare room called the refectory. Only then Pieta said: "You know, Frère Emanuel, the fledgeling wasn't a pigeon."

"I'm not an ornithologist, Pieta. In my hands I felt its heart beat with the same love of life as us all."

They sat on a bench on one side of the long wooden table on which there was an aquarium that Gideon at first took to be a tank in which the monk kept his catch but, on looking closer, saw it contained various kinds of marine life, hardly any of which appeared edible. There were also several piles of books, suggesting that it was here, rather than in the library, that the friar did his reading. Beyond the glass tank, at the far end of the table, a plate, mug, knife and fork, were neatly placed.

"Did you hear that a new administration has taken over on the mainland?" Pieta said.

"News bulletins don't fall onto this table, and when I'm not fishing I'm looking through books where the news is centuries old."

"But you go to the Priory."

"For the Holy Offices, yes. But I don't meet any news-vendors on the way."

Gideon had not expected Pieta to speak so casually to the old recluse, with an affectionate familiarity, nor his half-teasing answers. For his part he could not address the old monk except formally.

"You know, Reverend Brother, that Prior Celestine thinks the independence of the island is threatened," Gideon ventured to tell him.

Frère Emanuel didn't answer immediately, and Gideon regretted not having left the conversation to Pieta. But then, just when he was, rather desperately, going to put the question in another form, the monk exclaimed: "A lot of my lobster pots are empty these mornings."

Gideon thought best to refrain from any comment, but Pieta enquired:

"Why is that?"

"Because of the toxic discharge from the foreign ships in the bay."

So news reached him after all, Gideon reflected, in a more direct, if submarine, way.

"They've some diabolical machines with them," Frère Emanuel added as an afterthought."

"And marines on board, as well."

"Is that what you've come about, besides bringing me your

bright blessing?"

"Yes. The Prior thinks Gideon should go to London to persuade an influential official there called Cusack, whom he knows from when he was here as a diplomat, to get his government to intervene."

"A rather distinguished-looking gentleman."

"You know him?" Pieta asked, without apparent surprise.

"I saw him when he visited his brother, Père Ignatius Cusack, our Master of Novices. Kindly give him my sincere good wishes."

Gideon, none of whose suppositions were proving correct, was now perhaps over-reluctant to come to conclusions. But Pieta immediately grasped that this was the friar's way of intimating his approval of the mission.

"You've cleared up our doubts."

"Doubts? After all, it comes back to your sick dove, or whatever it was, that, like the rest of us, wanted so much to survive."

"And shall we? What do you think, dear Frère Emanuel?"

The old monk turned over an hour-glass that Gideon hadn't noticed among the other objects on the long table.

"On the other hand," he said, pointing to some tiny flat ovaloid marine creatures at the bottom of the tank . . .

In his anxiety to follow the trend of the friar's thought that seemed to switch from one conceptual level to another, Gideon tried to determine from what former statement the 'on the other hand' introduced an alternative.

" . . . these I've come to believe are descended from the trilobites by a line that goes back through a series of submarine events, some of them astonishing upheavals, for five or six hundred million years, and have nothing to fear whatever happens."

"What about a nuclear war?"

"I've some brachiopod fossils, slightly older, I'd show you only I took them to the priory to help the novices meditate on

343

time and its measurement. Father Ignatius has them regulate their hours of study by one of these," he indicated the hour-glass "and I too have been refreshing my perceptions by such contrasts in simple temporal comparisons."

Gideon thought he began to grasp the principle behind the old monk's discursive method. He did not concentrate exclusively on one subject, especially an urgent one, but surrounded it with other completely unrelated ones — such as the hour-glass and the fossils — steeped it, so to speak, in solvents which might cause it to vanish or could reveal something about it which was hidden from a direct approach.

"What surprises me is that you know the difference between the tiniest molluscs which look all the same to me, and yet can't tell a thrush from a pigeon."

"We each have our element. I'm not an aerial being like you, dearest child. She floats at times, doesn't she?" Frère Emanuel turned to Gideon.

This unexpected turn in the talk was something that Gideon was unprepared for, being in the process of what he thought was elucidating some of the workings of the old monk's mind.

"Flies, as the dove," he said, looking at Pieta and seeing her in what he thought was all her loveliness, to which Frère Emanuel had just drawn his attention.

The monk shifted his glance from the hour-glass — what on earth was he timing? Gideon, who'd lost the thread of his earlier remarks, wondered — and looked from one to the other of his visitors. And although he bore the signs of extreme age, the skin deeply wrinkled across the forehead, stained and baggy under the eyes, pleated at the throat, his expressions at that moment struck Gideon as one of compassion, even of love, such as he had seen long ago on Lydia's as she'd stooped over the dying infant.

"Take your dove with you," the monk told him.

## THIRTY EIGHT

As there were still two or three days left before the appearance of the magazine without the Government pronouncement, they could fly to London from Aphrin without fear of arrest.

Pieta had never before been in the great city where they arrived in the evening, and was astonished at the mass exodus of the citizens which was of a magnitude beyond that of the rush-hours in Aphrin. This reminded Gideon, in a circuitous way, of what he'd been intending to ask her since the day before, as to why the old monk had let the sand run in his hourglass.

"When the light through the seaward window reaches a certain stone in the opposite wall, he starts his evening vigil, summer and winter."

"Weren't we interrupting it?"

"I don't think so. He withdraws his attention from outward or worldly matters, but that doesn't mean that he excludes visitors if he happens to have any, which is very seldom."

"The conversation went on."

"But didn't you notice the change in it, Gideon?"

"He started to talk about you."

"And took that strange look at us."

"What did it mean, darling?"

He thought he could use this endearment, as he dare not have before, in the light of that same look.

"He must have looked at the ailing bird like that before he let it out of his hands at the window of your flat."

Gideon had been too distracted, even sceptical, to notice

such subtle signs, but he believed Pieta. He was even ready to imagine they had flown out of his hands fully briefed on this mission that a few days earlier he would have seen as futile.

When Gideon telephoned Robert Cusack, he asked them to lunch at his South Kensington flat. Most of the leaves had fallen from the trees in the square as they walked from the bus stop, and Gideon was very conscious of the late autumn atmosphere of a London day with its special scents, sounds and shadows, that vividly recalled his time there with Kathy. They had gone a little out of their way for him to show Pieta the Geological Museum where he had worked and brought her up to the gallery where her sister had sometimes visited him and the bench near the cases of precious stones where, on night shift, he and Frank had discussed the situation in Failland.

Pieta lingered at a showcase in which was exhibited a fossilised section of mud excavated from the Thames estuary, on which were small indentations made by raindrops that had fallen, the notice said, during the pre-Cambrian era.

Gideon waited while she took her time at the exhibit. With the coming interview on his mind, he was impatient. Then he recalled what he'd observed of the old monk's way of dealing with important issues by placing them in a larger perspective.

He didn't think that Pieta had learnt how to do this from Frère Emanuel, or that he could so easily explain her delaying at this showcase. He had noted yesterday that, although he had been her spiritual guide and confessor, the young woman and the old monk were now on the same footing, each treating the other with affection as an equal.

"Come along, Pieta darling, we'll be late."

She turned and followed him out into Queensway, and Gideon was back in the present from a brief reminder of what it had been like to be strolling between the glass cases on a summer afternoon with the prospect of the coming evening with Kathy. And again, on the way up to the Cusack flat in the lift, he was momentarily being taken to one of the upper floors at the Aphra by Pieta.

A maid showed them into the livingroom where they were greeted by Robert Cusack and his wife, Joan.

Gideon, who, however poor in registering certain situations, was quick in his perception of the atmosphere in places, knew at once that he was on what he called to himself: the middle ground. He saw it as a sheltered, cultivated valley between high, show-capped peaks and beyond these, jungles and deserts and vast oceans with scattered tropical islands. Here was a kind of ideal norm, socially, politically, culturally, even sexually.

The area of this middle-ground, he reflected, was shrinking, invaded by those whom the revolution (in this quick impression he hadn't time to define what revolution he meant) had made more powerful, more ruthless, more corrupt and more arrogant in their stupidity. There wasn't time to come to a final conclusion, but he knew in his heart that it wouldn't be an assurance that what he valued — leave Pieta out of it — was being preserved in these last pockets or patches of civilisation.

As he listened to the conversation at lunch he wondered if it had been a mistake to come.

Joan Cusack was telling them how much she liked *Faillandia*, mentioning some of the articles — but not what Gideon thought were the really original and radical ones.

"There's nothing like it here, you know."

"It wouldn't have survived long with us were it not for the upheaval we were going through."

"Now that democratic law and order has been re-established, what will happen?" Cusack asked.

Did he not know why they were here? Had the Prior, in arranging the meeting, not told him? Or was this the diplomat's way of getting round to the subject?

"To the magazine, you mean?"

"The new Government made the publication in it of an official announcement and plea for support, which was printed in the daily press, a condition for allowing it to appear," Gideon explained.

"Yes, I've read it. Of course we get the main Faillandian

papers, with those of the rest of Europe, at the Foreign Office."

Gideon glanced at Pieta to indicate that it was now her turn.

"We've moved the magazine to Dominicus, but whether they'll honour the island's charter, nobody knows. You see, Mr. Cusack (shouldn't it have now been Sir Robert? Gideon wasn't sure), it's not just *Faillandia* that's a thorn in their side, even with the fall in its distribution, some supporters of Colonel Klotz have also taken refuge there."

Which ones? Certainly not Paul. Did she mean the Kemps? And, anyhow, Gideon didn't think that she need have said something that might give the impression that the island was a hive of political dissidents.

He saw that he needn't have worried, because Cusack was well-informed about the situation.

"I've just been in touch with our intelligence sources there, and these people you mention don't amount to any serious threat to the new administration. The Klotz regime seems to have collapsed from inside, rather than from armed hostilities, leaving the Colonel more or less friendless."

"He didn't inspire devotion."

Gideon was surprised at Pieta's remark. Yet, when he considered it, she was right. Klotz, unlike some national leaders, hadn't the gift of endearing himself emotionally to any large section of the populace. He was never photographed with children nor visiting homes for the elderly. There was no use going over all that again, but Gideon would never quite get over the moment when he had believed it possible that his idea of the Kingdom of Heaven could be brought here on earth with the help of a powerful ally. He and, he thought, Paul had been slow in seeing their folly.

"You want us to make it plain to the Faillandian Government that any intervention in the affairs of Dominicus would be seen by us as a contravening of the Charter of which the United Kingdom was the chief guarantor. Have I got it right, Gideon?"

Gideon, aware that he was being addressed, was, for a

moment, astonished at this sudden coming to the burning issue which he'd expected would be gradually and warily led up to by the diplomat.

His next reaction was momentarily one of pride that he, a figure of no particular weight in politics, should be involved in such discussions.

"That is just what we hoped might be possible, Sir Robert, for the island's freedom to be assured with that of the Priory with its long monastic tradition and independence of the Faillandian Hierarchy, which, as you know from a recent example, still hopes to impose some of its more puritanical precepts on the civil law. Then there is our magazine to keep a counter-current flowing to the conformism and timidities of the Faillandian press, as well as the island assembly that operates merely like the jury system here, and is changed periodically to prevent the corruption and collusion inherent in all the mainland parties."

Gideon took a swallow from his glass of wine. He was proud of his little speech which he thought had presented their case briefly and to the point. He glanced at Pieta but her eyes were lowered. He kept looking at her as long as he could without it becoming noticeable to their host and hostess, but, though she must be aware that he was awaiting some sign from her, she didn't look up.

Cusack was talking to him and, although he heard the phrases, several of which would have delighted him a few minutes earlier, now with his growing realisation of Pieta's reaction, they meant little or nothing.

All the same, he had to keep the conversation going and express their gratitude to Cusack for his promise to put the position to his Minister and suggest that a statement be sent to Failland, which he himself would draw up, in the form of an official *aide memoire* setting out the U.K.'s responsibilities in regard to Dominicus.

Wasn't this a lot to have achieved? And at a private lunch without long drawn-out talks. Had Pieta hoped for something more? Or had she only come with him because Frère Emanuel had asked her to, or, at least, told Gideon to take her with him. But if not as a help in putting their case, then as what?

Gideon did not put any of these questions to her until they were back in their hotel, aware that the answers might lead them into a conversation too serious to be started on the walk through the streets and continued in the subdued roar of the underground. It was only when they were in the hotel lift that the lunch was mentioned and then it was Pieta who said:

"You mustn't be angry with me for not warning you beforehand. I wanted you to see for yourself."

"Warning me?"

"Don't look so upset."

He wasn't really upset now that they were communicating again, though he might have looked glum sitting opposite her in the train.

"You like to spring things on me in the lift."

That was better, they were close and natural again.

"Like what?"

"Like when you first told me you had to go to hospital."

He came with her to her room, and as she lay on one of the twin beds he saw how exhausted she was, and that it was her, not himself, out of whom the visit to the Cusacks, had taken most.

"Why did you ever let me come here?"

"You were determined to after you'd talked with Daddy and I thought you had to see for yourself."

"See what exactly, Dove?"

"That we don't live, you and I, in the kind of place that can be protected by treaties and charters or by us finding sympathetic allies to have them observed."

"What about the magazine, if they take over Dominicus?"

"We'll return to Aphrin, where, of course, it'll be more difficult to bring out."

"And where you long to be, don't you, darling."

"It's our homeland, Gideon, with its precious graves:

350

Kathy's, Lydia's, Sabina's, Ellis', yes, and those of Nolla and Klotz too. And soon ours as well, and those of the people who were close to us through *Faillandia*, though most of them we didn't know. None of us were ever bound together by nationality in the political sense, but by a belief in a Promised Land, that we were setting out for together."

"Does being back in Aphrin mean more to you than *Faillandia*?

"The magazine wasn't our lives, but our way of showing faith in the future and inspiring some others, though not nearly all those who were reading it at its peak of popularity."

She was certainly taking the prospect of *Faillandia*'s disappearance lightly; Gideon remembered Frère Emanuel's comments on the passage in the Dutch theologian's treatise in which he argued that apparent failure was a part of all great endeavours if they were ultimately to bear fruit.

He found it difficult to accept such a metaphysical attitude. It was all very well for Pieta to say: 'It isn't our lives.' But, faced with its loss, he saw how much of *his* life it had been.

They fell silent and Gideon thought sadly that Pieta was asleep while the long night was still before him, with still so much unresolved. He decided to remain where he was and lay down on the other bed.

A little later when it was almost dark, Pieta switched on the light and started to read from what he recognised as the small paperback copy of the Gospels he'd often noticed beside her bed at the Aphra. He waited, not sure whether, as the circle of light left him in deep shadow, she knew he was still in the room. Then, a little later still, she said: "Listen to this," and started to read out.

"That very day two of them were going to the village named Emmaus, about seven miles from Jerusalem, and talking with each other about all these things that had happened. While they were talking and discussing together, Jesus himself drew near and went with them. But their eyes were kept from recognising him. And He said to them, 'What is this conversation you are

351

holding with each other as you walk?' And they stood still, looking sad. Then one of them, named Cleopas, answered him: 'Are you the only visitor to Jerusalem who does not know the things that have happened there in these days?' And He said to them, 'What things?' And they said to him, 'Concerning Jesus of Nazareth, who was a prophet mighty in deed and word before God and all the people, and how our chief priests and rulers delivered him up to be condemned to death, and crucified him. But we had hoped that he was the one to redeem Israel . . . ' He appeared to be going further, but they constrained him, saying, 'Stay with us, for it is toward evening and the day is now far spent.' "